I0892064

Approaches to Teaching Henry James's *Daisy Miller* and *The Turn of the Screw*

Approaches to Teaching World Literature

Joseph Gibaldi, series editor

For a complete listing of titles, see the last pages of this book.

Approaches to Teaching Henry James's *Daisy Miller* and *The Turn of the Screw*

Edited by

Kimberly C. Reed

and

Peter G. Beidler

The Modern Language Association of America
New York 2005

© 2005 by The Modern Language Association of America
All rights reserved
Printed in the United States of America

For information about obtaining permission to reprint material from MLA book publications, send your request by mail (see address below), e-mail (permissions@mla.org), or fax (646-458-0030).

Library of Congress Cataloging-in-Publication Data

Approaches to teaching Henry James's Daisy Miller and The turn of the screw / edited by Kimberly C. Reed and Peter G. Beidler.
p. cm. — (Approaches to teaching world literature ; 86)
Includes bibliographical references and index.
ISBN 0-87352-920-0 (alk. paper) — ISBN 0-87352-921-9 (pbk. : alk. paper)
1. James, Henry, 1843–1916. Daisy Miller. 2. James, Henry, 1843–1916. Turn of the screw. 3. James, Henry, 1843–1916—Study and teaching. 4. Women travelers in literature. 5. Governesses in literature. I. Reed, Kimberly Capps. II. Beidler, Peter G. III. Series.
PS2116.D33A85 2005
813'.4—dc22 2005009675
ISSN 1059-1133

Cover illustration of the paperback edition: *The Introduction*, by George Goodwin Kilburne (1839–1924). Sotheby's Picture Library, London

Published by The Modern Language Association of America
26 Broadway, New York, New York 10004-1789
www.mla.org

CONTENTS

PREFACE TO THE SERIES

In *The Art of Teaching* Gilbert Highet wrote, "Bad teaching wastes a great deal of effort, and spoils many lives which might have been full of energy and happiness." All too many teachers have failed in their work, Highet argued, simply "because they have not thought about it." We hope that the Approaches to Teaching World Literature series, sponsored by the Modern Language Association's Publications Committee, will not only improve the craft—as well as the art—of teaching but also encourage serious and continuing discussion of the aims and methods of teaching literature.

The principal objective of the series is to collect within each volume different points of view on teaching a specific literary work, a literary tradition, or a writer widely taught at the undergraduate level. The preparation of each volume begins with a wide-ranging survey of instructors, thus enabling us to include in the volume the philosophies and approaches, thoughts and methods of scores of experienced teachers. The result is a sourcebook of material, information, and ideas on teaching the subject of the volume to undergraduates.

The series is intended to serve nonspecialists as well as specialists, inexperienced as well as experienced teachers, graduate students who wish to learn effective ways of teaching as well as senior professors who wish to compare their own approaches with the approaches of colleagues in other schools. Of course, no volume in the series can ever substitute for erudition, intelligence, creativity, and sensitivity in teaching. We hope merely that each book will point readers in useful directions; at most each will offer only a first step in the long journey to successful teaching.

Joseph Gibaldi
Series Editor

PREFACE TO THE VOLUME

For contemporary teachers and students of literature, Henry James's writings offer exploratory expeditions into both aesthetic and social realms. His probing of what Leon Edel calls the "myth of civilization" in the context of American-European interaction plots a path through the tangle of intercultural cues and miscues (*Henry James: A Life* 716). With James's famous dictum that the artist should be one on whom nothing is lost ("Art" [*Literary Criticism*] 53), his psychological acuity allows James to frame some of the most intricate characterizations in the history of the novel. In addition, his stylistic and thematic evolutions parallel the movement from realism to modernism in Anglo-American literary history.

During the last half century, these (sometimes overlapping) Jamesian projects have loomed large in the college literature classroom; various themes have emerged as most central, depending on currents in literary theory and their pedagogical impact. The kaleidoscope of approaches to teaching James has resulted in what Susan M. Griffin calls "the variety of 'Henry Jameses' being taught—the last Victorian, the literary theorist, the realist, the gay writer" (Introduction [*Forum*] 211). Such a multiplicity of approaches may be salutary for teachers and students alike, given the strictures of the formalist approach popular a few decades ago, which, as John Carlos Rowe has shown, focused on James's stylistic difficulty as the defining element of his "greatness" as an author ("Henry James" 214). The pedagogical pleasures of diversity notwithstanding, this new variety demands from the instructor an understanding both broad and profound of how best to implement different methods in the classroom. For these reasons, then—James's enduring legacy as an artist and the wealth of approaches to literary studies that his works afford—we have prepared this volume.

Two of James's most frequently taught novellas offer great appeal to both students and instructors. Daniel Mark Fogel calls *Daisy Miller* the "prototypical 'international theme' story" and Daisy the character the "paradigm of the international 'American girl' " (Daisy Miller 8), a combination likely to appeal to college-age students. Yet Fogel points out that the novella raises other issues that engage us all as readers, issues "about the role of convention and stereotyping in the human community, about our vulnerability to self-deception, and about the proper relations between men and women and between parents and children" (8–9). Even though many professors and students find *Daisy Miller* to be an almost transparent work—accessible, entertaining, and easy to understand—it turns out to offer the sorts of interpretive challenges that many associate more readily with later James. Those challenges are foregrounded almost immediately as one begins another of James's novellas, *The Turn of the Screw*, so much so that readers may feel the interpretive ground dissolving under their feet as the novella progresses.

The same issues that Fogel delineates in *Daisy Miller* also appear in *The Turn of the Screw*, with its social-class tensions, its (possibly) radically unstable narrative, and its (possibly) horrific view of the parental and sexual relations among men and women, boys and girls. Add to those themes the fact that, as Terry Heller says, "the tale is generally agreed to be the greatest tale of terror written in English," and the appeal of this novella becomes even clearer (6). Students will likely be drawn to the issues that James explores in both novellas: the conflict between—and possibly misleading nature of—innocence and experience, the complications of sexual attraction, the pressure to conform to a set of expectations. They may well recognize the protagonists' predicaments as familiar ones—and some degree of identification with a literary character is often the first step a student takes in coming to appreciate and enjoy literature.

The themes and techniques embodied in these texts suggest issues that instructors may wish to confront in their scholarship or in the classroom, issues involving elements of James's fiction that set James apart from other authors: his sometimes dauntingly difficult style, his finely honed narrative points of view, his ground-breaking psychological development of characters, his involvement with philosophical trends as the brother of a great philosopher, his unusual place in both American and English literary history, and so on. As with any author, we can categorize these issues as relating either to the text or to the extraliterary context, but such categorizing implies that the two are essentially discrete and do not nourish or interrogate each other. The actual practice of teaching James indicates that the opposite is true: even as instructors prepare students for James's stylistic complexity, they may relate it to his great theme of the impossibility of knowledge. They may connect James's interest in the psychology of his characters to Freud's contemporaneous theories of how the mind works, or they may consider William James's contributions to philosophy as they discuss Henry's interest in the paranormal. On a more pragmatic level, instructors may have to defend their choice to teach James's work at all, as the James scholar Sheila Teahan did to some degree at her state university, where the "ideological climate" of the university labeled James as an "elitist white male aesthete who exemplifies the dubious values of an outmoded canon" ("Henry James" 242–43).

Any teacher of these texts, then, may benefit from the essays that follow, as a way to help students manage the difficulties of James's fiction as they enjoy the pleasures of his art. In preparing this volume, we wished to be descriptive rather than prescriptive in our choice of essays—that is, we sought essays from teachers who present perspectives with which we may not entirely agree but who approach the teaching of these works in ways both practical and provocative. Some essays complement each other; others contradict each other. Some essays should be useful to the instructor who is new to James or teaching a lower-division course; others are more suitable to the instructor with more experience in James studies or who teaches an upper-division or graduate-level course.

Many people played an important role in bringing this project to fruition, and we want to acknowledge their help. We are deeply grateful to Joseph Gibaldi, the series editor, for his ever-gracious assistance and encouragement. We appreciate the contributors of the essays for their patience, cooperation, enthusiasm, and creativity. The survey participants provided us with very useful suggestions and advice. Robert A. Wilson, then a doctoral candidate at Lehigh University, and Jennifer Hyest, a Lipscomb University alumna and current Lehigh graduate student, gave us valuable assistance in proofreading and fact checking, and we appreciate the help of the Lehigh University library staff. We thank Lipscomb University, including the provost, Craig Bledsoe, for his financial help; the chair of the English department, Matthew Hearn, and the English faculty for their collegial encouragement; and the computer specialist Michelle Putnam for her calm assistance with electronic issues. Finally, we are most grateful to our spouses, Jerry and Anne, for their constant support and understanding.

KCR and PGB

Part One

MATERIALS

Introduction

> Indeed, if the artistic value of such an experiment be measured by the intellectual echoes it may again, long after, set in motion, the case would make in favour of this little firm fantasy. . . .
>
> —Henry James, preface to *The Turn of the Screw*

Much of the information in this "Materials" section is drawn from survey responses sent us by college and university instructors in North America and Europe (the survey participants are listed after the notes on contributors). Because the scholarship on James's extensive oeuvre is flourishing, what follows is necessarily quite limited. We have chosen to recommend only a few books dealing generally with James or with a large number of his texts; instead, we focus on those that specifically treat *Daisy Miller* or *The Turn of the Screw*. Further bibliographic suggestions occur in the essays of this volume. For more general reading on James and his works, the *MLA Bibliography*, found in most major libraries, offers an exhaustive list of scholarly works. The *Henry James Review* is an invaluable resource for those wishing to remain current in James studies.

Background Readings

For general background reading, respondents to our survey recommended a number of articles and books. Some use works on literary theory or history that provide a context for their discussion of James. Such recommendations include Wayne Booth's *The Rhetoric of Fiction*, F. R. Leavis's *The Great Tradition*, and Peter Brooks's *The Melodramatic Imagination* and *Reading for the Plot*. Many consult Leon Edel's epochal biography *Henry James: A Life*; many also find Fred Kaplan's more recent biography helpful. R. W. B. Lewis's biography offers a perspective on James in the context of his large family. Philip Horne's *Henry James: A Life in Letters*, with his intriguing headnotes and explanatory footnotes, allows instructors and students alike to explore the biography through a large sampling of James's vast correspondence. Both Jonathan Freedman and Daniel Fogel have published companions to studies in James; Fogel's book offers an excellent bibliography of landmarks of criticism on James, from 1905 through the early 1990s. Robert Gale's *Henry James Encyclopedia* elucidates references to James's life and writings. Adeline Tintner's remarkable series of books on James and his society (such as *The Pop World of Henry James: From Fairy Tales to Science Fiction* and *The Museum*

World of Henry James) are engaging explorations of the way James incorporated various elements of his milieu into his fiction. Millicent Bell's *Meaning in Henry James* includes chapters on both novellas that should be helpful for both instructors and students. Mark Seltzer's *Henry James and the Art of Power* examines issues of power in James's culture and work.

The controversy over whether the ghosts are real in *The Turn of the Screw* has generated an overwhelming, often passionate, response in the century since the novella was published. Indeed, so contentious has the work's reception been that instructors new to this subject would do well to consult an overview, such as Robin P. Hoople's study of the criticism through the late 1980s, *Distinguished Discord: Discontinuity and Pattern in the Critical Tradition of* The Turn of the Screw; Hoople's work situates many of the most influential critics in a larger, historicized context. More recently, Edward J. Parkinson published on the Web his doctoral dissertation on the novella's critical reception (www.turnofthescrew.com). The Bedford first and second editions of the novella (ed. Beidler) contain a summary of the critical history, and the Norton Critical Edition (2nd ed., ed. Esch and Warren) provides a number of contemporary reviews as well as more recent analyses of both the novella and its reception. All these texts have a select bibliography of the criticism forming this debate. Although space here does not allow more than a few suggestions for those interested in the history of the reception of *The Turn of the Screw*, many respondents suggested the following texts as a way of examining with students the historical contours of the criticism, even if the instructors disagree with the conclusions of the critics. Respondents note the importance of Edmund Wilson's seminal article "The Ambiguity of Henry James" with its Freudian hypothesis that the governess is neurotic. They frequently mention Thomas M. Cranfill and Robert L. Clark's *An Anatomy of* The Turn of the Screw, which builds on this interpretation in an attempt to demonstrate the governess's growing madness as the story unfolds. Robert Heilman's refutation of the Freudian approach in "*The Turn of the Screw* as Poem," joined with apparitionist interpretations from such eminent critics as Leavis in "Reply to Bewley's 'Rejoinder,' " establishes an opposing position in the pro- and antighost debates that flourished between the 1930s and late 1950s. Dorothea Krook, one of the first critics to move beyond the either-or approach, suggests in "Intentions and Intentions: The Problem of Intention and Henry James's *The Turn of the Screw*" that James's text structures an essentially perfect ambiguity. Her position is embraced or expanded, often with differing conclusions, by more recent critics such as Christine Brooke-Rose in *A Rhetoric of the Unreal*, Shoshana Felman in "Turning the Screw of Interpretation," John Carlos Rowe in "Screwball: The Use and Abuse of Uncertainty in Henry James's *The Turn of the Screw*," and Paul Armstrong in *The Challenge of Bewilderment: Understanding and Representation in James, Conrad, and Ford*. In similar fashion, Terry Heller provides an interesting synthesis of the either-or debate in The Turn of the Screw: *Bewildered Vision*.

Not all the criticism on *The Turn of the Screw*, however, deals with the reality of the ghosts. The move in the 1960s toward accepting and celebrating the ambiguity of this text cleared the field for other perspectives and methodologies. Survey respondents recommended a number of more recent works, such as Martha Banta's engaging *Henry James and the Occult: The Great Extension*, which focuses on how James incorporated late-nineteenth-century interpretations of the supernatural into his aesthetic structure of human consciousness. T. J. Lustig argues in *Henry James and the Ghostly* that James's use of ghosts is a central, overarching metaphor that expresses the liminal nature of relationships and consciousness. Bruce Robbins in " 'They Don't Much Count, Do They?': The Unfinished History of *The Turn of the Screw*," Edwin Fussell in "The Ontology of *The Turn of the Screw*," and Graham McMaster in "Henry James and India: A Historical Reading of *The Turn of the Screw*" have developed intriguing Marxist interpretations through their investigations of the implications of class in the novella. Gender-related criticism includes Priscilla Walton's *The Disruption of the Feminine in Henry James* and Paula Marantz Cohen's "Freud's *Dora* and James's *The Turn of the Screw*: Two Treatments of the Female 'Case.' " Mary Poovey's *Uneven Developments: The Ideological Work of Gender in Mid-Victorian England* provides helpful information on gender issues in James's time—including an examination of the place of governesses. For those interested in the connection between *The Turn of the Screw* and gothic literature, David Punter's *Literature of Terror* is recommended.

Suggestions for background reading on *Daisy Miller* tend to be more general in scope, given the relatively straightforward reception history of this novella in comparison with that of *The Turn of the Screw*. Nevertheless, *Daisy Miller* did elicit a small storm of controversy when it was first published. Fogel's Daisy Miller: *A Dark Comedy of Manners*, which many respondents recommended for an excellent overview of the novella, contains a chapter on the contemporary reaction to the text. Instructors also point to Virginia C. Fowler's *Henry James's American Girl: The Embroidery on the Canvas* and Vivian Pollack's anthology of essays on *Daisy Miller* and *The Turn of the Screw* as good sources for students and instructors. Last but not least, a large number of respondents turn to James himself, in his prefaces to his works. Some use the preface to the novella in question; others use his collected prefaces in *The Art of the Novel* as a way of helping students understand James's theories of writing, of literature, and of art.

The Texts in the Classroom

The constellation of possibilities for situating these two texts in the classroom is a frequently shifting one, given the variety of ways in which they lend themselves to use. A few instructors assign one of the novellas in a freshman composition course, finding that students are interested in its plot and thus motivated to explore different rhetorical strategies to write about it. Many respondents put one of the novellas on literature survey syllabi for sophomores—both American and British, given James's importance in both national literatures. In the greater diversity of upper-division courses, the possibilities become even more interesting. One of the two novellas often appears in syllabi focusing on post–Civil War American literature, the American novel, or (esp. *Daisy Miller*) American realism. *The Turn of the Screw* not unsurprisingly appears in courses on the gothic, literature and decadence, and literature and sexuality or gender. In these courses, instructors place it alongside such diverse texts as Edgar Allan Poe's "The Fall of the House of Usher," Nathaniel Hawthorne's *The House of the Seven Gables*, Joyce Carol Oates's "The Accursed Inhabitants of the House of Bly," Charles Brockden Brown's *Wieland*, Kate Chopin's "Desiree's Baby," Stephen Crane's *Maggie*, Sigmund Freud's "The Uncanny," and works by Oscar Wilde and by Walter Pater. Other instructors use the novellas in courses or seminars on modern fiction, film and literature, and literary theory and criticism.

Teaching Resources

Many survey respondents recommend using film adaptations. Peter Bogdanovich's *Daisy Miller* (1974), Jack Clayton's *The Innocents* (based on *The Turn of the Screw*; 1961) and Ben Bolt's *The Turn of the Screw* (1999) are most commonly cited, although instructors encourage their students to watch these films with a critical eye. (For those who need more information about film adaptations of James's works, Susan M. Griffin's *Henry James Goes to the Movies* contains an exhaustive filmography by J. Sarah Koch as well as excellent essays on these adaptations.) Some instructors use recordings or videos of Benjamin Britten's opera *The Turn of the Screw* for yet another example of an interpretative stance regarding the novella.

Instructors have found the Internet to be useful. The invaluable Henry James scholars' Web site (www2.newpaltz.edu/~hathaway) has a plethora of links, including those to e-texts of both novellas, scholarly articles, concordances, and background information on James and his works. Several respondents noted that the Internet is also a good source for photographs of James, his family and friends, and sites associated with him and his works.

Editions

The respondents to our survey use a variety of editions of these two novellas in their classes. Obviously, those who assign *Daisy Miller* in a survey course use the edition in their textbook; those who assign it in other courses tend to choose either the Dover Thrift edition or the Penguin Classics edition. Because James heavily revised *Daisy Miller* between the novella's original appearance in 1878 and the New York edition of 1909, instructors adopting it must choose which version to teach. For more information about the issue of James's revision of his works, teachers may wish to consult David McWhirter's *Henry James's New York Edition: The Construction of Authorship*. Many instructors prefer the original edition of *Daisy Miller* to the substantially revised New York edition; because Penguin Classics uses the original and is easily available, we have chosen to use the Penguin edition for this volume.

Most who teach *The Turn of the Screw* use either the Bedford Case Studies in Contemporary Criticism edition or the Norton Critical Edition (both now available in second editions). Both use the 1908 New York edition of the novella; unlike *Daisy Miller*, *The Turn of the Screw* did not undergo dramatic revision between its appearance in *Collier's Weekly* in 1908 and its inclusion in the New York edition ten years later. A number of instructors use the Bedford edition of *The Turn of the Screw* because of its review of the critical reception of the text as well as the five essays that explicate contemporary critical theories in its context. (Note that there are differences between first and second edition in the essays.) Because several of the essayists in this MLA volume discuss specifically how they use the Bedford edition, all references to *The Turn of the Screw* are from it. But some respondents recommended the Norton because of the relatively large number of critical essays provided and the helpful section on textual variants among the various versions, so we provide here a chart showing page correspondences of the Bedford and Norton second editions.

Page Conversion Chart for the Bedford and Norton Second Editions of *The Turn of the Screw*

Bedford	Norton
Prologue	
22	1
23	1–2
24	2–3
25	3
26	3–4
27	4–5
28	5–6
Chapter 1	
29	6–7
30	7–8
31	8
32	8–9
Chapter 2	
33	9–10
34	10–11
35	11–12
Chapter 3	
36	12–13
37	13–14
38	14–15
39	15–16
40	16
Chapter 4	
41	16–17
42	17–18
43	18–19
44	19–20
Chapter 5	
45	20–21
46	21–22
47	22
48	22–23
Chapter 6	
49	23–24
50	24–25
51	25–26
52	26–27
53	27–28
54	28
Chapter 7	
55	28–29
56	29–30
57	30–31
58	31–32
Chapter 8	
59	32–33
60	33
61	33–34
62	34–35
63	35–36
Chapter 9	
64	36–37
65	37–38
66	38–39
67	39
Chapter 10	
68	39–40
69	40–41
70	41–42
71	42–43
Chapter 11	
72	43–44
73	44–45
74	45
Chapter 12	
75	45–46
76	46–47
77	47–48
Chapter 13	
78	48–49
79	49–50
80	50–51
81	51
Chapter 14	
82	51–52
83	52–53
84	53–54
85	54–55
Chapter 15	
86	55–56
87	56–57
Chapter 16	
88	57
89	57–58
90	58–59
Chapter 17	
91	59–60
92	60–61
93	61
94	61–62
Chapter 18	
95	62–63
96	63–64
97	64–65
Chapter 19	
98	65–66
99	66–67
100	67–68
Chapter 20	
101	68
102	68–69
103	69–70
104	70–71
Chapter 21	
105	71–72
106	72–73
107	73–74
108	74–75
109	75
Chapter 22	
110	76
111	76–77
112	77–78
Chapter 23	
113	78–79
114	79–80
115	80–81
Chapter 24	
116	81–82
117	82
118	82–83
119	83–84
120	84–85

Part Two

APPROACHES

Introduction

Virtually all literary texts feature characters whose qualities, actions, and motives are open to conflicting interpretation. But few authors so insistently foreground the issue of epistemology as Henry James does. The assumptions that Winterbourne and others make about Daisy in *Daisy Miller*, the ontological status of the ghosts and the nature of the governess in *The Turn of the Screw*—all are interpretative puzzles that the readers of these texts must immediately confront in order to make sense of the narrative. No wonder that all the essays in this volume embrace, as their underlying pedagogical method, issues of interpretation by using the various questions they raise.

The essays in the first section, "Contexts," thematize and contextualize pedagogy. Kristin Boudreau situates James as a modernist writer in her emphasis on the subjectivity of the narrative in *Daisy Miller* and *The Turn of the Screw*; she uses Williams James's writings to highlight his brother's belief that value and meaning are determined not absolutely but relationally and demonstrates ways to turn the difficulties of reading Henry James into the pleasures of indeterminacy. Using articles written by women for Victorian periodicals, Sean Palmer demonstrates a new-historicist approach to *Daisy Miller*: highlighting the linguistic constituents of political discourses on the modern woman that find correlation in the character dialogue of the novella, an instructor can help students identify the relation between political context and literary text. Kimberly C. Reed demonstrates how to use historical documents about governesses and ghosts to guide students in a (first) reading of *The Turn of the Screw* as a ghost story. Philip Horne draws on the parallels between James's life and the characters and events in *Daisy Miller* to show how biography can be used creatively in the classroom. By focusing on issues of social class in *The Turn of the Screw*, Robert Andrew Wilson suggests ways of helping students ask innovative questions about the novella.

The section "Classroom Strategies" provides practical suggestions for how students can tackle the problems of interpretation. Peter G. Beidler argues that a consideration of the historical situation of the governess as a teacher of students is a natural way to engage modern-day students with *The Turn of the Screw*; he provides a list of questions that can elicit a vigorous discussion. Collin Meissner acknowledges the difficulty of teaching James to undergraduates but argues that this very difficulty proves to be a pedagogical advantage. The parallel he draws between the failure of the characters in both novellas to understand what is happening and the same failure of teachers and students reveals the shortcomings of readers' interpretive strategies. Gert Buelens, teaching *Daisy Miller* to European students, argues that giving them broad questions and fewer preconceived notions about which answers are right allows the teacher to share the students' experience more closely—and to mirror the interpretative puzzle that the novella presents. Nicolas S. Witschi likewise writes of teaching James in a European setting. He draws on the response of his German university students majoring in English, who were interested more in misreadings of the Europeans in *Daisy Miller* than in misreadings of Daisy (the traditional American concern), to suggest how teachers can use contemporary reviews, letters, and essays that reflect culturally and historically specific reader responses. Greg W. Zacharias demonstrates how the inherent dramatic quality of James's fiction, with the attendant importance placed on the reader's interpretation of the action, invites teachers to model dramatic readings for and with their students.

The essays in "Theory and Intertextuality" provide more-specific suggestions on using theoretical and intertextual approaches. Pericles Lewis shows how surveying older approaches to *Daisy Miller* and then studying more-modern approaches can allow instructors to demonstrate the multiplicity of critical schools in an accessible way while doing justice to their complexity. Sheila Teahan assigns *The Turn of the Screw* alongside a number of theoretical texts as a way of questioning the distinction between literature and theory and demonstrating how the novella both dramatizes and thematizes the problematics of reading. In her course on the gothic, Diane Long Hoeveler pairs *The Turn of the Screw* with a retelling of James's story by Joyce Carol Oates. She argues that teachers can use the voyeurism, exhibitionism, oedipal desire, and mourning in both tales to show how Oates throws a bright—and frightful—light on what is shadowed in James's story. Michelle E. Moore assigns Shoshana Felman's often reprinted essay "Turning the Screw of Interpretation" to show students how different traditional critical perspectives find themselves reflected in the text of the governess's narration. According to Moore, Felman's essay is valuable because it strives to preserve the ambiguity of the text without reenacting earlier analyses.

A wide range of classroom strategies appears in the section "Gender and Sexuality." Eric Savoy outlines a method by which teachers can demonstrate to their students that the natural desire to find the one right interpretation of *The Turn of the Screw* leads readers to ignore aspects of the text that do not fit their reading. A close look at rhetorical devices helps students locate the queer James, moving from the analysis of individual passages to an examination of deconstructive, psychoanalytic, and queer approaches. Dawn Keetley explores the fantasies, politics, and laws that surround the concept of motherhood, arguing that the governess embodies fears about the all-devouring, (literally) suffocating mother as well as the mother substitute. She shows how anxieties about surrogate mothers from the late Victorian era continued to shape the discourse of mothering through the twentieth century. Warren Rosenberg, teaching *Daisy Miller* at an all-male college, suggests how to help students recognize that gender powerfully shapes and often distorts the way we see the world, sometimes with tragic consequences.

Teachers looking for ideas about teaching James in a course on composition will benefit from the essays in "James and Composition." Marian Kelly demonstrates how to take advantage of the heated critical history of the reception of *The Turn of the Screw* in introducing students to analytic writing. The governess's reading of and writing about her situation become a model of how *not* to read and write. Sallie Duhling and Patricia Worrall, at a two-year college, encounter students with a wide range of skills in reading and writing. Duhling approaches *Daisy Miller* from a formalist perspective in her grammar and composition course; in her introduction-to-literature course, Worrall introduces her students to more contemporary critical approaches through *The Turn of the Screw*. Anna Despotopoulou shows how *The Turn of the Screw* can be used to teach the structure of composition, grammar, and reading skills to students for whom English may not be the first language. That the text can be the basis for either an apparitionist or nonapparitionist approach hones critical reading skills. Students also examine Jamesian ambiguity as it functions grammatically and structures the novel.

In the final section, "James and Film," Mark A. Eaton finds that Peter Bogdanovich's version of *Daisy Miller* draws its viewers into James's world and simultaneously reveals new attitudes about gender and sexuality during the 1970s, when the film was made. Using the film with the text, Eaton argues, allows students to become more sophisticated cultural critics. Monika Brown shows how to use film adaptations of *The Turn of the Screw* in any literature course, presenting a sequence of activities for the classroom as well as an annotated bibliography of films and related resources. Finally, Sue Sorensen outlines pragmatic strategies for drawing attention to the clarity of James's visual sense as a way of helping students cope with his sometimes difficult style. After her students perform close readings of certain passages, she shows key scenes from film adaptations of the text so that they can see how filmmakers have interpreted James's ambiguity.

Many of the essays in this volume overlap in their treatment of the two novellas. The sections go from general to specific, but instructors may have a pedagogical interest that suggests a different grouping. For example, those interested in James and theory may wish to look at the essays by Lewis, Teahan, Savoy, Meissner (who provides a provocative caveat about the reliance on any interpretative stance), and Moore. James's place in literary history is the focus of Boudreau's and Hoeveler's essays. Social history is foregrounded by Palmer, Reed, Witschi, Eaton, Keetley, and Beidler (the last two espouse quite different interpretations of the governess). Close readings, whether done by the New Critics (sometimes known as formalists) or in support of other literary theories or approaches, are featured to some degree by Horne, Zacharias, Savoy, Buelens, and Sorensen. Cross-cultural perspectives appear in the essays by Despotopoulou, Buelens, and Witschi.

The texts of *Daisy Miller* and *The Turn of the Screw* are too rich to receive their full due in this volume. Nevertheless, we hope that all instructors, from those new to James to those who are established Jamesians, can find in these pages provocative, engaging, and entertaining suggestions for teaching his works.

CONTEXTS

The Difficulty with Plain Answers: Introducing Modernism by Way of Henry James

Kristin Boudreau

There is a cartoon by Max Beerbohm that I like to use when introducing my students to Henry James: "A Nightmare, Mr. Henry James Subpoenaed as Psychological Expert in a *Cause Célèbre*." The exasperated lawyer, cross-examining the expert witness, explodes at James: "Come Sir, I ask you a plain question and I expect a plain answer!"

The illustration provides the perfect introduction to James and to the modernist preoccupations found in his works, early and late. For one thing, by placing James in the role of psychological expert, Beerbohm indicates James's prominent place in the late-nineteenth-century developments of the novel. As Michael Levenson has shown, with the breakdown of certainty that came in the wake of intellectuals like Marx, Darwin, Nietzsche, and Freud, modernist writers looked to the individual consciousness as the only source of permanence in an otherwise fluctuating world. "Traditional justifications of value had lapsed," he writes, "but this is seen less as a cause for regret than as an opportunity." These writers turned to subjectivity in order to represent, through limited point of view, what had once been more simply and fully conveyed by the omniscient narrator. For the moderns, as Levenson notes, "human subjectivity [would] become the foundation and support for a range of threatened institutions" (13). Henry James, whose brother William coined the phrase "stream of consciousness" in his 1890 *Principles of Psychology* (1: 239), was devoted to explorations of consciousness in his narrators and central characters and came to be known as the psychological novelist par excellence.

CROSS-EXAMINING COUNSEL: "COME SIR, I ASK YOU A PLAIN QUESTION AND I EXPECT A PLAIN ANSWER!"

Fig. 1. "A Nightmare, Mr. Henry James Subpoenaed as Psychological Expert in a *Cause Célèbre*." Caricature by Max Beerbohm. Courtesy of the Henry James Collection (#6251-K), Clifton Waller Barrett Library, Albert and Shirley Small Special Collections Library, University of Virginia Library

The other way in which this cartoon provides an appropriate and useful introduction to James has to do with Beerbohm's joke about plain answers. Students of James are generally relieved to learn that they are not the only ones to find his prose obscure and difficult. Indeed, they are often as frustrated as Beerbohm's lawyer when they seek the meaning embedded in James's language. A representative line from the governess-narrator of *The Turn of the Screw* reads, "This was not so good a thing, I admit, as not to leave me to judge that what, essentially, made nothing else much signify was simply my charming work" (42). The word "simply" renders this line better than any parody of James (and there are many), for it flies in the face of the obscurity produced by the governess's contorted prose and multiple negatives.

James's own obscure prose is better than any parody, because most parodies (including Beerbohm's "Mote in the Middle Distance," a late-Jamesian account of Christmas morning) suggest that style is simply something slapped on top of content. Instead, as I try to show my students, form and content are intricately related. That the governess has difficulty describing her feelings is not because James was addicted to obscure prose but because he was saying something about her psyche, about her inability to confront difficult feelings. Like the hysterics described in Joseph Breuer and Freud's 1895 *Studies on Hysteria*, James's governess does not want to face consciously what she already knows unconsciously, but she is often betrayed by her language. Breuer and Freud write that hysterics often express their unacknowledged thoughts through hysterical symptoms that symbolize verbal expressions (179). We might want to keep in mind the insights of William James, who believed that all truths are largely determined by the temperament of the subject who registers them. William James laughed at the rationalist, who believes "that life transacts itself in a purely logical or epistemological, as distinguished from a psychological, dimension, and [that] its claims antedate and exceed all personal motivations whatsoever" (*Pragmatism* 102). If the psyche observing the world helps shape the truth of that observation, then it seems clear that form (the words we choose, the cadences or contortions of our language, its relative clarity or density) cannot be extricated from content. And the more opaque the prose, the more irresistibly we are drawn to the medium of language and consequently to the character who forms the words we read. The governess's obscure language demonstrates the impossibility, for a modern sensibility, of plain answers.

Allon White's excellent book *The Uses of Obscurity* helps make this point. White puts modern obscurity in the context of "that momentous shift when certain deep, discursive regularities (clarity, coherence, sincerity, objective representation) began to crack and slide in the 1870s and 1880s" (1–2). For him, the opacity of modern prose does not merely cover up the meaning beneath the linguistic surface; that meaning is constituted in part by the density of the language: "How a thing is obscured in a text is itself significant. It carries meaning such that, to believe only the 'clear' truth 'behind' the difficulty to be the 'actual' meaning, is to produce a partial (and inadequate) reading" (19). It is important to me that my students understand obscure prose not as something that gets in the way of what a text means—an ongoing preoccupation for English majors—but rather as something they must recognize and begin to talk about. Why, I ask them, might this passage be deliberately dense? And so we plunge into the most difficult passages in *The Turn of the Screw* in order to talk about what White calls the "uses of obscurity."

What is true for prose style is also true for plot; thus the questions we ask of the difficult *Turn of the Screw* might also be asked of the relatively transparent *Daisy Miller*. Despite its lucid style, *Daisy Miller* is another tale that refuses to divulge its secrets. Certainly these are not the only James texts that can profitably be taught in a course on James or on modernism. What I say here applies to nearly any work of James, early or late. Like many of his fictions, these two tales help students understand that their uncertainty about what a character signifies derives from the novelist's larger interest in psychology. This uncertainty attaches not only to main characters but even, in many cases, to the disembodied narrators whom students are often tempted to trust. The narrator of *Daisy Miller*, for instance, introduces Winterbourne, the man through whose sensibility we come to know Daisy:

> I hardly know whether it was the analogies or the differences [between European and American resorts] that were uppermost in the mind of a young American, who, two or three years ago, sat in the garden of the Trois Couronnes, looking about him, rather idly, at some of the graceful objects I have mentioned. (48)

In this opening scene, we get an impression of a narrator who, although his judgment may not always be accurate, is engaged in an earnest effort to give us the entire truth of his story, even down to the idle thoughts of his main character.

When I ask my students whether, judging by this opening scene, they can regard the narrator as reliable, most say they can. They point out that, not being part of the action, he has no interest in distorting the facts. On occasion a student might draw back, particularly when invited to look closely at those opening paragraphs, and then one or two students might consider the narrator with some of the suspicion that Winterbourne comes to direct at Daisy. My skeptical students often refer to the same passage, which introduces Winterbourne:

> He was some seven-and-twenty years of age; when his friends spoke of him, they usually said that he was at Geneva, "studying." When his enemies spoke of him they said—but, after all, he had no enemies; he was an extremely amiable fellow, and universally liked. What I should say is, simply, that when certain persons spoke of him they affirmed that the reason of his spending so much time at Geneva was that he was extremely devoted to a lady who lived there—a foreign lady—a person older than himself. (48)

What does this narrator know about Winterbourne, and why won't he reveal it frankly? In refusing to name what he only hints at, is he saving Winterbourne's reputation or damning it? Is Winterbourne's character at issue here? Might it prevent Winterbourne from seeing Daisy as she really is? If so, are readers justified in evaluating this unnamed narrator as well? In his penchant for gossip, does he reveal motives that might compromise his ability to tell the story accurately?

I ask my students, finally, whether accuracy is ever fully possible. If perception and judgment are based on interest and involvement, is it not likely that even the most self-effacing narrator will intrude briefly into the action? Why does James introduce this unnamed narrator, giving him a personality and some definite preferences, if narrators are simply a value-free means of telling a story? The question of Daisy's character—the question that looms at the center of this novella—depends entirely on the question of

Winterbourne's character, which we can know only through the presentation of this murkier (but undeniably interested) character, the narrator.

Still, readers generally like to know what a text means, and in this novella about Daisy's character, my students expect that they will find answers by the end. Is she innocent or corrupt? When Winterbourne wonders how Daisy feels about having been cut from her social circle, he cannot make up his mind whether she is incapable of perception and reflection or whether "she carried about in her elegant and irresponsible little organism a defiant, passionate, perfectly observant consciousness of the impression she produced" (106). The difficulty of deciding between these mutually exclusive points of view (and they are positions between which Winterbourne vacillates wildly) is the difficulty of all intersubjective relations: we can never really know what another person is feeling or thinking. Even on the last page of the novella, when we might expect the question of the eponymous heroine's character to be settled, we confront only more questions. Some time after Daisy's death, Winterbourne concludes that she "would have appreciated one's esteem" (116). The meaning of this conclusion is no clearer to Winterbourne's aunt, to whom he delivers it, than it is to James's readers: the aunt asks for clarification, and Winterbourne does not answer her. Would it matter if we knew for certain Winterbourne's final conclusion? Perhaps not, for James chose to end this novella with his maddeningly insinuating narrator, hinting at "the most contradictory accounts" of Winterbourne's future actions and motives (116).

I ask my students to read the entire novella before our first class meeting so that they can know the outcome and begin to feel frustration with the lack of plain answers before we begin our discussion. It does not take much debate over the ending before the class arrives at some consensus that we cannot know Daisy in any absolute sense; we cannot know whether she is essentially innocent or corrupt. James gives us no direct insight into her consciousness; we know her only by her actions and her words, which are, as Winterbourne discovers, mystifyingly inadequate. If we cannot answer the question of Daisy's character, though, we can pose other, perhaps more fruitful questions. I would hate for my students to conclude that the lesson of *Daisy Miller* is that there is no truth in the world or that any meaning we wish to impose on the text is equally acceptable because equally unverifiable. I focus our discussion, instead, on Winterbourne, about whom James does give ample information. For one thing, in his radical oscillations between admiration and contempt for Daisy, Winterbourne demonstrates to us that he is a man who enjoys plain answers; he wants to assign Daisy to a type:

> Poor Winterbourne was amused, perplexed, and decidedly charmed. He had never yet heard a young girl express herself in just this fashion; never, at least, save in cases where to say such things seemed a kind of demonstrative evidence of a certain laxity of deportment. . . . He felt that he had lived at Geneva so long that he had lost a good deal; he had

> become dishabituated to the American tone. Never, indeed, since he had grown old enough to appreciate things, had he encountered a young American girl of so pronounced a type as this. Certainly she was very charming; but how deucedly sociable! Was she simply a pretty girl from New York State—were they all like that, the pretty girls who had a good deal of gentlemen's society? Or was she also a designing, an audacious, an unscrupulous young person? (57)

Perhaps we do not condemn Winterbourne for wanting desperately to know how to evaluate Daisy, because we share that wish with him. But he gains the sympathy if not the admiration of most readers when he avoids reaching a conclusion about Daisy, when he remains susceptible to being "amused, perplexed, and decidedly charmed"—when he acknowledges, that is, that he does not know.

Unfortunately for Winterbourne, our sympathy for him is short-lived: he is also a man who likes to be right, and in his willingness to act on this preference he loses his reader's regard. The passage quoted above ends when Winterbourne refuses to maintain his perplexity, instead deciding the matter by consigning Daisy to a type, the "pretty American flirt":

> He had never, as yet, had any relations with young ladies of this category. He had known, here in Europe, two or three women—persons older than Miss Daisy Miller, and provided, for respectability's sake, with husbands—who were great coquettes—dangerous, terrible women, with whom one's relations were liable to take a serious turn. But this young girl was not a coquette in that sense; she was very unsophisticated; she was only a pretty American flirt. Winterbourne was almost grateful for having found the formula that applied to Miss Daisy Miller. He leaned back in his seat. . . . (57–58)

His body language tells all: imagining he has found a plain answer, he loses interest and reclines as if to proclaim his satisfaction. And he reaffirms this conclusion repeatedly: when he decides "that [Daisy] had no more surprises for him" (101) and when, at the climactic scene at the Colosseum, he concludes "with a sort of relief" that Daisy is "easy to read," a woman "whom a gentleman need no longer be at pains to respect" (111).

However helpless we may be to ascertain Daisy's true character, James's tale prompts us to reach an opinion about the character of Winterbourne. He does not like the sensation of bewilderment, wanting comfortable conclusions. He would rather draw a hasty and perhaps incorrect conclusion about Daisy than be charmed, mystified, and taken off guard by her. He wants above all to enjoy the confidence that he is right, even if he must oversimplify his evidence to do so. Daisy may be a flirt, she may be immodest, and she may not inspire the admiration of her readers—these are all points my students feel compelled to discuss, and they are right to, even if they cannot reach any certain conclusion. After reflecting on Winterbourne's character, however, they nearly always decide that he is too smug to be attractive.

I ask my students to imagine a world that holds no surprises. Would a world where everything is thoroughly knowable interest us? What would it mean for the objects of our observation if we were always sure that we understood them through and through? How engaging would either the seeing subject or this phenomenal world be if mystery were not a regular part of life, if existence were transparent? For James, as Paul Armstrong has demonstrated (*Challenge*), the world is valuable only when it is bewildering.

Granting that we are not all alike in this regard, I try to put James's attraction to mystery in a larger intellectual context, one that reaches beyond his temperament. The moderns confronted and represented a world that had, for better or worse, lost its clarity. No longer confident that they could know all, they began to understand reality as subjective, contingent, and liable to dramatic changes. A pessimist might conclude, like the speaker of T. S. Eliot's *Wasteland*, that we "can connect / Nothing with nothing. / The broken fingernails of dirty hands. / My people humble people who expect / Nothing" (*Complete Poems* 46). Another sensibility might see the human predicament differently. The speaker of Wallace Stevens's "The Snow Man" finds it nearly impossible to regard the neutral landscape and see "the nothing that is not there"—to avoid projecting one's affect onto the world one beholds (line 15). In proportion as we distort the neutral reality that we observe, we prove ourselves to be living, sentient beings. Only a person with "a mind of winter" could do otherwise (line 1).

Of course, to acknowledge the influence of affect and experience on interpretation is not to accept all beliefs as equally true. Some versions of reality may in fact be more useful—or less dangerous—than others. William James suggested that a healthy tentativeness about our conclusions might prevent us from enforcing our views of the world when the consequences of doing so are clearly destructive:

> The "absolutely" true, meaning what no farther experience will ever alter, is that ideal vanishing-point towards which we imagine that all our temporary truths will some day converge. Meanwhile we have to live to-day by what truth we can get to-day, and be ready to-morrow to call it falsehood. (*Pragmatism* 100)

Reading *Daisy Miller* in the context of the pragmatist's response to modern uncertainty, my students eventually turn their attention from the question of Daisy's meaning in order to consider Winterbourne's method of judgment. They need not conclude, as I think both Jameses did, that complacent people are the greatest villains, but I do wish them to evaluate Winterbourne's ethical judgments. William James demonstrated the pragmatic method by asking what difference it would "practically make to any one if this notion rather than that notion were true?" (26). In this spirit, we might ask what difference it makes when one sees the world as Winterbourne does.

The question of judgment is vitally important as well in Henry James's later tale, *The Turn of the Screw*. In this apparent ghost story, where the consequences of what a thing means are undoubtedly much greater, James gives us no plainer answer than in his earlier tale. Here he dramatizes how the very attempt to decide unequivocally what a thing means leads to violence. Winterbourne's need to imagine Daisy as a clearly legible type reappears as the governess's willingness to endanger her charges in order to prove the truth of her suspicion. Though she claims to ache for "proof" that Miles is a guilty child (96), we see that she will accept the most questionable forms of evidence. Taking the "silence" of her charges to be "systematic," she charges that "*Never*, by a slip of the tongue, have they so much as alluded to either of their old friends" (76). Negative proofs assume the authority of positive proofs, because the governess wishes to be confirmed in her suspicion—though readers should be careful of accepting her account of the goings-on at Bly. More alarming, the more ambiguous the signs around her become, the more insistently she interprets these signs—particularly silences and empty spaces—as incontrovertible evidence of the children's corruption: "the element of the unnamed and untouched became, between us, greater than any other" (78). When she refers to the boat that Flora has taken to the far end of a pond, she might as well be referring to larger signs: "Our not seeing it," she insists, "is the strongest of proofs" (99).

Even before we understand the consequences of the question, before we understand that the death of Miles raises the stakes of the question, readers of this tale want to know whether the ghosts are real or only the hysterical imaginings of a sheltered governess. Here we are reminded of Winterbourne's inability to decide what Daisy represents: whether she is an American innocent or a wicked girl. Critics of *The Turn of the Screw* have debated the authenticity of the ghosts since the novella was first published, and once again there seems to be no plain answer. As anyone who has taught this text already knows, students often point to evidence that supports the claims that the ghosts are real (how else could the governess so accurately describe Quint at their first encounter?) or the claim that they are not (nobody else sees what the governess sees). James would have been amused by this ongoing critical debate, for he characterized the novella in his 1908 preface as "pure romance" (Preface to *Turn* [Beidler (2nd ed.)] 184). Since, according to Nathaniel Hawthorne, James's great predecessor, romance is the "neutral territory . . . between the real world and fairy-land, where the Actual and the Imaginary may meet, and each imbue itself with the nature of the other" (36), the question of whether the ghosts are real or delusional seems beside the point and irresolvable in any case.

In the context of our discussion, moreover, the debate only replicates the struggles over truth that James dramatizes in *Daisy Miller* and again, to more sinister effect, in *The Turn of the Screw*, where the governess's determination to get to the truth ends tragically for her charges.

I allow my students time to argue over the evidence and try to determine the answer to what seems to them the central question. After they discover that, once again, there is no "plain answer" to this absorbing question, I once again turn the discussion. If we cannot know whether the ghosts are real, can we begin to ask about the process whereby we try to make such a judgment? What does it mean to judge, and are some methods of judging more acceptable than others? As in *Daisy Miller*, this question takes us to the character of the person who constitutes our primary source of information.

As Winterbourne, whose conclusions we depend on for our interpretation of his story, is introduced by the narrator, the governess is introduced to us by two interested parties: Douglas, the man who was in love with her, and the unnamed narrator, who clearly feels some connection to Douglas. From Douglas we get a character reference: the governess was an "agreeable woman," "worthy of any [position] whatever" (24). But if we trust this reference at the beginning of the tale, we are likely to rethink our confidence by the end, when the death of Miles signals the consequence of the governess's judgment.

As we discuss truth and William James's belief that it must remain provisional, I find that the governess's near confession in the final scene is pivotal to our conclusions about her narrative. As the governess is badgering Miles for a confession, she experiences her first sensation of uncertainty:

> I seemed to float not into clearness, but into a darker obscure, and within a minute there had come to me out of my very pity the appalling alarm of his being perhaps innocent. It was for the instant confounding and bottomless, for if he *were* innocent what then on earth was I? Paralysed, while it lasted, by the mere brush of the question, I let him go a little. (119)

Her noble doubt is only momentary; unable to bear the implications of her mistake, she insists on her reading, as if the act of forcing it on Miles will make it true. When Peter Quint reappears to her and the "bewildered" Miles "glar[es] vainly over the place and miss[es] wholly . . . the wide overwhelming presence," she admits to being "so determined to have all my proof that I flashed into ice to challenge him." The result, as we know, is "the loss I was so proud of" (120), the disappearance of Quint but also, inevitably, the death of Miles. Shoshana Felman contends that "by the very act of forcing her suspect to confess," the governess commits the crime she has been investigating: "it is nothing other than the very process of detection which constitutes the crime" ("Grasp" 205). For James, we are never more in danger than when we become confident that we know what a thing means.

Unlike *Daisy Miller, The Turn of the Screw* is linguistically dense and elusive. Students want to know what really happened at the end of the novella: Is Miles in fact dead? Does he die of fear, of suffocation? Does Peter Quint kill him, or does the governess? And are we to read his death as a triumph over evil (his soul is now safe, according to the governess) or as a tragedy (he died because she was deranged)? I encourage my students not to feel inadequate as readers simply because they cannot discern a clear meaning. Rather, they should consider why the governess fails to depict this final scene plainly. In other words, they should look for meaning in the text's very obscurity. What motives might she have for using elusive language here and throughout her tale? The larger rhetorical question connects this novella to a wider context of modern writers: if the tale dramatizes the dangerous effects of certainty, why should its author depict the tale in a language that makes things clear? If the novella pits itself (again, in the words of William James) "against dogma, artificiality, and the pretence of finality in truth" (*Pragmatism* 28), why might an emphatic and deceptively lucid prose not suffice?

When I teach Henry James or modernism, I use one or both of these texts, one relatively lucid and the other dense and obscure, to discuss James's modernity. *Daisy Miller* is an excellent way of introducing students to James, because, although it is much easier to read than stories written in James's later style, all his later modernist preoccupations—particularly with truth, point of view, and consciousness—can be found there. William James, worrying in 1907 over the imperialist consequences of moral and epistemological certainty, argued in *Pragmatism*, "The world is full of partial stories that run parallel to one another, beginning and ending at odd times. They mutually interlace and interfere at points, but we can not unify them completely in our minds" (67). William James did not wish to evade the spectacular collisions enacted by contradictory truths, but he did acknowledge that "the greatest enemy of any one of our truths may be the rest of our truths" (38). The same can be said for his brother the novelist. In ethical, narrative, and epistemological terms, both *Daisy Miller* and *The Turn of the Screw* demonstrate how value and meaning came to be determined, for modernists generally and for Henry James in particular, not absolutely, as they were in previous generations, but relationally. The discovery of multiple truths makes for the impossibility of a plain answer, but it also makes the world richer. This discovery means—alas for the overworked student!—that one cannot meaningfully skim a text; indeed, even a single reading proves insufficient. James's fiction consistently demonstrates Wayne Booth's insight: "First readings are almost always inadequate. Every truth proclaimed by any human being is sure to be at best fragmentary, correctable by further truth to be discovered on down the road" ("He Began" 250). The challenge for teachers of James is turning the difficulties of reading him into the pleasures of indeterminacy.

The Dialogism of Modern Women: A New-Historicist Pedagogical Approach to *Daisy Miller*

Sean Palmer

Those who embrace a new-historicist approach to teaching literature have always been confronted with the practical difficulties of bringing history into the classroom. The preeminent challenge has been to cope with a lack of historical awareness among students; quite often instructors become overburdened by having to convey both history and literature through what students see as a less effective lecture format (Thomas 509). Such a format detracts from the benefits of a collaborative pedagogy; students may feel unable to participate in informed classroom discussions without relying exclusively on the instructor's historical knowledge. In New Critical or reader-response approaches to teaching literature, they feel empowered, being encouraged to construct interpretations of literary texts based on discovering correlations between fictional characters and their own personal experiences. But in a historicist approach based on the lecture format, students are prompted to construct interrelations between character and context—the basis of historical analysis—by relying on the instructor's presentation and interpretation of the events, people, and language that comprise the historical context of the work. In short, the professor's construction of context becomes totalizing, determining in large part how students interpret. The pleasure and sense of independence that they feel when they analyze literary texts by relating to literature on a personal level may be superseded by emotionless, historical strictures imposed upon them from on high.

There are, of course, strategies for circumventing this use of historical context, of what the literary critic Mikhail Bakhtin would invariably refer to as a monologic context. Such strategies promote interpretive flexibility or empower students to devise multiple interpretations of a particular work of literature, as Dorothy Kehler suggests in "Teaching *Romeo and Juliet* Historically" (84). As an instructor who shares Kehler's objective of raising student awareness of the possibility of plural interpretations of a literary text through the use of history, I introduce here a new-historicist pedagogical approach that moves away from treating context as monologic.

By offering an alternative to the lecture format, I strive to get students involved in the process of creating historical contexts through the use of a course pack composed of primary sources whose language and themes can be interpreted in more than one way. My role in this approach is to facilitate the historical discoveries of the students, while they construct context and establish correlations between historical documents and the work of fiction under analysis—in this case, Henry James's *Daisy Miller*.

Material should be selected for the course pack for *Daisy Miller* in a way that does not compromise the historical integrity of the work. Establishing correlations between the plight of American women during the 1990s and James's treatment of Daisy Miller, for example, would certainly provoke lively classroom discussion about issues of sexual discrimination but would keep students from engaging in depth with women's social repression of the 1870s and perceiving the subtle and unique ways that the novella challenges it. Jerome McGann suggests that the relation between literary text and historical context begins with establishing a correlation between a work's publication date and an event of the same historical juncture—a war, for example (191). Since we are, after all, concerned here with exploring social conventions that are manipulated rhetorically to fulfill a political agenda over time and not with an event that occurs at one point in time, we cannot achieve in the selection of documents for our course pack and in our analysis of *Daisy Miller* the kind of precision associated with McGann's historicist approach. Nevertheless, following McGann's emphasis on the importance of examining the context of the reception history of a work, we can discover a variety of sources for the signifiers that mark these conventions, enabling us to formulate the selection criteria for the course pack.

Daisy Miller's reception history includes James's response to a famous female journalist and woman of letters, Eliza Linton. In 1878, Linton wrote James, expressing her determination to learn the intention behind his portrayal of Daisy Miller: "Did you mean us to understand that Daisy went on in her mad way with Giovanelli just in defiance of public opinion, urged thereto by the opposition made and the talk she excited?" (qtd. in Van Thal 123). James responded to Linton by denying any desire to promote scandal: "In this sense I fear I must declare that she was not defiant, in the sense you mean." He continued to placate Linton by suggesting that Daisy Miller was not in the least aggressive but rather "an unsuspecting creature being sacrificed as it were to a social rumpus" (124, 125).

This exchange alerts us to a historical event in which James participated and that resonated throughout the 1870s, when *Daisy Miller* was conceived and written: the "girl of the period" controversy. In 1868, Linton launched a comprehensive critique in the form of articles appearing in the *Saturday Review*. In "The Girl of the Period," she pointed out that young women were conducting themselves in ways that challenged Victorian modesty and propriety; their conduct undermined the notion that men and women were assigned separate spheres of influence based on gender difference. Nancy Fix Anderson observes:

> Deliberate or not (and it probably was), [Linton's] article certainly did create an earthquake of outraged public reaction. Victorian patriarchs, seeking to protect their women not only from useful employment and personal responsibility but also verbal attacks, were incensed by the

> criticism. So were women's rights advocates, who resented the exaggerations and unfair implications of the caricature. (121)

The reaction shows the extent to which constructions of women in print culture at this time engaged directly with the political agendas of women's rights advocates and their opponents. James responded to this controversy in a review article entitled "Modern Women" (appearing in the *Nation* in 1868) by defending the women that Linton had caricatured (23).

This review article of 1868 cannot, of course, be directly tied to *Daisy Miller*—there is no biographical evidence to suggest that James wished to continue the "girl of the period" debate through his fiction—but the controversy, lasting well into the 1880s, provides us with the opportunity to choose documents for the course pack from the period of the controversy and from the years immediately preceding the publication of *Daisy Miller* (Helsinger, Sheets, and Veeder 181). Anderson, for example, argues that Linton continued to write about the same issues anonymously throughout the 1870s (124). Merle Bevington says that the controversy was so intense that it enabled Linton to release her collection of essays in 1883, under the title *"The Girl of the Period" and Other Social Essays* (112). Traces of the controversy also appeared in articles written by authors and journalists with whom both Linton and James were acquainted. Justin McCarthy was one writer who appropriated and challenged many of the terms of Linton's earlier constructions of the modern woman (e.g., in his "American Women and English Women," appearing in 1870). Indeed, immediately following *Daisy Miller*'s publication, James acknowledged McCarthy in a letter to Thomas Perry as a "great Journalist" (Edel, *Henry James: Letters* 2: 275). James reviewed Albert Rhodes's *The French at Home* in 1875 ("Albert Rhodes"), the same year that Rhodes published "Shall the American Girl Be Chaperoned?"

Since my objective in teaching *Daisy Miller* is to acquaint students with the possibilities of interpreting its female characters through a historical context, a context that offers many constructions of the modern woman, articles written by Linton, McCarthy, and Rhodes should be selected, on Bakhtin's principle of dialogism. When such articles are assembled to form a course pack, they should contain words and signifiers that reveal the extent to which they are, as Bakhtin would have it, "entangled, shot through with shared thoughts, points of view, alien value judgments and accents" that cannot ultimately be stabilized (276). The articles that constitute the course pack are, therefore, selected on the basis of the extent to which they deploy and redeploy shared signifiers and shared words that are used to present differing, sometimes contradictory, constructions of the modern woman. What makes Linton's work particularly appropriate for this course pack is not only that she was a prolific author of periodical articles but also, as we shall see, that her method of argumentation was often contradictory (Helsinger, Sheets, and Veeder 104).

While the selection relies on the instructor's ability to identify the contradictory uses of signifiers in the primary historical material, it also depends on themes supported by equivalent signifiers in the novel. Such signifiers and themes will enable students to establish multiple correlations between the historical documents and the actions, dialogue, and points of view of the characters of *Daisy Miller*. The themes that serve as an organizing principle in my course pack are the modern woman and fashion, the modern woman and slang, mother-daughter relations and the modern woman, and the modern woman as American girl. Other themes can be found in Linton's vast oeuvre as it appeared in the *Saturday Review*. Citing the selections of the course pack as they concern these themes, I will attempt to demonstrate how students can explore the possibilities of history that lead to discovering multiple interpretations of the novel based on their analyses of character in *Daisy Miller*.

Linton's "The Girl of the Period" (1868); two anonymous articles but arguably written by Linton, entitled "Woman and the World" (1868) and "The Exclusiveness of Women" (1870); and Justin McCarthy's "American Women and English Women" enable students to create a historical context concerning women's rights and fashion that, in turn, allows them to produce readings of Daisy Miller, Mrs. Walker, Mrs. Costello, and Winterbourne that both support and refute women's rights. "Girl of the Period" defines women's fashion as an expression of feminine power on the level of personal freedom; Linton associates provocative dress not with selflessness and modesty but with selfishness in a woman "whose sole idea of life is plenty of fun and luxury." This article can be regarded as supporting women's repression by repudiating women's right to choose what they wear in public, rejecting their "extravagance of fashion" (340). An extension of this position is offered in "The Exclusiveness of Women," where the modern woman's selfishness is both an economically destructive expression of power and a bid for personal control over her husband: "There is scarcely a husband of the good and domestic kind who does not suffer under the exclusiveness of his wife, and whose life is not impoverished by her determination to be his sole source of pleasure and interest" (242). While these two constructions of the modern woman and fashion argue that self-determination in dress must be taken from women, there are those who endorse extravagant fashion and its significance for women's emancipation. "Woman and the World" is critical of women's extravagance of dress but acknowledges their right to self-determination, attacking men or husbands who pressure women to dress extravagantly:

> What woman owns that what she really does is to mould herself as much on the monster's model as she can. According to her own account, she puts nature's picture of herself into the hands of this imbecile, invites him to blur it as he will, and lets him write under the daub "Ego feci." . . . As he refuses to be attracted by modesty of dress and manner, she apes the dress and manner of the demi-monde. His indolence, his triviality, his worldliness become her own. (479)

Men are "monsters," "imbeciles" who create repressive social conventions that force women to dress extravagantly. Extravagant dress is exposed as signifying an expression of men's power over women, an exposé that seems aimed at raising the political consciousness of women who dress for men. Women are encouraged to recognize how they are being manipulated to behave in a way that testifies to their lack of self-autonomy.

McCarthy sees extravagant fashion as signifying social progress and the nascent social emancipation of women, of which he clearly approves. Contrasting the "gorgeous colouring and costly dressing" that characterize the dress of the American woman with the conservative drab of English women, he notes that "there is almost everywhere more vividness and variety of tone in the character of the former than of the latter. The latter may symbolize Law, the former Liberty" (25).

Using fashion to establish a correlation between political context and literary text, students will find that Mrs. Costello's pointing out to Winterbourne that Daisy Miller dresses extravagantly may indicate a connection between James's text and "The Girl of the Period" and "The Exclusiveness of Women." Of the Millers, Mrs. Costello begins by commenting that "[t]hey are very common. . . . They are the sort of Americans that one does one's duty by not—not accepting." She reinforces this judgment by noting with sarcasm Daisy's tendency to overdress: "She has that charming look that they all have . . . I can't think where they pick it up; and she dresses in perfection—no, you don't know how well she dresses. I can't think where they get their taste" (62). For both Linton and Mrs. Costello, dress becomes a means for preserving feminine respectability and servility.

Mrs. Costello's character as constructed from Winterbourne's point of view also enables us to establish a correlation between "The Exclusiveness of Women" and James's text. Winterbourne offers a critique of Mrs. Costello: "She admitted that she was very exclusive; but, if he were acquainted with New York, he would see that one had to be" (62). The use of "exclusive" here suggests a correlation with "The Exclusiveness of Women." Also, in observing that Mrs. Costello is preoccupied with her status as a widow, we cannot help but wonder whether she was responsible for her husband's death, whether her selfishness and tireless pursuit of wealth created the stress that led to his demise. Winterbourne's comment that Mrs. Costello's description of the respectable social circles of New York as hierarchical is "oppressively striking" (62) suggests that he perceives her, in endorsing such a society, as equally oppressive, domineering, and exclusive. Yet his observations of her exclusiveness do not prove a correlation between James's text and the political strategy of "The Exclusiveness of Women," for Daisy herself strives to emulate what would oppress her; she too wishes to become exclusive.

Still, Winterbourne's impression of Daisy evokes both Linton's contradictory approach to women's rights, as indicated in "Woman and the World," and McCarthy's article. It is, after all, Daisy's dress that captivates Winterbourne, that draws him to her and in part sustains his loyalty in the face of the harsh criticisms launched by Mrs. Walker and Mrs. Costello. In Winterbourne's first impression of Daisy, "[s]he was dressed in white muslin, with a hundred frills and flounces, and knots of pale-coloured ribbon. She was bare-headed; but she balanced in her hand a large parasol, with a deep border of embroidery; and she was striking, admirably pretty" (51). The frills and flounces suggest to us that she is dressed immodestly, provocatively, and exclusively, presenting an effrontery of fashion—and Winterbourne embraces her for doing so. His approval of her display evokes the woman, according to Linton, who "mould[s] herself" to "the monster's model." Students then see how a text, through this example of signifiers associated with fashion, can accommodate many political strategies without promoting one in particular. Indeed, Winterbourne's approval of Daisy can be regarded as an endorsement of McCarthy's celebration of the "liberty" of the American woman: her emancipation through dress from the social law that McCarthy points out is a characteristic of the drabness of Englishwomen.

Selecting Linton's "The Girl of the Period," "The Tyranny of Mothers," "The Modern Mother," and Rhodes's "Shall the American Girl Be Chaperoned?" for the purpose of constructing a context for a discussion of mother-daughter relations and the modern woman enables students to investigate the causes of the immodest behavior associated with the modern woman, causes that reveal the political biases of the commentators in their support for or repudiation of women's self-determination in society. The mother-daughter relationship is the central contradictory signifier in assembling these documents, since it was regarded by these commentators as a means of preventing or perpetuating the construction of the modern woman as immodest or free. Mothers were expected to protect their daughters from the aggressive advances of unsuitable men and to prevent their daughters from pursuing men at social functions by chaperoning or escorting them. In these four articles, mothers are criticized for being both too lenient and too strict with their daughters, thereby promoting their freedom and repression simultaneously. At once endorsing and refuting the immodesty associated with the modern woman, these articles allow students to identify a plurality of motivations for Daisy's immodest behavior as they make correlations between the articles and Daisy's relationship with her mother.

"The Girl of the Period" does not explore the mother's role in the daughter's immodesty; rather, Linton blames the daughter exclusively for embracing the immorality of modern society. Here, mothers become victims of their daughters:

> It was all very well in old-fashioned times, when fathers and mothers had some authority and were treated with respect, to be tutored and made to obey, but [the daughter] is far too fast and flourishing to be stopped in mid-career by these slow old morals. (340)

"The Modern Mother" offers the kind of political reversal for which Linton was notorious; shying away from attacking the daughter, this article promotes the mother's active surveillance of her daughter to protect her daughter's chaste reputation by foiling her efforts to behave flirtatiously:

> Mamma, occupied in her own well-seasoned coquetries, or absorbed in the chances of her deep "finesse" winning the trick, lets the girls take care of themselves, and would think it an intolerable impertinence should a friend hint to her that her place of chaperon included vigilant personal guardianship, and that she would do better to keep her daughters in her own charge than leave them to themselves. (109)

A stinging indictment of the daughter is superseded by an equally harsh condemnation of the mother's failure to take social responsibility for her daughter's moral education. Ineffective chaperoning will leave girls, according to this writer, to "parade the streets, dressed in the most startling and meretricious costumes of the period" (109).

"The Tyranny of Mothers" also criticizes mothers—but this time for being too repressive in their surveillance. Of particular note here is the discussion of the timid mother; her tyranny is the "greatest trial to young creatures full of life and energy" (211). The method of surveillance undertaken by her is to instill in the daughter an overpowering fear of independence, of venturing out unescorted; admonishing the daughter not to appear in public lest she contract smallpox is one such tactic of control.

A similar political strategy, though a contradictory one, appears in Rhodes's article. He says that "a chaperone, however, naive she may be, is better than none at all to guard even a wicked woman" but rests his position on the assumption that American men are so predisposed to protect American women, that they themselves often act as effective chaperones:

> It has been said that our young men can safely be trusted not to take advantage of long tête-à-tête with young women to do anything they would not do in the presence of mothers; but it is better not to have too much confidence in masculine rectitude under such circumstances. (453)

Offering such advice, Rhodes appears concerned to protect young American women, who suffer from a "boldness of innocence" and are naive about the objectives of the rake. He thereby contradicts his tepid warning against American men. Employing an anecdote of the typical American girl's inappropriate behavior at a party, he describes what would be avoided with an effective chaperone:

> In half an hour [the young woman] is probably flirting with one of them in an obscure corner of the stairway, or under the folds of a window

> curtain, knowing nothing of him except his name. He may have many vices, and a reputation that would not for a moment bear examination. (457)

Students are now provided with a variety of contextually based motivations they can assign to Daisy for her conduct, but these motivations do not lead to a stable and final interpretation of the text. While the dialogue and descriptions of flat characters establish the correlations between James's text and these documents, the dominant and changing point of view of Winterbourne preserves the work's interpretive flexibility.

Daisy's description of her mother lets students establish a correlation between Mrs. Miller and the timid mother presented in "The Tyranny of Mothers." Immediately before Daisy and Winterbourne's visit to the Château de Chillon, Daisy explains her mother's "slow and wavering" approach (67) to meet them:

> It isn't for me; it's for you—that is, it's for *her*. Well; I don't know who it's for! But mother doesn't like any of my gentlemen friends. She's right down timid. She always makes a fuss if I introduce a gentleman. But I *do* introduce them—almost always. If I didn't introduce my gentlemen friends to my mother . . . I shouldn't think I was natural. (68)

The key signifier here is "timid," an adjective foregrounded in "The Tyranny of Mothers" to describe a particularly sinister form of repressing young women. Another element of this article, the attempt to control the girl of the period through the use of medical threats, is evoked later in the story when Mrs. Miller articulates her commitment to Dr. Davis, whom she hails as a preeminent medical authority. She deploys that authority to keep Daisy from walking the streets unchaperoned: "You'll get the fever as sure as you live. Remember what Dr Davis told you!" (85). The above description of Mrs. Miller from Daisy's point of view, however, can also be seen as an appropriation of the mother's voice, testifying to Daisy's boldness as both Linton's girl of the period and the American girl, free-spirited and highly mobile, as endorsed by McCarthy. Indeed, the girl of the period is echoed in Daisy's unabashed commitment to violating the principles of social convention she outlines for us here and to which, she stresses, her mother clings. Daisy will not allow her mother to protect her or chaperone her.

The assumptions of "The Tyranny of Mothers" and of Rhodes's position on chaperoning the American girl seem supported by Winterbourne's changing demeanor toward Daisy. Rather than go back to the hotel with her mother, Daisy speaks briefly with Mrs. Walker and receives permission to bring Giovanelli to the party; she then meets him unescorted. Consistent with Rhodes's contradictory belief that the mother should chaperone the daughter but that many American men can assume this responsibility, Winterbourne attempts to protect her respectability forcibly: "Pray understand, then . . . that I intend to remain with you." He receives a harsh reprimand from the bold, aggressive American girl: "I have never allowed a gentleman to dictate to me, or to interfere with anything I do" (88). Daisy's desire to challenge Winterbourne's effort to protect her subverts the correlation between James's text and Rhodes's political strategy, for it undermines the construction of Winterbourne as effective chaperone. That construction is undermined also by the ambiguity of his objectives: we cannot say for certain whether he is trying to protect Daisy or to watch over her so as to keep her for himself.

Mrs. Walker's relationship with Daisy and Winterbourne is also evocative of Linton's "The Modern Mother." Mrs. Walker, in response to Mrs. Miller's negligent conduct as chaperone in failing to accompany Daisy forcefully back to the hotel, comments to Winterbourne:

> She's very crazy! . . . Did you ever see anything so imbecile as her mother? After you had all left me, just now, I could not sit still for thinking of it. It seemed too pitiful, not even to attempt to save her. I ordered the carriage and put on my bonnet, and came here as quickly as possible. Thank heaven I have found you! (91)

Mrs. Walker is highlighting Mrs. Miller's unwillingness to subject Daisy to the moral instruction and supervision associated with the convention of chaperoning. Yet this reading cannot be ultimately sustained, as Mrs. Walker's criticism of Daisy and her mother during Mrs. Walker's attempt to force Daisy into the carriage away from Giovanelli is answered rather coldly by Winterbourne: "I suspect, Mrs Walker, that you and I have lived too long at Geneva!" (94). Winterbourne can be seen as supporting Daisy as the liberated modern American woman here in his indictment, expressed in geographic terms, of Mrs. Walker's and his commitment to European social conventions.

Another provocative signifier that leads students to arrive at a variety of interpretations of Daisy's character through Winterbourne's construction of her is that of the American girl. With Linton's "Women's Weapons" and "The Wild Women" and McCarthy's article, the instructor can provide them with many interpretive options. In "The Wild Women," Linton argues against women's participation in politics, suggesting that the women of New York, the geographic location associated with Daisy Miller's character, produced

> inarticulate howls and claims for equality which have only tried by experience to show us what female capacities for work are, so we may now add that the more we know of female debates, and female conventions, and female meetings, the more we see that they are only an accidental form in which the one universal feminine temper displays itself. (14)

The universal temper characterizing the wild women of America is associated with the "vanity, scandal, immorality and bickering of [their] tea-tables" (14).

Linton's position appears to have been reversed in "Women's Weapons," for instance, when it is suggested that American women should be feared:

> The female politicians in America have shown that they can beat their best male competitors with their own tools [. . . that] if there were any arms special or restricted to woman, [this restriction] will evidently henceforth be [an] anachronism. (441)

This position is shared by McCarthy when he endorses the exploration of the great question "being put to proof" in America, "whether woman may be trusted to follow her own impulses, obey her own principles, walk her own way in the social world." He suggests that "American women have used their freedom so wisely and well, that their far off sisters are likely to become more and more captivated and encouraged by example" (33). The boldness of the American girl, Daisy's immodesty, and her wish to confront social conventions become symbols of both her political inefficacy and her empowerment.

Another theme that can be used to explore the relation between political context and literary text is the modern woman's use of slang, a signifier foregrounded to achieve opposite political effects in Linton's "The Girl of the Period" and McCarthy's "American Women and English Women." In Linton's article, the use of slang indicates a social rebelliousness in young women that must be quashed if they are to marry:

> All men whose opinion is worth having prefer the simple and genuine girl of the past, with her tender little ways and pretty bashful modesties, to this loud and rampant modernization, with her false red hair and painted skin, talking slang as glibly as a man, and by preference leading the conversation to doubtful subjects. (340)

McCarthy, by contrast, sees slang as an endorsement of women's social freedom. He contends that he "would rather hear an English woman break into a little word of forcible slang, as such women will do occasionally, than hear her spoil our pure and noble Saxon speech." Spoiling such speech for McCarthy means "over-refining" language through the use of euphemism and consequently supporting a "superficial gentility" (30).

Daisy's use of slang through the novella, coupled with Winterbourne's oscillating point of view concerning her character, enables students to read James's text from the positions of both Linton and McCarthy. In her discussion with Winterbourne over Randolph's lack of interest in visiting castles, Daisy does not use the proper singular form of the verb *to do*: "He says he don't care much about old castles" (59). In another example, she assesses her brother's refusal to obey her mother, pointing out to Winterbourne that Randolph is "real tiresome" rather than "really tiresome" (69). Her propensity to use adjectives where adverbs are appropriate signifies her association with two opposing political strategies: Linton's critique of the modern woman for violating linguistic manifestations of social control or convention and McCarthy's celebration of modern women using slang as a means of social resistance. Winterbourne's refusal to reproach Daisy for this use of slang, his silence, and the absence of a domineering point of view here preserve the dialogic nature of the text.

Silence also alerts students to an alternative focus for analysis: the subtle ways in which historical context can be evoked in a literary text. Thus, this pedagogical method emphasizes interpretive flexibility and shows that the historicist approach does not stifle creativity but rather encourages it.

a position. Examining the excerpts from Maria Edgeworth's book from 1798, *Practical Education* (Edgeworth and Edgeworth), we find that Edgeworth warns parents about the dangers of allowing their children too much proximity to servants:

> The language and manners, the awkward and vulgar tricks which children learn in the society of servants, are immediately perceived, and disgust and shock well-bred parents. . . . [T]he habits of cunning, falsehood, envy, which lurk in the temper, are not instantly visible to strangers, they do not appear the moment children are reviewed by parents; they may remain for years without notice or without cure.
>
> (Edgeworth 124)

Edgeworth goes on to note with approval that the governess, far from being regarded as a servant, had come to be treated more as a "friend and companion of the family" (126). However, she worries about those parents who wish to make the governess their constant companion. "If a governess attends the card table," asks Edgeworth, "and the assembly room; if she is to visit, and be visited, what is to become of her pupils in her absence? They must be left to the care of the servants" (126–27).

I ask my students to consider how this stern admonition against leaving children in the servants' care presents a thorny problem for James's governess, who might be expected to have some familiarity with Edgeworth's book since it was frequently reprinted in the nineteenth century. They note first that Edgeworth warmly welcomes the governess into the family as an equal; but, given that the governess must function as both educator and a sort of parent, she has no choice but to leave the children in the care of servants at times. The line that Edgeworth draws between servants and governesses does not escape students: while they approve of her egalitarian view of governesses, they are taken aback by the sharpness of her tone regarding servants. They may point to Douglas's description of the servants at Bly as "the best people [the master] could find to look after [the children]" (27). A careful reading of Douglas's prologue reveals his emphasis on the respectability of the servants, so much so that one of his listeners, hearing that the previous governess died, wonders how she met her end and asks, sarcastically, if the death was "[o]f so much respectability?" (28). The governess's problem is not really whether to leave the children with the servants; it is how to determine the servants' respectability. This question is the crux of the matter as she learns more and more about Peter Quint and his influence. The students and I spend some time identifying passages in the novella that demonstrate the governess's evolving attitude toward the servants, especially toward Mrs. Grose, as well as her conception of Quint. Her belief that Quint seduced Jessel and corrupted the children shows the bourgeois distrust of servants that Edgeworth articulates, yet her reliance on Mrs. Grose as a "counselor," "colleague," and

"The Hideous Obscure": Historical Backgroun of *The Turn of the Screw*

Kimberly C. Reed

When I teach *The Turn of the Screw* in an upper-division English class, usually one on Victorian literature, I often find that my students are not well equipped to understand the historical situation of the governess in nineteenth-century Britain, nor do they recognize the cultural background of ghostly narratives. Directing their attention to various contextual documents about governesses in mid-nineteenth-century Britain enriches our discussion of the literary text by awakening students' interest in the historical situation of women in general and in educated single women—such as governesses—in particular. In addition, their growing awareness of the liminality of the governess's position in the family and in society provides a natural springboard for considering the function of the ghost story in Victorian fiction, for they come to realize that both governesses and ghosts were often condemned to what James's governess calls "the hideous obscure" (112).

The contextual documents provided in the Bedford edition of *The Turn of the Screw* (2nd ed.) supply students with a variety of selections about Victorian governesses and ghost stories. I assign the "Cultural Documents and Illustrations" section of the Bedford to be read before the students start the novella itself. I follow Wayne Booth and others in categorizing reactions to this novella as "straight," "ironic," and "mazed" (Booth, "He Began" 244, 246, 248), and my goal in teaching this text is to lead my students through those categories in that order. Therefore I very much want the students who are encountering *The Turn of the Screw* for the first time to read it at first as a straightforward ghost story (244). Only after they have read the historical documents and the novella (and after we have had the sorts of discussions described below) do I assign the selected critical essays included in the Bedford edition as a way of showing them how their initial reading can be repeatedly destabilized. My purpose in having students study these historical documents is twofold: to help them develop an appreciation both for the difficult situation of the governess and for the form of the Victorian ghostly narrative and to predispose them to read the novella as a ghost story. In this essay, I focus on some issues raised in these documents that the literary text articulates, echoes, or complicates. I wish only to suggest points of discussion rather than detail the extended answers that my students and I have formulated, since individual instructors will want to direct the discussion according to their own pedagogical agenda.

As we begin our study of the historical situation of the governess, I raise three themes that emerge from reading the documents: the danger of well-bred children's mixing with servants, the spirit-crushing servitude of the profession of governess, and the religious background of women who sought such "friend" (34, 35, 41) complicates this issue—especially viewed in tandem with her often condescending attitude toward the housekeeper.

Anna Jameson, in an 1846 essay, vigorously rejects Edgeworth's optimistic reading of the governess's relation to her employers, stressing instead the humiliation of her position. Jameson argues that "the occupation of governess is sought merely through necessity, as the *only* means by which a woman not born in the servile classes *can* earn the means of subsistence" (130). My students observe that she maintains the social distinction between servants and governesses, but her passionate diatribe against the conditions that she claims break the spirit of these young women shocks the reader with its candor if not outright cynicism. The woman who with the best will and intentions becomes a governess must, Jameson says, "break down completely, under the crushing influences which [meet] her at the very outset, and for which she [is] in nowise prepared" (132). Jameson addresses such women directly, advising them that "the best preparation is to look upon the occupation to which you are devoted (I was going to say *doomed*) as what it really is,—a state of endurance, dependence, daily thankless toil . . ." (132). After reading that excerpt, I draw my students' attention to a section in the novella when, almost as a riposte to Jameson's warning, the governess writes of her honeymoon-like period with her pupils: "It was all the romance of the nursery and the poetry of the schoolroom. . . . [I]nstead of growing deadly used to them—and it's a marvel for a governess: I call the sisterhood to witness!—I made constant fresh discoveries" (42–43). What, I ask, would be the reason for the governess's insistence on this almost Eden-like state, especially when read alongside contemporary documents that suggest the opposite? This question often leads to a fruitful discussion of the governess's desire to exonerate herself from any suspicion that she mishandled the mysterious events at Bly, a desire so all-consuming that it likely serves as the impetus for writing her manuscript.

The idea of holding a position so difficult that it can break one's spirit appears again in Jameson. While advising the future governess on the proper attitude toward her career, Jameson also admonishes the mother of the family to have patience with her young employee:

> [S]he will be presumptuous, perhaps, or perhaps she will be nervous and over-anxious. . . . Give her all the benefit of your better knowledge of your children's characters; let no maternal vanity interfere with your truth in this respect; encourage her to refer to you. . . . (131)

I ask my students to explore the connections between Jameson's beliefs and the governess's experiences. They note the parallels between Jameson's description of the goodwill that many young women innocently have at the beginning of their careers and the governess's sense of being called to help first the uncle, then the children in their life at Bly, as when the governess writes, "I now saw that I had been asked for a service admirable and difficult; and there would be a greatness in letting it be seen" (53). Yet the absence of any parental figure means that this governess will not be able to benefit from the wisdom of motherly guidance. Indeed, as the parent figure and the "supreme authority," as the uncle would have it (27), she must navigate an unplotted course: that of both governess and parent. I discuss the concept of liminality and ask my students how the governess's role reveals itself as doubly liminal. They find that she straddles the line between outsider and trusted caregiver and the line between trusted caregiver and parent. In retrospect, she realizes that she was "lifted aloft on a great wave of infatuation and pity," writing, "I found it simple, in my ignorance, my confusion, and perhaps my conceit, to assume that I could deal with a boy whose education for the world was all on the point of beginning" (37). This description, coupled with her sense of her beginning at Bly as a "succession of flights and drops, a little see-saw of the right throbs and the wrong" (29), mirrors Jameson's prediction that a new governess will be presumptuous, nervous, and overanxious.

In other passages regarding the lives of governesses, Mary Maurice writes about the financial necessity that forced many clergymen's daughters into this profession. "They are trained," Maurice writes, "by the constant exercise of self-denial, to do good to the parish in which they dwell, and they shed a living light, the reflection of the truths their father teaches" ("Many" 134). Students find an obvious connection between this passage and the governess's observation about her new life at Bly: "I learnt something—at first certainly—that had not been one of the teachings of my small smothered life; learnt to be amused, and even amusing, and not to think for the morrow" (38). More to the point is the question of how the governess's upbringing in a clerical family relates to her compelling, even obsessive, sense of duty in ridding Bly of evil spirits. Shortly before her first vision of Quint, she applauds herself for fulfilling the master's commands or, to adopt Maurice's words, for denying herself and doing good: "It was a pleasure . . . to reflect that by my discretion, my quiet good sense and general high propriety, I was giving pleasure—if he ever thought of it!—to the person to whose pressure I had yielded" (38). Maurice also warns of the danger a governess runs if she is attractive, for she may become the "corrupter" of her charges, or how her desire for admiration may make her seek the father's attention ("There Is" 135). The analogies between Maurice's warnings and the behavior of the two governesses in this novella can give rise to a discussion in the classroom about precisely who corrupts whom. For example, does the governess's religious upbringing, one apparently embedded in her family's very structure, prompt the governess to envision Quint and Jessel as corrupters, while she serves as what Maurice calls "living light"? Or is the governess the corrupter—a possibility that she herself confronts at the end of the tale, when she writes about Miles, "there had come to me out of my very pity the appalling alarm of his being perhaps innocent. It was for the instant confounding and bottomless, for if he *were* innocent what then on earth was I?" (119)? Do the ghosts seek her, as we might assume from Quint's staring at her from the tower, or does she seek them, as when she wanders through the house in the middle of the night and finds Quint on the stairs or when she searches for Flora, knowing she will also find Jessel?

Just as students have little knowledge about governesses, they also tend to be surprised to learn how widespread the interest in ghost narratives was in the late nineteenth century. I use the excerpts from ghost narratives in the Bedford second edition as a way of suggesting answers to questions that may appear to involve only the content of the text but often have to do with the accepted structure of the ghost narrative at this time. A close reading of the ghost narratives helps students understand some of James's motives in structuring this tale as he did as well as recognize the paradigmatic elements that appear over and over.

We discover that many of the details in James's novella already appeared in contemporary accounts of ghostly encounters. I ask my students to list the elements from the excerpts that they recalled when they read the novella. In almost every excerpt they report finding common elements: the narrators vouch for their personal reliability and emotional stability, they point out their courage in handling these frightening confrontations, and they bitterly resent the haunting of their homes or the possession of their bodies.

One document that my students find particularly intriguing is the circular from a group known as the Cambridge Ghost Club, an establishment formed by researchers from Trinity College, Cambridge, in 1851 (Westcott 144). This circular apparently attempted to impose order on the potential chaos of recorded ghost sightings, laying down rules that narrators were to follow. Its author, Reverend B. F. Westcott, requests that narrators suppress names but vouch for the accuracy of the narrative. In addition, the narrator should give "particulars as to the observer's natural temperament, (*e.g.* sanguine, nervous, &c.,) constitution, (*e.g.* subject to fever, somnambulism, &c.,) and state at the time, (*e.g.* excited in mind or body, &c.)" (145). Not only do the authors of the rest of the excerpts of ghostly narratives follow Westcott's advice, but his rules may elucidate issues about the structure of *The Turn of the Screw*.

For example, after reading Westcott's circular, I ask students to think about why James bothered to include the opening frame, with the group of friends at a country-house Christmas gathering. Why does Douglas vouch for the governess's character with such devotion? Why does she fail to give her name or the family name of Miles and Flora? The emphasis on what Westcott calls the "natural temperament," "constitution," and "state" also suggests why the governess has an obsessive desire to establish the righteousness of her position. She writes:

> I scarce know how to put my story into words that shall be a credible picture of my state of mind; but I was in these days literally able to find a joy in the extraordinary flight of heroism the occasion demanded of me. (53)

Just as the governess is determined to show her rectitude, so is she sure of her courage, a virtue that is echoed in several of the ghostly narratives. Mrs. Vatas-Simpson, author of one of these excerpts, speaks of sitting up with her friend "L." (possibly the governess) and realizing that she has "no feeling of security with only women in this big, grim, and hollow-sounding house." Nevertheless, she says, "we have had our courage put to the test, and most decidedly it has not been found wanting" (153). Mrs. G., author of another narrative, writes that after several encounters she "feared nothing and no one" (159). I point out to my students that, however else we may interpret the governess's attitude toward Quint and Jessel, she certainly does not lack courage, if we understand courage to be the control or mastery of fear. "I had plenty of anguish after that extraordinary moment [of confronting Quint on the staircase]," she writes, "but I had, thank God, no terror. And he knew I had n't—I found myself at the end of an instant magnificently aware of this" (67). Indeed, so proud is she of her courage that she sees it as a crucial part of her arsenal against the supernatural encroachers. I ask my students to speculate about the origins of that courage: was it likely imbued in her as the child of a clergyman? Is she a religious fanatic who seeks danger, or is she someone to admire?

Finally, we look at the resentment against the ghosts that so many narrators express in their narratives. William T. Stead collected stories about ghosts and edited a journal called *Borderland* in which he published various narratives of supernatural encounters (163). In one volume of this journal, he wrote of a young British army officer who came to see him, desperate to be rid of the spirit possessing him:

> He spoke quietly, with simple earnestness, as of a man caught in the grip of a mighty, invisible force which was bearing him irresistibly down into the abyss against which it was in vain even to struggle. . . . "I am afraid I am [lost]; at least he says so. He says that he will do me all the evil he can while I live, and that after, I am to be damned."
>
> (164–65)

The "abyss" echoes Miles's "cry of a creature hurled over an abyss" as he struggles with the governess at the end of the story—until his heart, "dispossessed," has stopped (120). My students and I look for occasions when the governess uses the verb "possess" to describe the desire of Quint and Jessel for the children—and her consequent hatred of the ghosts. We find that her much-vaunted courage feeds her own desire to possess the children: "I believe that no woman so overwhelmed ever in so short a time recovered her command of the *act*. . . . It was like fighting with a demon for a human soul . . ." (116–17).

The governess quickly comes to hate the ghosts for the terror that they unleash: "my equilibrium depended on the success of my rigid will, the will to shut my eyes as tight as possible to the truth that what I had to deal with was revoltingly, against nature" (111). Students may recall that the authors of the excerpts also rail against the upheaval caused by the hauntings. Mrs. G., a single mother with two small children, finds a house she likes, only to be driven out by ghosts; she tells her neighbors that because of her children's fear and resulting illnesses, she must leave (159). Mrs. Vatas-Simpson writes that her husband laughs at her story, "derides my credulity," but she nevertheless defends her observations with vigor and reason:

> It is useless to contend against facts. Nervous terrors and timorous imaginations have nothing whatever to do in suggesting the various appearances and the indescribable sounds which pervade the rooms, the corners, and the recesses of this great house. (154)

My students see how the historical narratives about governesses and ghosts in nineteenth-century Britain provide a scaffolding to explore James's text. In addition, they begin to understand the concept of liminality as applied to both ghosts and governesses. Both are marginalized, feared, threatening to the establishment, demonized or made into scapegoats, tortured—the list goes on, and it provides a useful transition to the next step of my pedagogical strategy, in which I assign students the critical essays in the Bedford second edition and begin destabilizing their first "straight" reading of the tale.

I wrap up this preliminary section of my classroom time on *The Turn of the Screw* by reading the excerpt from James's preface to the tale. He remembers being in a great country house one winter afternoon when the discussion turned to ghosts and ghost stories and especially to the low quality of contemporary stories:

> The new type indeed, the mere modern "psychical" case, washed clean of all queerness as by exposure to a flowing laboratory tap, and equipped with credentials vouching for this—the new type clearly promised little, for the more it was respectably certified the less it seemed of a nature to rouse the dear old sacred terror. (*Turn* [Beidler (2nd ed.)] 180)

As Sheila Teahan rightly points out, we must avoid assuming that the preface is "a transparent explanation of the text" and should instead read it " 'against' the text" ("I Caught Him" 361). My students and I, remembering the echoes that we have identified in the literary text, conclude that James knew at least some of the elements of these narratives and incorporated them into his novella. If those narratives were too hygienic for his tastes, too respectably certified, we agree that his mastery reveals itself in his imbuing them with—and transforming them into—the dear old sacred terror.

The Biography of *Daisy Miller*

Philip Horne

One of the main lessons of *Daisy Miller* is that interpretation is crucially shaped by context and by values. Winterbourne's crisis of understanding when dealing with Daisy is provoked by the unfamiliarity of her transatlantic milieu, while Daisy cannot fully comprehend the way in which her conduct is being judged. Given the gap of well over a century and the geographic distance of most American and other English-language readers from the setting—both temporal and physical—of the story, one of the most helpful things we can do for ourselves as readers, as well as for our students, is to fill in some of the contexts in which the action and its meanings play themselves out.

Obviously, there are all sorts of suggestive contexts in which the tale can be seen—as a prototype for the much more ambitious *The Portrait of a Lady*, for example, or, outside James's oeuvre, as a picture of the American girl at large that anticipates Anita Loos's *Gentlemen Prefer Blondes* (1925). Indeed, the kind of debate about American girlhood that it involves could be seen as pointing forward to movies like *Clueless* (1995) and *Legally Blonde* (2001), where questions of style and conduct are negotiated through an engaging comedy. One could consider the story in the light of James's own revisiting of it when he prepared the New York edition of his novels and tales, for which he heavily revised the text, in the autumn of 1908, and wrote a preface that is a fascinating if incomplete critical and autobiographical document. (The chapter on the story in my *Henry James and Revision: The New York Edition* reads it in this way.) But the approach I suggest here is more directly biographical—it draws, that is, on James's experience and interests up to and just after the publication of his story; it allows us to construct for ourselves the story of the story, telling us what James was preoccupied with at the time of writing *Daisy Miller*. Thus temporarily restricting our use of hindsight in working with the literature of the past allows it more profoundly and interestingly to challenge and refresh our sense of the world—showing where we came from, showing what has been lost as well as what has been gained (not, of course, that we can ever fully recover the past or fully escape our present concerns).

There has recently been much biographical speculation about James's sexuality, a subject on which there is an enormous amount of twenty-first-century interest and perilously little direct evidence. It would doubtless be possible to construct a speculative reading of *Daisy Miller* as an allegory of some kind of homosexual import: the true reason for Winterbourne's reservations about Daisy is his doubt about his own heterosexuality; his real attraction is to Giovanelli, not to Daisy (stranger arguments have been attempted); or Daisy's scandalousness, ostracism, and death are a figure for James's sense of the likely consequence of any exposure of his secret same-sex desire. The work, however, was not generally read in that way at the time, judging by the surviving evidence—though the story's own critique of Winterbourne's halfheartedness was echoed in readers frustrated by his lack of red-blooded passion, and versions of masculinity are indisputably at stake. Such queer readings risk forgetting the explicit focus of the story on the cultural differences between Americans brought up in Europe (Mrs. Costello et al. are not actual Europeans, it should be remembered) and American nouveaux riches from Schenectady and elsewhere with no education in European manners and culture. The short texts—travel essays, reviews, short stories, letters, chapters of autobiography—that I consider here offer ways back into the settings and milieus about which James was writing and the terms in which he saw them.

The sense of place in this story is not just an atmospheric setting against which an action occurs that could have occurred anywhere. Switzerland, where the first half of *Daisy Miller* is set, has meanings for James—it is Protestant, democratic, bourgeois, and somewhat repressive—that would not have been lost on most of his readers. He had a particularly strong basis for his sense of what difference it would make to his hero, Winterbourne, to have been brought up in Geneva, "the little metropolis of Calvinism," to have been "put to school there as a boy" (48). In the course of the James family's restless movements back and forth across the Atlantic during his upbringing, he and his elder brother, William, had for a time been "put to school" there themselves. The first chapter of Henry James's autobiographical *Notes of a Son and Brother* deals with the period of his boyhood spent there; his comments, which I lack space to quote here, help give body to what Winterbourne's background may have done for and to him. Vevey, where Winterbourne and Daisy meet in 1875 or 1876, was briefly mentioned in a travel sketch, "Swiss Notes," in 1872 (where, incidentally, James mentions the Victor Cherbuliez novel *Paule Méré*, which comes up again in the novella and is a source for it). And James records in the sketch that when he goes to the Byronic Château de Chillon, as Winterbourne and Daisy do, it is to find a large queue there already:

> When I went, Bädeker in hand, to "do" the place, I found a huge concourse of visitors awaiting the reflux of an earlier wave. "Let us at least wait till there is no one else," I said to my companion. She smiled in compassion of my naïveté, "There is never no one else," she answered. "We must treat it as a crush or else leave it alone."
>
> (*Collected Travel Writings: The Continent* 632)

James too, therefore, had gone with a female companion (possibly his friend Lizzie Boott) to this magnet for tourists, though with one much better informed and more alive to the cultural situation than Daisy. The growth of tourism, especially American tourism to Europe, was in fact a great cultural phenomenon of the time, stimulated by the increasing wealth of the United States. This tourism was one of the fundamental developments driving James's career, for he made much of his living as a writer at this period by giving accounts like "Swiss Notes" for American readers of the *Atlantic Monthly* or the *North American Review*—accounts of old Europe, but in particular of the lives and doings of Americans settled or traveling in Europe.

One can read James's travel writing as offering an informal education in European culture to his American audience, meeting a demand at the high end of the domestic cultural market (for the American consciousness of the Old World, see his 1877 tale "Four Meetings"). Had Daisy Miller, before her departure, read James on Europe with any understanding, one might say, there would have been no *Daisy Miller*. But you could come to Europe—many did—without the benefits of a prior immersion in high culture. The grand Roman sites of religious and cultural pilgrimage in the second half of *Daisy Miller* are sufficiently well known to attract not just the overrefined Winterbournes of this world but also its uncultivated Millers, who are probably not subscribers to the high-toned *Atlantic* but who have paid Eugenio to point them in the right direction. James's many evocative writings on Rome, mostly collected (and revised) much later in *Italian Hours* (1909), allow us to get a sense of the meanings for him of these common places of the tourist trail, where—they are both tourists, at their different levels of sophistication—Winterbourne encounters Daisy.

The young writer's initiation in the Eternal City in October 1869 shows a much less urbanely controlled James writing home to William in strikingly ecstatic terms:

> At last—for the 1st time—I live! It beats everything: it leaves the Rome of your fancy—your education—nowhere. It makes Venice—Florence—Oxford—London—seem like little cities of paste-board. I went reeling & moaning thro' the streets, in a fever of enjoyment. In the course of four or five hours I traversed almost the whole of Rome & got a glimpse of everything—the Forum, the Coliseum (stupendissimo!) the Pantheon—the Capitol—St. Peter's—the Column of Trajan—the Castle of St. Angelo—all the Piazzas & ruins & monuments.
>
> (Skrupskelis and Berkeley 116–17)

James himself, then, had gone there for the high touristic thrill, as part of his general intellectual education—though perhaps not without a thought to the eventual artistic returns on his investment of time and effort. As he told his friend Grace Norton in a letter a couple of weeks later, "My mind swarms with effects of all kinds—to be introduced into realistic novels yet unwritten" (Horne, *Henry James: A Life* 28). One of those "realistic novels" to introduce Roman "effects" was his first real novel, *Roderick Hudson*, in 1875, the greater part of which is set in Rome; another was *Daisy Miller*. In both the eponymous character sees Rome and dies—which may be one of the city's effects.

Given his passionate interest in the visual arts and the ulterior motive of seeking fictional material for later use, there is quite a contrast between James and the compatriots he saw around him in large numbers. As his friend the poet and statesman John Hay said in a fascinating and suggestive review of *Daisy Miller* (and a selection of reviews would be intriguing for students to analyze), James has learned "to look at his own people with the eyes of a foreigner" (Hayes 69). Just before going south to Rome, he wrote from Florence to his mother back home in Cambridge, Massachusetts, of "the Americans I have met":

> A set of people less framed to provoke national self-complacency . . . it would be hard to imagine. There is but one word to use in regard to them—vulgar, vulgar, vulgar. Their ignorance—their stingy, grudging, defiant, attitude towards everything European—their perpetual reference of all things to some American standard or precedent which exists only in their own unscrupulous wind-bags—and then our unhappy poverty of voice, of speech and of physiognomy—these things glare at you hideously. On the other hand, we seem a people of *character*, we seem to have energy, capacity and intellectual stuff in ample measure. What I have pointed at as our vices are the elements of the modern man with *culture* quite left out. It's the absolute and incredible lack of *culture* that strikes you in common travelling Americans.
>
> (Edel, *Henry James: Letters* 1: 152)

Writing within the family circle, James can freely express his disgust at the "vulgar, vulgar, vulgar" travelers he has seen with their closed minds and open mouths (Mrs. Miller and Randolph are comic examples); but even here he can, characteristically, turn appreciative. "On the other hand," he pivots to observe, "we seem a people of *character*, we seem to have energy, capacity and intellectual stuff in ample measure." America is the future. He recognizes that the terms he has been using are becoming superseded by the growth of a new force in the New World, that what were "vices" can be seen more neutrally, or positively, as just "the elements of the modern man." "Culture" can perhaps wait. In an 1872 letter to Charles Eliot Norton, brother of Grace, James famously remarks, emphasizing the trickiness of adjudication, "It's a complex fate, being an American, & one of the responsibilities it entails is fighting against a superstitious valuation of Europe" (Horne, *Henry James: A Life* 48).

The paradox, or epistemological difficulty, James is confronting—that of finding a standard by which Americans can be judged in a newly relativized world—emerges again in a more pro-American form when he finds himself taking the waters in Great Malvern in March 1870. The plain, stiff native Englishwomen tire him, he writes to William, by comparison with the American women he knows: "I revolt from their dreary deathly want of—what shall I call it?—Clover Hooper has it—intellectual grace—Minny Temple has it—

moral spontaneity." These attractive examples (from the highly educated circles he moved in—Americans are never simply "American") bring him closer to the "national self-complacency" that eluded him the previous autumn:

> I find myself reflecting with peculiar complacency on American women. When I think of their frequent beauty & grace & elegance & alertness, their cleverness & self-assistance (if it be simply in the matter of toilet) . . . my bosom swells with affection & pride.
>
> (Skrupskelis and Berkeley 149–50)

We can certainly find something of Daisy in this list of qualities. Indeed, the "moral spontaneity" James attributes to his beloved cousin Minny Temple is a crucial element in Daisy's attractiveness to Winterbourne, though it is also the feature, leading to mild defiance, that causes her ostracism by the American colony in Rome.

The connection of Daisy with the lively, discontented Minny Temple is worth pondering, not least as a case history of the transformations wrought by the creative imagination. Minny died on 8 March 1870, the day James wrote this letter from Great Malvern, and the shock of her sudden death (from tuberculosis) provoked in him a series of extraordinary, poetic, mournful, intimately meditative letters back across the Atlantic to those who had also loved her. The bereavement was a formative experience. The last chapter (13) of *Notes of a Son and Brother* is a moving portrait of Minny Temple, the prototype of so many of James's American heroines in Europe, concluding with her death: "We felt it together as the end of our youth" (James, *Autobiography* 544).

Other texts and documents cast light on James's preoccupations in *Daisy Miller*. In late 1870 the *Atlantic Monthly* published a tale by James called "Travelling Companions," a story set in Italy, beginning in Milan and moving south to Rome, with an all-American cast of characters: a male first-person narrator, who has lived in Germany; a beautiful American girl; and her businessman father. Much of it is less romantic action than travel writing, description of places and works of art, and it is apprentice work, carrying little conviction as a love story, but the plot resembles that of *Daisy Miller* in hinging on Americans' being inadvertently compromised by the application to their conduct of un-American criteria. As the heroine says of Italy, "It perverts our dear good old American truth!" (536).

Around the time of *Daisy Miller* there was a general debate in the United States, partly prompted by James's story, on the national, social, and moral questions raised by the unavoidable spectacle of Americans abroad and the contrast they made with European natives. Only a few months after *Daisy Miller* made its first appearance in the (British) *Cornhill Magazine* (it had been rejected by *Lippincott's* of Philadelphia, probably because of a perceived anti-American bias in its ironies), James published a reflective, provocative travel essay called "Americans Abroad." In the essay he emphasizes the national differences that make the issue so salient:

> Americans in Europe are *outsiders*; that is the great point, and the point thrown into relief by all zealous efforts to controvert it. As a people we are out of European society; the fact seems to us incontestable, be it regrettable or not. . . . We are the only great people of the civilized world that is a pure democracy, and we are the only great people that is exclusively commercial. Add the remoteness represented by these facts to our great and painful geographical remoteness, and it will be easy to see why to be known in Europe as American is to enjoy an imperfect reciprocity. (*Collected Travel Writings: Great Britain* 787)

American self-consciousness and sensitivity on the subject were extreme, and James draws attention to the basic cause, other than geographic remoteness, of the gulf between America and Europe: America is exclusively commercial and a pure democracy. The essay as a whole culminates in a prediction of American dominance: "the American in Europe may be spoken of as a provincial who is terribly bent upon taking, in the fullness of ages, his revenge" (792). The essay also helps explain why, aside from the story's literary power, American "society almost divided itself in Daisy Millerites and anti–Daisy Millerites," as W. D. Howells said in a letter to J. R. Lowell (Horne, *Henry James: A Life* 110).

Finally, in this survey of short texts forming a constellation around the novella, one needs to mention two notable letters written by James to intelligent British women in response to their comments on his international fiction. The critic Jane Dalzell Finlay (Mrs. Frank Harrison) Hill reviewed in 1879 the volumes in which *Daisy Miller* first came out in book form, praising it but protesting against the representation of English aristocrats in another story, "An International Episode," included in the same edition. James's eloquent retort on 21 March 1879, remonstrating with her "for your apparent assumption that in the two English ladies, I meant to make a resumé of my view of English manners" (103), is a warning to readers not to assume too much too quickly. Perhaps because of the controversial reactions to *Daisy Miller*, he insists on his right to represent sympathetic and unsympathetic characters of all types, classes, and nationalities without being taken as schematically offering a totalizing "resumé":

> A man in my position, and writing the sort of things I do, feels the need of protesting against the extensions of his idea in which, in many cases, many readers are certain to indulge. One may make figures & figures without intending generalizations—generalizations of which I have a horror. (104)

In October 1880, the figure of Daisy Miller also strayed into the sights of the extraordinary novelist and (by this time) conservative cultural commentator Eliza Lynn Linton, who was best known for her violently antifeminist articles collected as *The Girl of the Period* (1869)—which James had reviewed anonymously under its United States title, *Modern Women, and What Is Said of Them*, in 1869. Her letter to James is lost, but his unusually frank and full reply suggests that she had argued with a friend about *Daisy Miller*, taking the view that Daisy was indeed a bad flirt and "defiant." At any rate, James declares explicitly:

> Poor little D.M. was (as I understand her) above all things *innocent*. . . . The whole idea of the story is the little tragedy of a light, thin, natural, unsuspecting creature being sacrificed, as it were, to a social rumpus that went on quite over her head & to which she stood in no measurable relation. (122)

The full letter is fascinating, particularly since James's vindication of Daisy in it tallies with his review eleven years earlier of Linton's book attacking what she called the "Girl of the Period." That review is the last text I'd suggest for consideration alongside *Daisy Miller*, as it shows intense sympathy for the predicament of young women in modern society, especially vis-à-vis marriage. James sees the self-appointed judges of young women's conduct as reprehensibly ignoring the full picture of an "extravagant, superficial, and luxurious" society, the pressures that lead to an exaggerated concern with dress ("Modern Women" 24). And he makes a remark that might remind us of the thematic movement of his novella, with its turn of attention from Winterbourne's judgment of Daisy to our judgment of Winterbourne. In the climactic scene at the Colosseum, "He stood there looking at her—looking at her companion, and not reflecting that though he saw them vaguely, he himself must have been more brightly visible" (*Daisy Miller* [1986] 111). This scene echoes a gesture near the end of the 1869 review, where James declares, "When [women] present an ugly picture, . . . we think it the part of wisdom for men to cast a glance at their own internal economy" ("Modern Women" 25).

"And He So Dreadfully Below": Teaching Issues of Social Class in *The Turn of the Screw*

Robert Andrew Wilson

When a novella such as Henry James's *The Turn of the Screw* has been so dominated by critical debates and classroom discussions surrounding the psychology and reliability of its narrator, it may seem an unlikely text with which to teach issues of social class. Indeed, the cardinal debate over the ghosts' actual existence privileges discussions focusing either on the governess's individual drives or on the formal qualities of James's prose. Such concerns tend to exclude matters of social position and conflict or at the very least cast them into a secondary framework. But I propose that although such discussions do not emphasize the economic realities of the novella's characters, *The Turn of the Screw* makes for an excellent medium to introduce undergraduates to the dynamics of class relations. As students come to recognize how James's characters participate in a culture of economics, their inquiries may well lead them to ask innovative questions about other, more commonly recited aspects of the novella.

Of course, as soon as one begins looking at matters of social and economic class in *The Turn of the Screw*, class seems to pervade all character relationships: the wealthy but absent uncle from Harley Street whets the romantic and financial desires of a needy governess; the governess tries desperately to relate to the uneducated housekeeper Mrs. Grose; Flora and Miles, while of a privileged class, are dependent entirely on hired servants and governesses for their upbringing; and Quint and Jessel's evil appears to arise predominantly from their transgression of class boundaries. There are few major characters at Bly who can substantially interact with others of an equal class, the possible exception being Miles and Flora. By focusing on these relationships and the narrators who convey them to us, we might impress on our students a sense of what Fredric Jameson points out regarding James's aesthetic: "the degree to which point of view is also part and parcel of a whole ideology" (221).

What follows here is a series of talking points and questions that teachers interested in emphasizing the class dynamics of *The Turn of the Screw* can use to shape student discussions and writing assignments for the story. I try to show my students that the prologue of James's novella conditions its readers to understand the governess's narrative from the socially privileged point of view of her hiring family (notably because of Douglas) and thus to neglect the economic status of Bly's inhabitants. To give a sense of the anxieties of the genteel class over a governess who may present a threat to social stability, I direct my students to historical documents offering advice to and about governesses. From this information, students can then move to more politically informed interpretations of James's novella.

In my experience with teaching issues of social class, most American students, of various backgrounds and ages, recognize real divisions between economic classes, but many ultimately doubt that these differences can determine or shape their personal lives. Students think that who they essentially are lies outside the economic environment in which they live—that there exists a split between their psychical and their social existence. This assumption applies particularly to romantic relationships. As one of my students commented, "I'd marry the man I fell in love with whether he was a trash collector or on Wall Street. It doesn't matter." This statement suggests the belief that if we could strip away the clothing of class distinction—the paychecks and dividends of society, the culture of wealth or poverty—we would arrive at something human, something not defined by the economy. It is out of this romantic notion of what a person essentially is that one falls in love, not because of parts shaped by profession or social circle. The denial of economic reality and the valorization of romantic love hold particular importance in *The Turn of the Screw*; they emerge as the earliest ways of thinking about the governess's relationship with the man in Harley Street and also about her reasons for accepting the demanding responsibility of Miles and Flora.

The fireside audience of the story's prologue, to whom Douglas first reads the tale, latches on to the notion of idyllic romance as the governess's central motivation. Before the prologue narrator has even heard who the principal characters are to be in Douglas's story, he assumes that the governess is driven by love, that love has prompted her years of silence. The prologue narrator explains, "I see. She was in love," to which Douglas replies, "You *are* acute. Yes, she was in love. That is she *had* been" (24). Her love for the master in Harley Street also explains, for Douglas's audience, why the governess, who was "young, untried, nervous," would accept such "serious duties" at Bly: "The moral of which was of course the seduction exercised by the splendid young man. She succumbed to it" (28). The governess's presumed romantic motivation (an issue that critics often emphasize) intrigues Douglas's audience because, while it demonstrates her desire to rise in social rank, it also shows her willingness to serve the desires of her employer. Note that the audience seems to find quite charming the flirtation that the master of Harley Street extends to a member of his Bly staff—an instinct that the governess's narrative reproves when such class transgression occurs between Jessel and Quint.

This notion of romantic love masks what students often miss: the very real economic need of the governess in accepting the Bly position. Douglas explains the dilemma that she faces after the uncle's offer of employment: "She hesitated—took a couple of days to consult and consider. But *the salary offered much exceeded her modest measure*, and on a second interview *she faced the music*, she engaged" (28; my emphasis). The phrase "she faced the music" suggests not delight but a grim decision to address her poor resources and limited financial prospects. Despite this candid observation about the governess's economic need—the youngest daughter of a "poor country parson" (26)—Douglas's audience persists in reading her motivation as springing from "the beauty of her passion" for the man of Harley Street (28). Furthermore, the phrase "she engaged" embodies an ambiguity between love and lucre as, by the eighteenth century, *engaged* had developed both the sense of a servant's entering into an agreement for employment and the sense of betrothal. Thus, James's prologue invites an understanding of *The Turn of the Screw* as a love story as well as a ghost story, but both readings overlook issues of class difference and economic need.

More perceptive students may offer a conciliatory explanation of the governess's motives, that she falls in love at least in part because of her economic need. Douglas is rather explicit about the impressiveness of the uncle's "vast and imposing" house in Harley Street, which had been "filled with the spoils of travel and the trophies of the chase" (26–27). Among the impressive qualities of the master, those that make him a gentleman, are the possessions that allow him such grace and gallantry. The governess "figured him as rich, but as fearfully extravagant—saw him in a glow of high fashion, of good looks, of expensive habits, of charming ways with women" (26). Some of my students note here how the master's allure for women is built progressively on fashion, looks, and expensive habits, that extravagance produces charm. It may be that the governess's unconscious awareness of her financial need manifests itself in a romantic desire for the master, but in any case James's text makes clear that his desirability and appropriateness are based on the magnificence of his class, not on the benevolence of his character.

To engender a sense of the historical position that James's nineteenth-century English governess held, I assign students a selection of cultural documents from the Bedford second edition of *The Turn of the Screw*. The texts under the heading "The Victorian Governess" offer brief but insightful glimpses into the Bly governess's class. From these documents students can glean something of the complex social position that James's narrator refers to as a "sisterhood" of governesses (43). Teachers might ask students to read these documents, then to make a list of characteristics of the nineteenth-century English governess, and finally to locate passages in James's novella that resonate with these characteristics. Teachers might also assign the historical readings after their students have completed the novella, to ensure their direct experience of James's prose. But priming them first with background on the governess class gives them some of the knowledge that James's original audience brought with them to *The Turn of the Screw*; it demonstrates that the skills students develop in order to understand literature can be applied to a wide range of cultural artifacts; and it teaches them to examine the novella not as a work of art detached from the economic realities of the nineteenth century but rather as a work embodied by and engaged with the politics of its era.

Two selections by Mary Maurice, who wrote advice to governesses and their employers at roughly the time James's novella is set, show the governess position as one of expensive expectations but modest means. Maurice writes that many governesses were the daughters of either "affluent parents"—who

> brought them up with every indulgence and refinement, that wealth could bestow: . . . but a sudden loss of fortune, a failure in business, or death, has reversed the picture, and no alternative remains, but that they must support themselves, and no other way but this is open to them

—or "clergymen" (the case of the Bly governess) ("Many Were" 133). James's text resonates with this description when the governess comments on her "disturbing letters from home, where things were not going well" (43–44). We don't know the exact nature of the governess's family problems, but it is reasonable to suppose that they are financial. More pertinent is that the novella minimizes concern with the governess's family in order to direct our attention to the Bly–Harley Street family. The governess herself transfers her class and family identifications when she adopts Miles and Flora as her children: "But with this joy of my children what things in the world mattered?" (44). We are not expected to worry about the poverty and problems of the governess's family; as the governess identifies with Bly over her Hampshire origins, we are meant to worry only about the woes of the wealthy.

Maurice further warns of the deleterious effects a governess might have on a household. To justify a "strong prejudice against governesses," families are warned of "[f]rightful instances" of governesses who corrupt children's "innocence and purity" and engage in "pilfering and theft" ("There Is" 134–35). Elizabeth Missing Sewell's selection from *Principles of Education*, which warns of a governess's underpreparedness to teach, performs similar work:

> [G]overnesses are continually recruited from these penniless, ignorant, yet well-born and well-bred young girls. What is to be done with them? . . . Must our children necessarily be taught by superficial or under-bred governesses? Alas for English society if it is to be so! (136)

I ask students to note the use of "English society" as somehow distinct from those who are penniless and ignorant. Both nineteenth-century advice books and James's story minimize concern with the governess and her family in their emphasis on the problems of the hiring family. Our attention is almost exclusively pulled to the problems of the privileged class—the upbringing of Miles and Flora—at the expense of understanding the governess's origins and position. Maurice's and Sewell's construction of governesses paints them as sympathetic figures whom we might pity in their fall from affluence but should guard against as creatures who covet the wealth and family of their employers.

James's governess distances herself through erudition and speech from the "homely" exclamations of Mrs. Grose (76), but she does not entirely belong in the society that has employed her. The governess is of the privileged class but not in it.

Anna Jameson's 1846 essay describes the economic forces that contributed to the creation of the governess profession and pertinently explains how the governess's position lies outside rigid class distinctions. Governesses emerge from social relations that are "not natural, not necessary, arising out of a very luxurious and complicate[d] state of society"; they are an invention of the capitalist economics that has made necessary their assumption of parenting duties from a "simpler state of society" (129). Students might profitably compare this description with the condition set by the master of Harley Street that he never be contacted regarding Flora and Miles's upbringing. We are told that the "awkward thing was that [the children] had practically no other relations and that [their uncle's] own affairs took up all his time" (27). While we are left to speculate as to what exactly the master's "affairs" might be, they most certainly concern his financial undertakings and the "expensive habits" that the governess assumes him to possess.

It is no coincidence that only two years after Jameson published her essay on the governess class, Karl Marx and Friedrich Engels criticized the bourgeois middle-class family in the *Communist Manifesto*:

> On what foundation is the present family, the bourgeois family, based? On capital, on private gain. . . .
>
> The bourgeois claptrap about the family and education, about the hallowed co-relation of parent and child, becomes all the more disgusting, the more, by the action of modern industry, all family ties among the proletarians are torn asunder and their children transformed into simple articles of commerce and instruments of labor. (226–27)

The uncle's employment of the governess is clearly for reasons of "private gain": it enables him to continue to enjoy his rich lifestyle. More significant is what Marx and Engels's description reveals about the governess's proletarian identity (her need to sell her labor for wages). Because of the "luxurious" state of society that Anna Jameson describes, the governess is driven from her father's poor home—her family torn asunder—and made the instrument of labor in raising and instructing children who are not her own. Jameson clarifies this point with her direct address to governesses: "I have never in my life heard of a governess who was such by choice: and when you look about for a family in which to enter, not only you will not have the power to choose, but in all probability your circumstances are such, that you will not have the power to refuse" (132). The governess's engagement of the Bly position stems from wide-ranging economic relations and needs, not from the romantic inclinations of youth.

If Anna Jameson's essay presages better educational and economic opportunities for women, it also warns of the dangers of social confusion brought about by the class indeterminacy of the governess position:

> No social arrangements can violate certain natural and necessary premises with impunity, nor indeed without admixture of much evil. The relation which exists between the governess and her employer either places a woman of education and of superior faculties in an ambiguous and inferior position, with none of the privileges of a recognized profession, or places a vulgar, half-educated woman in a situation of high responsibility. . . . (131)

The liminal status of the governess afloat between distinct positions of wealth or servitude must bring about "more or less of evil consequences" (131). What Anna Jameson's text assumes—an assumption that James's narrators share—is that class identity is essential and intrinsic to a person's character and cannot be changed through social action. Class is based on a "natural and necessary" premise, a premise to be violated by social arrangements only at the expense of producing "evil" outcomes. Better to keep the well-bred woman behind the veil of wealth and proper society, while the vulgar poor are locked in their prison of servitude. By this logic, violation of class boundaries is morally corrupt.

James's governess and Mrs. Grose share the moral coding of sacrosanct class boundaries in their figuring of Quint and Jessel as evil spirits. The ghosts have returned from the dead to continue their corruption of Miles and Flora, and that corruption is based on the contravention of social status. Quint and Jessel's own damnation and subsequent threat to the children—"They're lost!" cries the governess (59)—stem from their disrespect for the inviolability of separate class positions, "base menial" servant and governess (62). Indeed, class transgression seems to be the ghosts' principal sin, as Mrs. Grose discloses to the governess the extent of Quint and Jessel's relationship:

> "There was everything."
> "In spite of the difference—?"
> "Oh of their rank, their condition"—she brought it woefully out. "*She* was a lady."
> I turned it over; I again saw. "Yes—she was a lady."
> "And he so dreadfully below," said Mrs. Grose. (58)

Mrs. Grose views Miss Jessel as "infamous" when she was alive (58) and a "horror of horrors" as a ghost (57), because Jessel lowered herself through her sexual association with Quint and allowed Miles to spend so much time with the servant. What made Quint so deplorable was his disrespect for the limitations of his humble position. As Mrs. Grose exclaims, "He did what he wished" (58). Mrs. Grose, who admonished Miles that she "liked to see young gentlemen not forget their station" (62), and the governess thus become the defenders of social order. Where the governess declares her battle with the undead to be "like fighting with a demon for a human soul" (117), the evil that the ghosts present comes from their seduction of Miles and Flora away from the "natural and necessary premises" that Anna Jameson describes of proper class relationships.

From the Maurice, Sewell, and Jameson documents, students will find that the governess class was one filled with complexities and internal divisions—not to mention with the cultural anxiety stemming from its placement between lower and upper classes. By emphasizing such information and asking questions about how the governess's position might influence her narration of the tale, teachers provide their students with a mode of inquiry that allows them to examine the story's most often raised issues—the threat of the ghosts, the narrator's reliability, the fates of Miles and Flora—through a political-economic lens.

The classic strategy of reading the apparition scenes of the story for evidence of ghosts or delusion takes on new proportions when matters of class are scrutinized. I ask students, When the ghosts appear, does James's text give any sense of the class to which either the governess or the ghosts belong? Just before nearly every appearance of Quint or Jessel, the governess fantasizes about herself belonging to the Bly pedigree or is reminded of her exclusion from it. Before Quint's first appearance, she writes, "I was giving pleasure—if [the uncle] ever thought of it!—to the person to whose pressure I had yielded" (38). As she desires to meet the uncle on one of her afternoon walks so that he might recognize the good work she has been doing as his hire, Quint appears in the uncle's stead (39). When Jessel first appears, it is as the governess moves to retrieve a "pair of gloves that had required three stitches and that had received them—with a publicity perhaps not edifying" (44). Why is the mending of the gloves "not edifying"? Is it because the governess is after all a woman poor enough that she must sew her own gloves? Jessel's first appearance by the lake occurs as the governess pretends to be some "remarkable person or thing" in the children's games due to her "happy and highly distinguished sinecure" (54). With Quint's appearance on the stairs, the governess imagines Quint, "the low wretch," turning to disappear as though on "receipt of an order" (68). Her will in confronting him at this moment has seemingly restored the hierarchical order and reminded the ghost of his position in it. With these scenes (and others), a ghost's appearance is linked to the governess's awareness of how classes should properly interact at Bly. When the governess discusses Mrs. Grose's belief in the spectral sightings, she refers to Mrs. Grose's deference to her "more than questionable privilege" (50). This "privilege" is at once her unique ability to see the ghosts and her questionable status as the mistress in charge of Bly.

During her first days at Bly, she describes the building as "half-displaced and half-utilized," seemingly another of the master's trophies. But here, rather than the uncle who abdicates his responsibilities, the governess is in charge: she declares, "I was strangely at the helm!" (33). "Strangely," because she should not be at the helm: Miles and Flora's parents or at least their uncle should oversee her handling of the children's education and upbringing. The governess's unmanaged responsibility is precisely the type of situation that social commentators such as Maurice, Sewell, and Anna Jameson warn against, leaving the children of the hiring family too open to neglect and abuse. Bly is a society without a proper ruling class, with only the governess to masquerade as the face of authority.

Students might derive a sense of her odd authority at Bly by examining the early scenes in which she adjusts to her new environment and the moments during which she delays deferring to the uncle over what to do with Miles and Flora. Following her introduction to Flora, for instance, the governess comments on her own "admiration and wonder" as she sits at supper with "four tall candles" and her pupil (31). She is clearly not accustomed to the lavish accoutrements—the four candles, her "large impressive room," the "figured full draperies"—that she is now afforded (30). With this scene in mind, students might ask if the desire to prove her ability to take on the responsibilities of the command of Bly—and perhaps prove her romantic suitability for Harley Street—explains why she forgoes summoning the uncle. She justifies having not written to the uncle and states that Mrs. Grose "did n't know—no one knew—how proud I had been to serve him and to stick to our terms" (78). The governess's comment regarding her sense of "the liberality with which [she] was treated" at Bly is telling, given the story's conflicted uses of the word "liberal" (30). "Liberal" comes from the Latin *liberalis*, meaning "worthy of a free man," and was associated with the arts and sciences of a superior social station, as opposed to the servile and manual work of the servant class. For the first time, the governess is being treated not as the daughter of a poor Hampshire clergyman but with the "liberality" of Bly's genteel class. Yet, as she moves from her "small smothered life" into the "space and air and freedom" that her station at Bly accords her (38), she remains haunted by the notion that she does not fully belong there.

Another figure who masquerades above his scripted station is of course Peter Quint, who wears his master's stolen clothes, seduces the governess Miss Jessel, and spends inappropriate amounts of time with Miles. At Quint's initial appearance, the governess's first "sane inference" is that "some one had taken a liberty rather monstrous" (42). Here, "liberty" means the invasive and inappropriate behavior of a wayward traveler trespassing along the crenellations of Bly (a description perhaps not too distant from the governess's position). When she discloses "what was hideous at Bly" as challenging even "the most liberal faith," for which she cares little, it seems an affirmation of an orthodox religiosity (66) that affirms a "natural and necessary" relation between class divisions. We are told that Quint's wickedness comes from his willingness to adopt the visage and privileges of Bly's ruling class. When Mrs. Grose declares, "Quint was much too free" (51), the governess must be reminded of her own tenuous class position.

Students should examine closely the governess's conversation with Mrs. Grose as they piece together Quint's ghostly presence at the end of the fifth chapter. Mrs. Grose utters, "But if he is n't a gentleman—," which the governess finishes, "What *is* he? He's a horror" (47). It is as though the only other possible condition that someone in Quint's place might be, if he's not a gentleman, is to be an abomination. The "horror" remains that Quint had been dressing up and acting as a gentleman. In response to the governess's impression of Quint as an actor, Mrs. Grose explains that the master's "waistcoats" had gone missing and suspects Quint of wearing them (49). Exactly what makes Quint's acting as a gentleman so deplorable? Would we hold the same prejudices against people today who act above the station they were born into? Students will likely see the class tensions surrounding not only Quint but also the governess as the social and economic politics of the nineteenth century, not of their own era.

Thus, while the governess describes Bly at one point as a "theatre after the performance" (80), the estate seems filled with multiple actors donning the costumes of a class not fit for them. What initially gives the phantom Quint away is that he does not wear a gentleman's hat, a shibboleth of the genteel class. The governess's failure to save Miles suggests that she was ill prepared for her role as stewardess of Bly. Misplaced servants, without the tethers of a definite social order to restrict them, cannot be remade by simply adorning themselves with the trappings of gentility. The Bedford edition of the novella also contains Bruce Robbins's Marxist essay (quite accessible to college undergraduates), which offers a more redemptive view of James's text than what I offer here, by emphasizing "a vision of social equality to which [the governess] is utterly blind" (343 [2nd ed.]). Surrounding *The Turn of the Screw* with historical documents covering the governess class suggests a view of James's narrative ultimately suspicious of any such equality. The apprehensive culture of nineteenth-century economics remained deeply troubled over the threat of the working class's adopting the vestments of mobility.

As students examine the story's moments of class consciousness and debate to what extent *The Turn of the Screw* represents the interests of the gentleman class, they might reasonably want to know how this issue informs the more common questions of the narrator's reliability and the ghosts' authenticity. Teachers might point out—and suggest as a writing topic—that consideration of class can support both the apparitionist and hallucinationist views. If Quint and Jessel are spirits returned from the dead, might they not be looking for revenge on a social order that forbade their relationship? If the ghosts are figments of the governess's troubled mind, do they not spring from her uncertainties about masquerading with the powers of a privileged class to which she does not belong? As students answer these questions for themselves, perhaps they will come to see how the economic landscape influences both James's characters and their own lives.

CLASSROOM STRATEGIES

The Governess as Teacher in *The Turn of the Screw*

Peter G. Beidler

Perhaps not noticing that *The Turn of the Screw* is about a teacher and her students, too many of us teachers fail to exploit a series of discussion and writing topics that will let our students connect to it in quite personal ways. Too often we encourage our students to leap immediately to a discussion of whether the ghosts are real or the governess is mad, subjects about which many college-age readers have little knowledge or experience of their own, and even less about nineteenth-century views of those subjects. I suggest in this essay that in teaching the story we should start with a subject area that younger readers do have personal background in and experience with: the motives and effectiveness of teachers who are charged with educating young people. Examining the governess through her role as teacher can let us later encourage our students to augment their own experiences with a knowledge of the condition of the governess in nineteenth-century England and to read James's text with more attention.

The governess at Bly is, centrally, a teacher of two pupils. We read through the daunting scholarship on *The Turn of the Screw*, however, without getting any but the vaguest notion that the young woman who takes up her duties as the governess of Flora and Miles is their teacher. We learn all sorts of other things by reading in that scholarship: she is a madwoman, she is a murderer, she is a sexually repressed psychopath, she is a sadomasochistic haunter of children, she is a pathological liar, she is jealous of Mrs. Grose, she hallucinates two ghosts into existence, she is a bad mother who viciously exploits Miles and Flora, driving one crazy and causing the death of the other. Alternatively, we read that she is a loving young woman who has surrogate motherhood thrust upon her by a set of circumstances she cannot control and that she is a bulwark of good protecting them from evil in the form of the prowling spirits of Peter Quint and Miss Jessel. But almost no one talks about the governess as a teacher or about Miles and Flora as her pupils. Discussing the effectiveness of the governess's teaching methods and her pupils' roles as learners will quickly take our students to the larger question of the general reliability of the governess and the accuracy of her record of the events at Bly. From that familiar territory we can then lead our students into less familiar territory, such as the reality of the ghosts and the sanity of the governess. If the governess's role as a teacher seems generally to be a positive one to today's generation of students, then they may be inclined to trust her version of the strange happenings at Bly. If the behavior of the two young students toward their new teacher seems awkward or unlikely or suspicious, then readers may be inclined to think that Miles and Flora have been and still are influenced by beings other than her. Alternatively, if our students see the governess as an incompetent or irresponsible teacher, and if they see Miles and Flora as innocent pupils endangered by their association with her, then they will distrust her vision. In either case, students' views on the effectiveness of the governess's teaching methods and practices can provide a useful platform from which to introduce other important issues in *The Turn of the Screw*.

I urge that teachers who wish to present any or all of the following questions to students should try hard not to direct their students' answers by revealing their own view of the governess. Students might want to consider these ten questions in class, in small-group discussions, or in short reaction papers assigned before class discussion:

1. *Is the governess wise to want Flora to get to know her as a person before the actual lessons begin?* The governess says:

> I reflected that my first duty was, by the gentlest arts I could contrive, to win the child into the sense of knowing me. I spent the day with her out of doors; I arranged with her, to her great satisfaction, that it should be she, she only, who might show me the place. She showed it step by step and room by room and secret by secret, with droll delightful childish talk about it and with the result, in half an hour, of our becoming tremendous friends. (32)

Is it pedagogically sound that a teacher be a friend to her pupils, that she give Flora a chance to get to know her as a person, and that she give Flora the opportunity to show her around Bly? Or should the governess have moved more immediately to Flora's schoolroom lessons? It is sometimes said of teachers that "you only get one chance to make a first impression." Does the governess make the right moves to make a good first impression on Flora?

How do you think you would react to the "gentle arts" of a teacher like the young governess who wants to become your friend before she becomes your teacher?

2. *Is the governess right to desire and approve of Miles's "fond familiarity" with her?* What are we to make of her response to his addressing her as "my dear"?

> "You know, my dear, that for a fellow to be with a lady *always*—!" His "my dear" was constantly on his lips for me, and nothing could have expressed more the exact shade of the sentiment with which I desired to inspire my pupils than its fond familiarity. It was so respectfully easy. (83)

Is a "fond" and "easy" relationship between a teacher and a student desirable? Why does the governess like it when Miles calls her "my dear"? Does it make a difference that he is a boy of ten and she a woman of twenty? Have you ever addressed one of your teachers as "my dear"? If not, might that be because customs and student-teacher protocol have changed in the last 150 years?

3. *Is the governess right not to inquire into the issue of what Miles did to get himself expelled from his school?* To the headmaster's letter she replies, "Nothing at all." To Miles's uncle, she says "Nothing at all" about it. To Miles himself, she says "Nothing at all" about it (37). Is she wise to make no reference to the matter to anyone except Mrs. Grose? Would a better teacher have found a way to confront the issue, or are some things in a student's past best left unexplored unless the student raises them? Consider the effect when she finally does ask Miles directly, "What happened before? . . . Before you came back?" (94). What is the outcome, in the last chapter, when she finally does ask him point-blank, "Is that [stealing] what you did at school? . . . Was it for that you might n't go back?" (118)? Does Miles's resulting death make us wish that she had challenged him directly months earlier, or, alternatively, that she had not challenged him now? Is it any of the governess's business why Miles was expelled from his boarding school? Should Miles's uncle, rather, have been the one to take the matter up with the headmaster? The headmaster, after all, had sent the letter to the uncle, who had forwarded it unopened to the governess.

4. *Does the governess care about Miles and Flora?* Good teachers, even if they are taskmasters, do care about their students. Is the governess concerned more about their welfare than her own? To what extent is her desire to be a successful teacher connected to her desire to impress their uncle, on whom she has a crush? Does she seem like the sort of woman who would care about her pupils whether or not she also cared about their official guardian?

5. *How smart is the governess?* Are we to take her at her word when she speaks about how much more Miles knows than she does? "Lessons with me indeed," she says, "that charming summer, we all had a theory that he was to

have; but I now feel that for weeks the lessons must have been rather my own" (37–38). Is she just being modest? Do good teachers learn from their students? Keeping in mind that Flora is eight and Miles ten, how are we to account for their scholarly sophistication? "They performed the dizziest feats of arithmetic," the governess tells us, "soaring quite out of *my* feeble range, and perpetrated, in higher spirits than ever, geographical and historical jokes" (95). Are we to believe that Miles learned so very much at school and that Miss Jessel had taught Flora so much? Or are we to assume that it is less that the children are so smart than that the governess, though twice their age, is so far less smart or educated than they are? Or is there some other explanation for the smartness of Miles and Flora? Might it come, for example, in some way from the prowling spirits of Quint and Jessel?

6. *To what extent should the governess broach forbidden subjects with her pupils?* There is specifically the matter of the possibility of the return of the dead: "Forbidden ground was the question of the return of the dead in general and of whatever, in especial, might survive, for memory, of the friends little children had lost" (79). Who determines that that subject is forbidden? Is it a good idea to keep it so? What happens when the governess finally does directly raise the forbidden subject with Flora on the other side of the lake? Would the governess have been better off not asking Flora directly, "Where, my pet, is Miss Jessel?" (101), and thus raising the specter of the former governess? What has been your experience with teachers who talked with you directly about subjects your society considered inappropriate, such as sexual conduct, insanity, drug addiction, and child abuse?

7. *Should the governess have been more suspicious of Miles's motives in offering to play the piano for her?* "[H]e came round to me," she tells us, "and asked if I should n't like him for half an hour to play to me" (96). She comes to see that during that entrancing half hour Flora sneaks off to the other side of the lake for what the governess thinks is a meeting with Miss Jessel. What is a teacher's proper role when a student makes such an overture? Should a teacher be less gullible, more suspicious of the motives of pupils? If you were a teacher, would you have been taken in by an eager pupil who wanted to impress you with a musical feat? What do you think Miles's motives were in entrancing his teacher by playing the piano? Whatever you think those motives were, do you think you would have seen through them?

8. *Do you think the governess oversteps her bounds as a teacher?* At the end of the story she tries to get Miles to tell her about some of his earlier activities with Peter Quint. She feels, in that scene, as if she is "fighting with a demon for a human soul" (117). Is her proper province Miles's mind, not his soul? Would she have done better to leave Miles, whom she feels is smarter than she is, to his own devices? Is *The Turn of the Screw* the story of a teacher who strayed into territories that she should have known were off-limits to her? Should she have stuck with reading and art and mathematics as her proper province? How do you think the story would have ended if she had *not* tried

to meddle with Miles's soul? Would it have had a happier ending for Miles?

9. *How would you compare the governess's effectiveness as a teacher with that of Miss Jessel, her predecessor as the teacher of Flora?* In your answer, deal only with what we can know, mostly from Mrs. Grose, about Miss Jessel's behavior when she was in charge at Bly. Which of the two would you rather have had as your teacher, the present governess or Miss Jessel?

10. *Would you want your children to be the pupils of the governess?* Would they find her inspiring, frightening, or dull? Would they be as eager to please her as Miles and Flora first are, and as eager to get free from her as they become? Is she just the sort of loving teacher you would hope to find for your own children, or do you fear that she would harm them physically or psychologically?

The point of these questions is obvious: to give students reading a complex and difficult work a basis for understanding the governess through her occupation as a teacher of pupils. Most students encountering *The Turn of the Screw* will bring to it at least a dozen years of their own experience as pupils themselves and their own experience with at least two dozen different teachers. Their own experience, then, can provide a way into the story and a basis for assessing the fundamental reliability or unreliability of the young woman whose recollections of the events at Bly are our primary source of information about her, about her pupils, about Mrs. Grose, and about Quint and Jessel.

Our students will, of course, be aware that their own experiences as pupils in home, public, or private school classrooms will have been different from those of Miles and Flora, who were privately tutored in their own home by a series of teachers hired to teach only them. It is important that our students be reminded, however, that what they know about teachers needs to be augmented by an understanding of the governess's own situation. They need to be reminded that this story was written before the end of the 1800s and is set a half century before that, before the middle of the 1800s. The situation of teachers was much different then.

Current students should be informed that, while the role of governess had its roots in earlier centuries, it grew to importance in England in the nineteenth century in response to two needs. First, governesses helped mothers educate their children, particularly their daughters. At around age ten, upper-class English boys were typically sent off to boarding school, where they learned independence and various skills for getting along in the world. There were a few schools for girls, but almost no girls were actually sent to school. Their education was considered to be less important than the education of boys, and their parents generally considered it safer for them to remain under the protection of their families. Mothers had the major responsibility for educating their daughters, but circumstances often made it desirable for them to hire a governess. Before there were sophisticated methods of birth control, some women had many children, and their preoccupation with babies and younger children often required that they have help with educating the older ones. In addition, many of the young mothers in a rising middle class found that social and philanthropic duties interfered with their maternal duties. It became a matter of status for upper-class and, increasingly, middle-class families to hire young "ladies" to come into the home to relieve the mothers of some of the day-to-day duties of teaching their daughters. Of course, when the biological mother died, as does the mother of Miles and Flora, a substitute mother in the person of a governess was required. Only under the most unusual circumstances would such a woman at so young an age as the governess at Bly have been given complete authority to make all decisions about the education and general welfare of her charges. Only rarely would a twenty-year-old woman have been given the responsibilities of motherhood quite so abruptly, with so little training, so little experience, and so little guidance from a parent or guardian.

The second need that the institution of governess filled was for a means of self-support for the grown young women in middle- or upper-class families that could not support them. The profession of teaching gave such women their only opportunity to earn a respectable living. Being a governess almost always meant being poor to start with, and it usually meant staying poor and dying poor. In *What Maisie Knew*, published at about the same time as *The Turn of the Screw*, James emphasized the poverty of governesses. Maisie hears her mother say of the pretty governess Miss Overmore, "I take her because she's a lady and yet awfully poor" (20). Maisie knows that her other governess, Mrs. Wix, is also poor: "She knew governesses were poor; Miss Overmore was unmentionably and Mrs. Wix ever so publicly so" (27). The profession of governess was never a lucrative profession, but it was an honorable one. A woman who got a job as governess to a good family could hold her head high enough while she did virtually the only work that was considered acceptable for single women of the middle or upper class. As a private governess she got a place to live, meals to eat, and a small stipend. The young governess at Bly is apparently offered a generous stipend to entice her to accept the position: "the salary offered much exceeded her modest measure" (28). Most governesses were paid pitifully little, and much of what they were paid they typically had to send home to help support their families.

The employment situation for governesses in mid-century England was precarious indeed. For one thing, as Kathryn Hughes puts it in her excellent *The Victorian Governess*, "for much of the nineteenth century, the supply of governesses far exceeded the demand" (37). According to Hughes, "middle-class women whose families were not able to offer them a home were left with no alternative but to earn their living in the schoolroom" (118).

We should imagine the governess in *The Turn of the Screw*, then, as very much in need of the job she takes at Bly. She has had, after all, no previous experience as a teacher and so no employment references whatever. It tells us something about her precarious situation that she was in competition for the position at Bly with others, including several to whom the job had been offered but who had turned it down because of the "main condition" imposed by the uncle:

> That she should never trouble him—but never, never: neither appeal nor complain nor write about anything; only meet all questions herself, receive all moneys from his solicitor, take the whole thing over and let him alone. She promised to do this. . . . (28)

Modern readers, knowing that there are now many career paths open to young women, sometimes question the governess's motives for taking the position at Bly, with its strange conditions and mysteries. They need to be reminded that, with no employment alternatives and no previous experience as a teacher, the twenty-year-old daughter, one of several children of a Hampshire parson, would have had to take almost anything that was offered and agree to almost any stipulations. Students sometimes question the governess's motives for her subsequent decision to keep her promise by not communicating with the uncle when Peter Quint and Miss Jessel appear on the scene and threaten Miles and Flora. These readers should be reminded that she needs a positive report from the uncle if she wishes to have a successful career as a governess after leaving Bly. She can ill afford to abandon a job she desperately needs, to break her promise to the man who hired her, or to risk alienating the man on whose recommendation the next job will depend. Although she feels an emotional attachment to the handsome gentleman-uncle who has hired her, it is for practical reasons that she must keep her promise.

At the first frightening appearance of Quint on the tower, the time when the governess might most logically have thought of quitting the job at Bly and going back to Hampshire, she gets "disturbing letters from home, where things were not going well" (43–44). If things are not going well at home, it is safe to assume that the governess's father, a poor country vicar, is in no position to welcome her back. She is, then, trapped in the strange job at Bly. She must either ride it out or commit occupational suicide. Her employer could dismiss her with no explanation if he became displeased with her performance. According to Hughes, "even a woman in full possession of her youth and spirits could find herself facing dismissal without warning: an overstocked market allowed employers to indulge sudden fancies and dislikes without any inconvenience to themselves" (169).

The cultural background section of the second Bedford edition of *The Turn of the Screw* provides nineteenth-century documents on governesses by Anna Jameson, Mary Maurice, Elizabeth Missing Sewell, and Maria Abdy. These might be assigned for students interested in pursuing further the historical situation of the governess in the nineteenth century. (Readers interested in such assignments may want to have a look at Kimberly Reed's essay in this volume.)

Students should also, of course, be encouraged to read with great care the text of the story itself. If they do, they will find that, whatever the questionable circumstances of her employment, the governess who moves from a vicarage in Hampshire to a country estate in Essex thinks of herself as a teacher. She refers to Miles and Flora as her "pupils" some twenty times, and she clearly envisions her role, at least initially, as that of a person who teaches.

There is, furthermore, textual evidence that she takes her teaching role seriously. When she first meets the lovely Flora, she thinks that to "watch, teach, 'form' little Flora would too evidently be the making of a happy and useful life" (31). The governess speaks early on of her initial fears that the life of a teacher would be a boring one, but also of her coming to see what a joy it is to work with two such delightfully apt pupils:

> The attraction of my small charges was a constant joy, leading me to wonder afresh at the vanity of my original fears, the distaste I had begun by entertaining for the probable grey prose of my office. There was to be no grey prose, it appeared, and no long grind; so how could work not be charming that presented itself as daily beauty? It was all the romance of the nursery and the poetry of the schoolroom. I don't mean by this of course that we studied only fiction and verse; I mean that I can express no otherwise the sort of interest my companions inspired. How can I describe that except by saying that instead of growing deadly used to them—and it's a marvel for a governess: I call the sisterhood to witness!—I made constant fresh discoveries. (42–43)

The governess teaches her pupils many subjects. She has Flora working on her penmanship "in the schoolroom with a sheet of white paper, a pencil and a copy of nice 'round O's' " (34). We find various references to music lessons and theatrical productions that she has Miles and Flora engage in. She teaches literature, including the "fiction and verse" she mentions on page 42, but also the stories of "Mrs. Marcet" (70)—that is, Jane Marcet, who in the 1840s was the still-living author of several readers and textbooks for young children. Later Miles makes reference to the children's having read with their governess some tales about knights, presumably of the Arthurian sort: "The true knights we love to read about never push an advantage too far" (96).

The governess also apparently gives the children lessons in elementary French: "I was invited . . . to repeat afresh Goody Gosling's celebrated *mot*" (79). That last term *mot* is French for "word" or "witty saying" and probably refers to an often repeated anecdote in which one of the wives in the Hampshire village of the governess's childhood had made a clever retort to someone. That she teaches writing also is suggested by the fact that she has Miles and Flora compose letters, "charming literary exercises," to their uncle (82). The governess teaches other subjects as well. She gets into arithmetic, to judge by her reference to multiplication tables. After all, "nine-times-nine" (70) represents reasonably sophisticated arithmetic for pupils of eight and ten. She also apparently teaches at least the rudiments of astronomy, navigation, and world geography. She gives pedagogically creative lessons in geography, allowing the pond or small lake at Bly to represent an inland sea just off the Black Sea in southwestern Russia: "as we had lately begun geography, the lake was the Sea of Azof" (54). The governess's lessons are effective enough because little Flora is soon at work constructing a makeshift little sailboat to launch on the imagined Sea of Azof. (For an extended discussion of that scene, of the Freudian freight the toy sailboat has been made to bear, and of a pedagogical source for such a toy, see my essay "With Holes.")

By being asked to think seriously about the governess's role as a teacher, our students will have begun with familiar reference points—teachers and students—rather than being thrust directly into more unfamiliar topics, such as nineteenth-century attitudes about ghosts and madness.

My experience as a teacher is that no matter how they interpret the governess and her reliability as a narrator of the events at Bly, students find themselves increasingly angry at the selfish uncle in Harley Street who abandons his responsibilities by hiring as the caretakers of his niece and nephew men and women whom he scarcely knows. These students can be encouraged to wonder why, in his brief interview with the naive young parson's daughter, he does not ask a single question about her teaching philosophy, her educational background, or what subjects she will teach Miles and Flora. They will easily see that he says nothing of what his own educational goals for them are. If they think about that interview, usually students come to see that the uncle is selfishly eager to pay a naive, needy, and inexperienced young teacher too much just to get her to take his niece and nephew off his hands.

Some students who follow this line of thinking come to see the tragedy of this story as one caused not by a bad governess who fails to save Miles and Flora but by their bad uncle who does not care enough about them to try to save them. This uncle has no qualms about whom he hires to guide his charges so long as she will leave him alone. When he finds one who is desperate enough to take almost any job she can get, he flirts with her to get her to do his bidding and exacts from her a promise never to bother him about any problems that arise with his niece and nephew. Students who think about the uncle will come to see that the real flaw of the young teacher he hires is not that she misjudges the children or the spirits of Quint and Jessel, not that she is an imperfect mother surrogate for Miles and Flora, but that she does not at first see that their handsome uncle cares far more about his own selfish tranquillity than about the education or even the safety of his niece and nephew.

The Matter of Perception: American Girls and English Ghosts

Collin Meissner

> "Here comes my sister! . . . She's an American girl."
>
> "My father ain't in Europe; my father's in a better place than Europe."
> (*Daisy Miller* 50, 54)

> So I saw him as I see the letters I form on this page. . . .
>
> I suppose I now read into our situation a clearness it could n't have had at the time. . . . (*The Turn of the Screw* 41, 115)

Surely it is comforting to know that there never was a time when the seemingly implicit simplicity of the above quotes, the first two from Daisy Miller's younger brother, Randolph, the second two from the governess in *The Turn of the Screw*, was simple. Anyone who has taught Henry James, at any level, has inevitably met the confused stare of students caught in the disconnection between the words on the page and what those words are supposed to mean. It is small comfort to know that James more often than not met that same stare in the eyes of his contemporaries, including his brother William, surely a close and intelligent reader, who suggested that Henry "say a thing in one sentence as straight and explicit as it can be made, and then drop it forever" (*Letters* 277). Even a simple sentence from *Daisy Miller* like "She's an American girl" is so freighted with meaning in the story that the prospect of teaching Henry James can be daunting. But taking James up in the classroom can be invigorating. It is for good reason that he was known to his contemporaries as "the master." Surely then, we should welcome his lesson.

Approaches to teaching, or reading, or coming to understand Henry James are as various and disparate as they are abundant. In fact, he has so often functioned as the medium through which different critical schools have demonstrated their method and has been so thoroughly read, dissected, and then put back together that when we now read his fiction, we can no longer be sure we've got it—"it" signifying some premium on meaning or understanding. Ironically, for James, bringing his audience to this position of reflective bewilderment is exactly what "it" is all about. The notion of provoked reflective bewilderment is an especially important position in the experience of a James text, because it represents the interpretive moment when one finds the kind of openness or freedom James believed was necessary for any kind of real understanding to take place. Not surprisingly, readers become frustrated when they discover that James invariably leads them toward a moment of interpretive failure and that the failure is a step in the right direction.

Teaching or coming to understand James is, then, strictly speaking, an act of resignation and release. Unlike many other kinds of fiction, James's work doesn't respond to or unveil itself for a particular theoretical approach; rather, his fiction inevitably reveals the shortcomings of all invested positions, beginning with the invested identity of the reading subject. To this end, his fiction often functions as a magic mirror, showing to the reading subject the inevitable insufficiency of an interpretive strategy. I have remarked elsewhere how "it may seem paradoxical to say that the failure of understanding becomes the medium for understanding" (32); it still strikes me that James would be comfortable with this enigmatic assessment. Time and again his writings arrive at the same conclusion. One thinks here of his remarks about the nature of reality from his preface to *The American*: "the real represents to my perception the things we cannot possibly not know, sooner or later, in one way or another" (1062–63); or his comment, in his essay "The Art of Fiction," about the unfathomable nature of experience: "experience is never limited, and it is never complete; it is an immense sensibility, a kind of huge spider web of the finest silken threads suspended in the chamber of consciousness, and catching every airborne particle in its tissue" ([*Literary Criticism*] 52); or his explanation in the preface to *Roderick Hudson* that one of the major difficulties with "representation" is that "experience" spreads "round us in a widening, not in a narrowing circle" (1039). The point here is double: on the one hand, the multitude of interpretive avenues in and out of James make him an ideal author for reflective reading and classroom discussion; on the other, what we could call the protean nature of Jamesian hermeneutics renders easy answers or conclusive statements of meaning impossible, a warning James himself gives in his preface to *The Turn of the Screw*. The passage is worth unfolding in its length, since it offers a period to the many sentences conferred on this most bewildering of ghost stories:

> What, in the last analysis, had I to give the sense of? Of their being, the haunting pair, capable, as the phrase is, of everything. . . . What would *be* then, on reflexion, this utmost conceivability?—a question to which the answer all admirably came. There is for such a case no eligible *absolute* of the wrong; it remains relative to fifty other elements, a matter of appreciation, speculation, imagination—these things moreover quite exactly in the light of the spectator's, the critic's, the reader's experience. Only make the reader's general vision of evil intense enough . . . and his own experience, his own imagination, his own sympathy . . . and horror . . . will supply him quite sufficiently with all the particulars. Make him *think* the evil, make him think it for himself, and you are released from weak specifications. . . . There is not only from beginning to end of the matter not an inch of expatiation, but my values are positively all blanks save so far as an excited horror, a promoted pity, a created expertness—on which punctual effects of strong causes no writer

> can ever fail to plume himself—proceed to read into them more or less fantastic figures. (*Turn* [Beidler (2nd ed.)] 185–86)

So then, how does one go about teaching *Daisy Miller* or *The Turn of the Screw*? Although some twenty years separate the 1878 publication of *Daisy Miller* from the 1898 publication of *The Turn of the Screw*, teaching these works as companion pieces is a valuable way of illuminating the complexities of James's art. Indeed, one could say that the two novellas represent interanimating sides of James's belief in art's capacity to educate and direct the "high and helpful, and, as it were, civic use of the imagination" (Preface to "The Lesson of the Master" 1230). The unifying thread here is James's constant and conscious effort to write stories in which perceiving characters are made to confront experiences or interpretive situations that exceed their capacity for control or understanding. Think of Winterbourne's revolving misinterpretations of Daisy Miller or the governess's catastrophically imposed and deadly interpretation of the world at Bly. It is not only that these characters suffer a kind of hermeneutic failure in their contextualized experiences. The revolutionary aspect of James's work lies in how perceiving consciousnesses function as a medium that draws readers into the work and forces them to go through the very same trial and confront, in the end, interpretive frailties that invisibly shape one's conception of reality and that were heretofore completely unknown to the reading subject. This is likely the reasoning behind James's development of the center-of-consciousness narrative technique. That perspective, as we know, places readers not only within the text struggling to forge meaning from the events observed but also, to borrow language from Paul Ricoeur, "in front" of the text where the events being read become interlocutory as they reverse the escapism inherent in reading and allow readers to be read by themselves (93). James characterized this reversal as the enjoyment of the privileged position of being both the subject reading and the object being read. In other words, stories like *Daisy Miller* and *The Turn of the Screw* are powerful fictions not only because of their formal sophistication but also because at a fundamental interpretive level they are fully real, in the sense that readers live through the experience of them as something more than fictional. Ineluctably, readers of James become readers of themselves. What more valuable classroom experience can one imagine?

Daisy Miller offers an effective and yet manageably complicated example of the inherent dangers of preconceived interpretive positions and their negative effect on daily life. An initial scene from this story shows by extension not only how well James's fictions describe the personal and cultural situations embedded in their narratives but also how tensions and ambiguities often direct the process of interpretation both inside and outside the text. From the beginning *Daisy Miller* subtly encourages readers to affiliate with Winterbourne: he occupies the role of protagonist, and he gives the impression of aesthetic and intellectual refinement. Yet the text simultaneously discourages readers from affiliating with Winterbourne: he seems just a little too Europeanized for James's American audience. The tension between trust in and suspicion of Winterbourne's capacity to read and judge a situation mounts through the text and is played out in the revisions of understanding we see Winterbourne undergo on each successive encounter with the American girl. As both a reading and classroom encounter with James's method, the initial meeting between Daisy and Winterbourne is especially fruitful, because it suggests how knowledge, experience, and understanding are malleable, and their malleability has distinct personal, social, and even political consequences, which can be measured in terms of the exercise of power.

Students opening *Daisy Miller* find a protagonist James imbues with just enough of a positive impression that when Winterbourne is caught off guard by his inability to categorize Daisy Miller as fitting this or that type of person and unable to figure exactly what Randolph means by saying, "She's an American girl," they often feel comfortable with Winterbourne's clinical assessment that "she was only a pretty American flirt" (58). This is the encouraging aspect of the text's intrusion into the reader's consciousness. But students are always a little uncomfortable with the assessment, because it comes at the tail end of a series of reflections in which Winterbourne has tried out various categories of "women" for Daisy, including the "exceedingly innocent" (57), the "very unsophisticated," the "great coquettes," and the "dangerous, terrible women," and concludes with the diminutive and infantalistic "she was only" as a preface to the undignified kind of concluding male nod and wink that the "girl" was just "a pretty American flirt" (58). Students are also troubled by Winterbourne's assessment precisely because it lacks any kind of critical, experiential, or even knowledgeable foundation and reveals itself as a desperate attempt at control. James ensures that we address our suspicions; live through them, as it were; and come to understand the exact measure of public and private consequence that results when an American man feels, after clinical observation, he's found just the right spot for his "American girl." As the narrative has it, "Winterbourne was almost grateful for having found the formula that applied to Miss Daisy Miller" (58).

But rather than provide a reading of Winterbourne for his audience, James restrains himself and offers instead opportunities to read him. He thus draws his readers into a debate not only with the story's protagonist but also with themselves. If asked why we want to trust Winterbourne's judgment, we point to his urbanity and intelligence. But the text stops us in our interpretive tracks: "Winterbourne," we are reminded, "had lost his instinct in this matter" of what Daisy Miller was, "and his reason could not help him" (57). It is disconcerting to find that the reason we feel drawn into a trusting relationship with a character turns out to be so naively imperceptive on both parts: on ours for misreading, on his for skimming to categorize. As it turns out, Winterbourne lacks the experience necessary for judgment. James forces us to ask what has happened here, then allows us just enough information to figure it out with close reading: Winterbourne's knowledge is exposed as relying on external formulas. His understanding is based on a need for control as opposed to an acceptance of openness. Readers stumble onto his interpretive shortcomings precisely because James allows them first to commit the same judgmental errors, then gives them the opportunity to get beyond formulaic modes of understanding. This prompting of interpretive growth is a strong example of how James cultivated fiction as a fully interactive medium.

Because the theoretical sophistication of this example is so muted by the text's immediacy and seeming simplicity, the example can function as a window onto aspects of reading and understanding James, or fiction, or even how understanding works more generally. Readers are effectively led to check the why and how of interpretation. If it takes them a little time to recognize Winterbourne and themselves in Winterbourne, their knowledge of his aunt, Mrs. Costello, is immediate and clear. When she categorizes the Millers as "very common, . . . the sort of Americans that one does one's duty by not—not accepting," no one for a moment assumes that she has got it—no one, that is, except the entire expatriate American population hovering in the background pointing fingers at and whispering about the Millers (62). Later, when we find Winterbourne in the midst of an interpretive seizure, "angry at finding himself reduced to chopping logic about this young lady" and "vexed at his want of instinctive certitude as to how far her eccentricities were generic, national, and how far they were personal" (107), James has brought our interpretive skills far enough along that we easily recognize the problem as residing in the inherently limited capacities of a methodology that categorizes and controls knowledge instead of opening itself up to the world's myriad potentialities. As one of James's international stories, *Daisy Miller* functions brilliantly as a vehicle to show the process of understanding, how assumptions operate as interpretive weapons whose overt and covert actions have drastic and even tragic consequences. In the end, the story shows that Daisy Miller, the girl from Schenectady, has no chance simply to be, if for no other reason than that her manner of being exceeds the ability of her compatriots to understand. In that collision, their lack of imaginative openness is shown by James to be far more lethal than the Roman fever that takes her life.

The end of *Daisy Miller* shows a more soberly wise Winterbourne on the other side of his experience; he has come, although too late after all, to understand Daisy not as a naive flirt but as a young woman wronged and one to whom he had done an injustice. The text also forces its readers to recognize the challenge of understanding. Despite what he has come to understand, despite acknowledging what he has witnessed as the lethal consequences of having "lived too long in foreign parts," Winterbourne finally lacks the strength to accept the responsibilities of his insight (116). James doesn't allow his readers to exercise such a luxury; nor, given the example, are they so prone.

Students of James have no difficulty recognizing how the consequences of interpretive assumptions are complicated and intensified in *The Turn of the*

Screw. Indeed, ambiguity was a motivating factor in the story's composition, a point, as we've seen, James makes in the preface and one he stressed even earlier to the story's publisher, Sir John Mackenzie: "So long as the events are veiled the imagination will run riot" (Edel, *Conquest* 214). Given that James exploited for the purposes of his fiction's energy what he knew would be any reader's assumptions, reading *The Turn of the Screw* with an eye to seeing how the story examines the process of interpretation will teach us a lot about understanding and reading and about understanding and reading Henry James.

In opening the novella, readers are immediately confronted by the narrative's multiple frames; these open up to a well-handled, successively copied, and likely unreliable manuscript produced by a woman who was under extreme duress during the events narrated and may well have been insane then and at the time of scribal recollection. Thoughts like this should provoke questions about narrative reliability and the trustworthiness of experience; they should raise suspicions about the value of any claimed empirical proof. To ask what this story means is to ask students a very complicated question. One might begin by asking questions such as the following: According to the story, do ghosts exist? Is Peter Quint walking the grounds of Bly? Has Miss Jessel returned for something she has no right to claim? In the realm of interpretation opened up by the narrative and for the purpose of provoking discussion, these interesting questions should set the reader on guard. But questions such as, How does James manipulate our sense of understanding?, Is James playing with our need to control meaning by way of interpretation?, and How does this text provoke us to allow our imaginations to run wild? Is it by limiting our perspective and undercutting the value of empirical comforts? are more powerful hermeneutic tools. They take us far into James's sense of how representation, understanding, and consciousness work to expose our construction and conception of reality. While the first set of questions serve to initiate discussion, they are limited by the governess's terms of disclosure. The second set of questions begin to theorize about understanding and interpretation as processes that are always under the pressure of influence and whose outcomes are never neutral. More specifically, they bring us into direct contact with James's belief that aesthetics was a live and active and even aggressive vehicle that could intervene positively and productively in the larger arena of human affairs.

As with *Daisy Miller*, I think it profitable to proceed from a seemingly simple to a far more complicated example. Predictably, the simple is anything but. After all, when the governess attempts to impose a manner of empirical proof on her narrative, saying that she "saw [the ghost of Peter Quint] as I see the letters I form on this page," James undercuts the sureness of her comment by having her remark how "then, exactly, after a minute, as if to add to the spectacle, he slowly changed his place" (41). Readers who take the narrative at face value understand that the ghost's change of place was from one physical space to another. From her perspective, this phrase is a factual representation of what occurred. But, as many commentators have pointed out, the governess's inscriptions on the page are recollections mediated not only by time and circumstance but also by the act of writing. As such, her narrative is always already suspect and calls attention in its very construction to her capacity to know and her determination to write a story that explains her experience as empirically verifiable—even though that experience can only be subjective and is thus unreliable. In other words, her authority as author is undercut by the intention of her authoring action. For students wrestling with the narrative, the casual suggestion that something as remarkable as the appearance of a ghost could be corroborated empirically in the same manner and with the same certainty as one's vision of letters formed on a page raises serious questions about the reliability of the printed word and the capacity of the perceiving consciousness to understand anything without the aid of a conceptual apparatus. James uses the governess's remark "as I see the letters I form on this page" as an ambiguous prompt to and not the final source of meaning. In the end, whether ghosts walk the grounds of Bly is a subjective matter yet also a belief whose consequences can be measured in terms of fictional or factual amusement (the "story had held us, round the fire, sufficiently breathless" [22]) or literal or figurative death ("his little heart, dispossessed, had stopped" [120]). That both interpretations apply is remarkable, but never for a moment should we misread the gravity of James's ambiguity.

From its opening sentence to its concluding scene the story exploits two contradictory impulses: the feeling that we should suspend judgment and the belief that judgment is required. For classroom purposes the tension between these impulses is enormously valuable, because in moving from the acceptance of the former to the resistance of the latter one can cover the entire ground of Jamesian hermeneutics—or the entire field of art's power to shape individual and cultural values, as James understood these realms. No reader of *The Turn of the Screw* misunderstands the lethal consequences of the governess's actions or how her interpretation of what she perceives to be the reality at Bly influences and determines those actions. In no significant way is it hard to imagine how her psychosexual and literary imagination contribute to and manipulate her interpretation of experience, a dynamic relation that has received immense critical attention. As readers we are thus equally amused and surprised when at one moment we read that the governess felt it "would be as charming as a charming story suddenly to meet some one . . . [who] would stand before me and smile and approve" and find almost immediately that her "imagination had, in a flash, turned real," that this wished for figure "did stand there!" (39). For James the point is not that it happens but why and how it happens, in the sense of what is going on at the level of interpretation. Amid all the complexities of the text; despite all the ambiguities, which play havoc with our ability to know what to think; and despite how the governess acts like an overzealous, overinvested, overdetermined, and out-and-out bad reader of every piece of evidence that comes her way, she also serves beautifully as an example of what good reading or an open approach to understanding requires, precisely because she doesn't deploy any of their strategies. One can therefore use *The Turn of the Screw* as a heuristic of the interpretive process. As the governess reads volumes into the slimmest of clues and goes so far as to shape or impose on reality so that her story will be more undeniably real, we readers carry the text's words from here to there, place this one against that, and come up with a meaning we then step back and pronounce as evident and proved on the basis of our reading. Our interpretation ends up being a hermeneutic circle: we see what we expect, and we believe what we see. Ghostly meanings and interpretive positions have this in common: by necessity they are always evanescent, yet their consequences matter. For this reason, how we get from belief to understanding and from understanding to action is worth serious consideration.

In *The Turn of the Screw* James shows how completely the governess's need for interpretive control influences her perception. Critics have offered numerous and compelling explanations, both cultural and psychological, of how she became so determined; but in the end, the story always returns us to the question of interpretation. The governess effectively puts Bly in a state of lockdown in her effort to control not only the appearances and disappearances of the ghosts but everyone's perception at the estate. She says, "Here at present I felt afresh—for I had felt it again and again—how my *equilibrium* depended on the success of my *rigid will*, the will to *shut my eyes as tight as possible to the truth* that what I had to deal with was revoltingly, against nature" (111; emphasis added). The words and phrases I have accentuated offer a kind of coda for this story and for James's larger aesthetic. The governess sees through "eyes" shut "as tight as possible," and her vision is the consequence of a will made "rigid," as though struggling against the possibility that the "truth" in question or under investigation could be anything other than something "against nature." Here interpretation is an act of aggression, intervention, violation, something one does to something or someone else; it is an intentional act of asserting control or mastery. That Daisy Miller does not fit a paradigm challenges Winterbourne and his contemporaries to interpret her; their act kills her as surely as does the Roman fever. The governess has her own paradigm, which involves her infatuation with the absent master, her literary imagination, and various levels of class conflict and contact. She interprets her experience at Bly; ghosts appear, and a young boy dies. It seems an understatement to say that she fails in her attempt to reach a state of "equilibrium," but her failure is James's way of offering the reader an opportunity. Readers who engage with *The Turn of the Screw* often find themselves imposing interpretations in order to achieve their own state of equilibrium: to square their sense of what the governess perceives and why. The disconnections that occur not only underscore the presence of multiple interpretations but also force readers to question why they value one kind of reading over another. The text shows us that we are not the governess but then asks us to explain why.

That readings of this text proliferate beyond even its many narrative frames accentuates James's belief that "experience is never limited, and it is never complete," that understanding depends on release and resignation and reflective bewilderment ("Art" [*Literary Criticism*] 52). Behind this remark, as *Daisy Miller* and *The Turn of the Screw* show, lies the deeper question of how we understand at all. Like most of James's fiction, these texts refuse to admit an interpretive deliverance from on high; they refuse the establishment of a vertical relationship between reader and authority figure. James prefers to show how meaning and understanding are the outcome of a struggle for possession, first in the text; then between the reader and the text; and then, more important, between the reader and the reader's consciousness. Not surprisingly, this struggle must not be won; it depends on a standoff—that is, on the establishment of an equilibrium. James's fiction never intends to clear up confusions or offer specific answers. *Daisy Miller* and *The Turn of the Screw*, much like *The Ambassadors* and *The Golden Bowl*, teach us that living with the tension of bewilderment or in that gap between ignorance and understanding, between control and release, is the point. As James would say, "Then there you are" (*Ambassadors* 365).

Teaching *Daisy Miller* Innocently

Gert Buelens

At my university, when instructors are considered for promotion, an element that works in their favor is the ability to demonstrate that their teaching is based on their research. The Ghent University administration assumes that the more advanced the research, the better the academic teaching. I am not at all convinced, though, that the quality of my teaching is always commensurate with that of my research. Actually, I suspect I am best at teaching material on which I have *not* yet published.

Take the junior course on Henry James that I taught in 1998–99. The syllabus comprised *Daisy Miller*, "The Real Thing," and *The Wings of the Dove*—texts on which I had not published—and two texts on which I just had—"The Beast in the Jungle" and *The Portrait of a Lady*. The size of the group, some eighty-five English majors, made lecturing the most obvious teaching mode. Now, one might expect that the greater the lecturer's expertise, the better the lecture. My experience is otherwise, and I do not think the reason is that I simply did not present my material well. Nor was the problem that the students lacked the requisite sophistication, though these were undergraduates. As juniors, they would already have been exposed to challenging literary texts (if not to James) and would have taken at least two courses in literary theory. Moreover, they were poised to start work on their senior thesis, a demanding 30,000-word research paper. Rather, the key reason why my classes on *Daisy Miller* and *The Wings of the Dove* were more successful is that I could more easily open myself up to the students' responses or occasionally pursue an interest that I had just discovered—without, as yet, having arrived at full conclusions. With the other texts, I wanted to lead up to the specific conclusions of my research.

For instance, with "The Beast in the Jungle" I was hoping to demonstrate to students not only that the conventional reading of this story as a tale of moral and sentimental blindness is flawed but also that Eve Sedgwick's influential interpretation of the hero's homosexual panic is really just as deplorably Romantic. I wanted to argue that a non-Romantic reading of this tale as a staging of interpersonal rhythms of mastery and surrender is much more persuasive. I had no more than two one-hour sessions in which to achieve all this in addition to establishing what the conventional reading was. I am not proud of the kinds of questions this pressure led me to resort to. We seem to have spent about half an hour considering the story's first sentence ("What determined the speech that startled him in the course of their encounter scarcely matters, being probably but some words spoken by himself quite without intention . . ." [277]). Some of my in-class questions on this text were embarrassingly factual (What is the grammatical subject of this sentence?); others were meant to be speculative but were really unanswerable, except by me, who knew where I wanted the argument to go (Why have an elaborate subject and postmodifier, only to deny in the main verb that their content matters?).

In hindsight, it seems obvious that broader, more overarching questions would have been more likely to stimulate active thinking in the students. For *Daisy Miller*, I had in fact given them five such questions to consider at home: What is the Roman fever literally, and what does it symbolize? Who is responsible for Daisy's illness? What was the relationship between Daisy and Giovanelli? How did Winterbourne regard Daisy? How did she regard him?

When I broached these questions in class, more than a dozen students contributed to what turned into a real discussion, which is unusual with Flemish students, who are shy, particularly when surrounded by eighty-five of their peers. Instead of sticking to the order of the questions as I had given them before class, I adopted a sequence that more closely corresponded with the experience of reading the story. I also made considerable use of additional questions to guide the students. Thus, with the first question, How did Winterbourne regard Daisy?, I asked them to tell me what they knew about Winterbourne. What is his nationality? his occupation? He is said to be "studying," but he keeps very vague about this to Daisy, telling her he's not in business but has certain "engagements" (48, 77; all quotations from the novella are from the Penguin reprint of the 1878 edition). How would the students assess his social class? (Class is left implicit, but his aunt, Mrs. Costello, certainly seems to consider herself as belonging to the first circles.) A particularly fruitful question is about Winterbourne's place of residence (to which he returns after he has taken Daisy to the Castle of Chillon). Another is, What do we learn about the nature of this place through the text? Geneva is crucially circumscribed early on as "the little metropolis of Calvinism" (48). I asked students to clarify this term for me: What is Calvinism? What is a Calvinistic philosophy? I expected not a technically precise account of the theory of predestination and the origins of Presbyterianism but something along the lines of how James was using the term here: to imply the sense of "Calvinistic" that a modern dictionary defines as "having very strict ideas about moral behaviour and tending to disapprove of pleasure or enjoyment" (*Longman*). I especially wanted to prod them about where, in the context of American studies, they had come across a similar philosophy. All these students had taken a required course with me the previous year, in which Puritanism figured prominently in the founding of New England. Thus I led them to see a link between Winterbourne's national roots and his current context and to understand his judgmental attitude toward Daisy as, in a curious way, both traditionally American and very European.

We then examined Daisy Miller herself, seeing of course that she is more clearly an American than Winterbourne, perhaps even the archetypal American girl. My Belgian students needed some instruction on the connotations Schenectady, Daisy's hometown, would have had at the time. I first answered negatively: she is not from New York City; no member of that city's high society, she would be totally unacquainted with its "minutely hierarchical constitution," of which Winterbourne's aunt reminds us (62). Neither is Daisy from Boston—a provenance that would have suggested a very different type of American girl (having intellectual interests, being combative on behalf of women's rights). Instead, she belongs to what Tony Tanner rightly calls the "provincial plutocracy—Schenectady in the process of taking over New York—she is the American girl of the future" (30). Daisy's father is too busy making money back home to join his family on their travels abroad, where they strike the likes of Mrs. Costello as "very common . . . the sort of Americans that one does one's duty [Calvin again] by not—not accepting" (62).

We were now better prepared to consider how Winterbourne regards Daisy. Some of the answers students offered were along the lines of, He likes her, He enjoys being with her—simple but accurate enough, especially when one also notes his doubts about her morality, that is, her sexual morality. Is she a "flirt" when she says, "I have always had . . . a great deal of gentlemen's society" (57)? Or is she just very innocent—as though it doesn't matter much to her whether a friend is a man or a woman? The narrator sums up Winterbourne's initial attitude nicely in saying that the young man was "amused, perplexed, and decidedly charmed" (57). A good additional question here is, Why does Winterbourne want to present Daisy to his aunt before Daisy and he go out together? It is a question that enables students to go to the heart of one crucial problem that this text presents: What is respectable behavior, and what are the rules that must be observed to live in accordance with it? Are the rules the same in Geneva, New York, and Schenectady? Are they the same from one decade to another? Back then and right now? Relevant passages from the text here are Winterbourne's hesitant question to his aunt, "You really think, then, . . . you really think that. . . . she's the sort of young lady who expects a man—sooner or later—to carry her off?," and Mrs. Costello's response, "You have lived too long out of the country. You will be sure to make some great mistake. You are too innocent." When Winterbourne returns, "My dear aunt, I am not so innocent," Mrs. Costello clinches the debate by asking, "You are too guilty, then?" (63–64). This exchange, I realized in discussion with the students, is actually a nice example of how Calvinism-Puritanism informs the moral texture of the tale: it is not just that one is either guilty or innocent—which would simply be an instance of moralistic black-and-white thinking—but that one is either too innocent or too guilty, meaning that one is guilty in any event.

We turned next to the trip to Chillon that Daisy and Winterbourne undertake (yes, we were making slow progress over the course of three one-hour meetings, but a good grounding in the nature of the problem that the text sets out to present is essential if students are to appreciate how the ending resolves it—or fails to resolve it, as the case may be). Winterbourne is unsure what to make of Daisy, unsure whether she is as "common" as his aunt claims

(62). This uncertainty causes him to look as "grave," according to Daisy, as if he were at a funeral rather than on a boat trip to a splendid castle (75). Confronted with this challenge, he claims that he "never was better pleased in my life," to which Daisy laughs out, "I like to make you say those things! You're a queer mixture!" (75–76). It is at a point like this that the value of teaching a text innocently appears at its clearest. My research at the time was very much around the issue of James and queerness: I had participated in the *TLS* exchange around Sheldon Novick's claims about a homosexually active James ("Henry James's Initiation"), I had published an article challenging Sedgwick's closet reading of "The Beast in the Jungle" ("In Possession"), and I had already written a draft of the queer reading of *The American Scene* that would appear a couple of years later ("Henry James's Oblique Possession"). Yet I had not hitherto reflected on the operation of the term "queer" in *Daisy Miller* and so did not feel the urge to impress on the students any conclusions of my own (as I had done with "The Beast in the Jungle"). Instead, I could afford really to listen to what the students thought the term meant here. They were not immediately inclined to talk about sexual connotations. Rather, they noted that "queer mixture" is here clearly an expression of Daisy's interest in Winterbourne, and we went on to observe that it conveys her delight in what cannot easily be caught or pinned down in any one category.

We were now coming to another of my five general questions and examining how Daisy regards Winterbourne. Her outburst at the end of the Chillon trip was a crucial discussion point here. Why does she charge him with being "horrid" when he announces his imminent return to Geneva? What does she mean when she says that what he calls "the last" she regards as "the first" (77)? How does each see the relationship that has sprung up between them? Who is the real flirt here?

Being left with only one one-hour session in which to address the three remaining questions, I had to make something of a jump to the party at Mrs. Walker's in chapter 4, which takes place after Daisy's refusal to get into this lady's carriage in order to escape from the allegedly cynical eyes of Rome and how those eyes assess her willingness to walk around unescorted with a Giovanelli. Picking up on the issue of who is the real flirt in this novella, I began by drawing attention to the exchange around "flirt" between Daisy and Winterbourne, where he announces "gravely" that he is "afraid your habits are those of a flirt," a point that she concedes with great alacrity: "I'm a fearful, frightful flirt! Did you ever hear of a nice girl that was not?" To which he is reduced to returning, "You're a very nice girl, but I wish you would flirt with me, and me only" (99). I encouraged the students to puzzle over this statement: what does flirting actually mean? Is it possible to flirt with one person and one person only? Why would it be better for Daisy to flirt with Winterbourne only? Would that be in her interest or in his? Has he not been provoked by her to reveal the nonserious nature of his intentions? (The lady in

Geneva seems to command his interest more permanently than does Daisy.) Be that as it may, for Daisy the simple fact is that Winterbourne is "the last man [she] should think of flirting with," since he is "too stiff" (as might be expected of someone with so cold a name) (99).

This exchange invites that simultaneity of interpretation that is often called (Jamesian) ambiguity. Daisy's response can be read both as a more than flirtatious interest in Winterbourne (as was already implied at the end of the Chillon trip by her insistence that this occasion was for her "the first" rather than "the last" in their relationship) and as a rich rejection of the social system that he supports. The system is most clearly represented by its twin pillars in the story: Mrs. Costello and Mrs. Walker. Daisy's charge that he is "too stiff" also ties up interestingly with Mrs. Walker's turning her back "straight upon Miss Miller" when Daisy attempts to leave at the end of the party (101). Winterbourne, we could conclude, is "too stiff" because he is too "straight" in his observance of the rigid rules by which Europeanized Americans organize their conduct.[1] Like his fellow expatriates, he is wholly unable to grasp the social semiotics of the behavior displayed by real Americans like Daisy Miller or real Europeans like Giovanelli. We arrived at this important conclusion when we considered the nature of the relationship between Daisy and Giovanelli, partly on the basis of the same exchange between Daisy and Winterbourne, where he cautions her against flirting with an Italian who may interpret her attentiveness as more than a noncommittal, mutual, amorous teasing: "he means something else." Daisy explains that she is not "flirting; we are too good friends for that; we are very intimate friends," which makes Winterbourne exclaim that "if you are in love with each other it is another affair" (100). This statement is wide of the mark, as Daisy's nonverbal response (blushing and getting up) amply demonstrates, causing him to "exclaim mentally that little American flirts were the queerest creatures in the world" (100). Lo and behold, here was the term *queer* again, this time applied by Winterbourne to Daisy and just at the point when she is calling him too stiff! I was really getting excited by these discoveries, some of which were actually made in class. Even if it was I who was doing the discovering, it still helped make these classes creative, something happening then and there, the students' own input (their responses to questions) playing a role in the process.

So here is the conclusion we had arrived at regarding the interpersonal dynamics in *Daisy Miller*: Winterbourne's straightness in playing by the social rules laid down by the Europeanized Americans, combined with his duplicity in wanting to continue his connection with the lady in Geneva while having a good time with this "little American flirt," blocks any chance of a real relationship with Daisy. We could now consider how it might be Giovanelli's greater queerness that enables Giovanelli to become Daisy's intimate friend. It struck us that for one thing he is heavily feminized in the text—think of "his decorative smile" (100)—and that his intimacy with Daisy in many ways resembles the sort that women friends share. For another, he is not as easily placed socially as Winterbourne and the Euro-Americans at first assume. Despite Winterbourne's preliminary estimate of him as "a music-master, or a penny-a-liner, or a third-rate artist" (89), Giovanelli turns out to be "a perfectly respectable little man. . . . in a small way a *cavaliere avvocato*" (103). He thus also meets the nonsexual connotation of the term *queer* that we had identified in our first session as constituting a major source of Winterbourne's initial attraction for Daisy, the "queer mixture" that defies easy classification, but that Winterbourne's later behavior in the story—stiffly observing the proprieties determined by Euro-American society—works to straighten out. The queer mixture that Daisy represents, of "innocence and crudity" (78) or "audacity and innocence" (90), cannot be enjoyed by Winterbourne, intent as he is on determining which of these two poles in fact applies. By contrast, the pleasure-oriented Giovanelli does not worry himself over such categories but simply counts himself lucky to adorn his day-to-day social life with this magnificently charming Daisy in a manner entirely similar to the way in which he decorates his buttonhole with an attractive almond blossom (108).

We had now covered enough ground to be poised to deal swiftly (there being only fifteen minutes left) with the final two questions. Although what the Roman fever is should be clear to any careful reader, in most editions a footnote spells it out. But asking the question beforehand ensures that students will look out for the information. The malaria that Daisy contracts may symbolize the ostracism she suffers at the hands of the Europeanized Americans; the illness, in this reading, is brought on by Winterbourne's chilling decision, on the basis of Daisy's presence with Giovanelli at the Colosseum at midnight, that she "was a young lady whom a gentleman need no longer be at pains to respect" (111). Not all my students had arrived at this idea, and the specific question of who is responsible for Daisy's illness led to a brief concluding discussion in which we covered such points as Daisy's recklessness, which causes her to take one risk too many (an idea that need not rule out the symbolic dimension of the illness); her confidence that she is healthy enough; her intention to take what are presumably quinine pills (112) and her abandonment of that intention ("I don't care . . . whether I have Roman fever or not" [113]) when she realizes to what extent Winterbourne has given up on her.

Looking back on the course, I believe that my success in teaching *Daisy Miller* was due to the fact that, as a cicerone to this text, I was more a Giovanelli than a Winterbourne: able to open myself up, queerly and innocently, to the seductive charm of the story instead of imposing on it such preconceived notions as my published research would have led me, all stiffly and all straightly, to adopt.

NOTE

[1]When I teach the course again, I should like to confront the students with Robert Weisbuch's reading of Winterbourne's stiffness as a diminution of his sexuality to a mere "phallic reduction of the Other" (74).

Daisy Miller and Reception: Lessons Learned Teaching Henry James in Europe

Nicolas S. Witschi

Every now and then, novice and veteran instructors alike experience the sort of moment that I had during my first day of teaching Henry James to a group of American studies majors in Germany. I was in my second week as a Fulbright professor at the University of Regensburg, teaching an upper-division seminar on American realism and naturalism, and the assigned reading for the day was *Daisy Miller*. No sooner had I finished asking for initial impressions of the story when one student fairly shouted out, "He's anti-European and anti-Catholic!" This not entirely inaccurate assessment of James did not surprise me nearly as much as did the force with which it was delivered. In my discussion notes for the day, I had written little reminders to myself about drawing the class's attention to issues such as character point of view, the beginnings of realism's narrative voice, and James's use of humor. But the other students in the class seized on the first speaker's emphatic assertion, and before I fully knew what was happening, I found myself moderating a rather heated discussion in which James's almost 125-year-old representation of an American in Europe was repeatedly criticized for the overgeneralizations and misinterpretations of its European elements. I was, of course, compelled then and there to rethink the day's lesson plan.

In a number of ways, my students and I had read two altogether different books. I was accustomed to thinking of James as an American author who wrote about American visitors to Europe, a notion that has become almost axiomatic in American criticism. With regard to *Daisy Miller*, this way of positioning James allows us to see his 1878 account of a Schenectady heiress's passage through the expatriate communities of Geneva and Rome as one of his earliest and most important international-theme narratives. It was in this framework that I had taught the text to my American students, and their mostly sympathetic responses to the book's title character were, I soon learned, largely conditioned by that critical assumption. My German students, in contrast, approached the story as being predominantly about European culture and people. For them, the tale's theme and content were distinctly more local than international, and they responded accordingly. (The question of when Germans, or for that matter anyone in Europe, do and do not self-identify as European, especially in response to American cultural aggressiveness, is an interesting topic but one better reserved for another time.) Despite—or perhaps because of—his affinity for European culture, James seemed clearly guilty of alternately idealizing and demonizing some of its aspects. Daisy Miller and Frederick Winterbourne, in this reading, are little more than unappreciative tourists.

Reflecting further on the matter, I have come to see that the difference in how my students on opposite sides of the Atlantic respond to the story boils down to the problem that confronts Daisy: the tendency of people only slightly outside her peer group to misunderstand and hence misrepresent her. The misfortune of being misread is a significant concern for many students in the United States; they repeatedly identify with this aspect of the text. However, by the end of the discussion in that German classroom, I learned that what concerned these readers was not Daisy's being misread but rather the American tendency to misread and misrepresent others. Daisy, of course, fails to recognize (or at least remains indifferent to) the subtle social cues of the world she has come into. Similarly, Winterbourne fails to appreciate not only Daisy's feelings for him but also his for her, a situation ironically communicated by the self-congratulatory tone with which he decides near the end that Daisy "had become easy to read" (111). Winterbourne is equally wrong in his reading of Giovanelli, a "subtle Roman" (115) to whom he at first mistakenly imputes less-than-gentlemanly motives, a point to which my German students were especially sensitive. That James's most significant European character in this story should be the subject of misrecognition also brings into focus the often edgy relationship that both Winterbourne and the Miller family have with the family's steward, Eugenio.

For some, misreadings of Daisy are central to the story; for others, the key issue is American misreading as a whole. Through it all, James weaves a story in which one's very life depends on the ability to read and recognize other people. In sum, the matter of response and reception stands at the heart of *Daisy Miller*. Building in part on the impetus generated by that first day with James in a German classroom, I have developed a number of approaches to *Daisy Miller*, and to the teaching of literature more broadly, that focus on reception in both historical and textual dimensions. In what follows, I sketch out several avenues that instructors may take, with *Daisy Miller* in hand, to explore with students how classroom responses to the text can be productively illuminated, complicated, and supplemented by the inclusion of materials that reflect culturally and historically specific reader responses.

When we look into the reception history of *Daisy Miller*, particularly as a means of evaluating both the novella's widespread popularity and its effectiveness as a literary work, the first important reader with whom we must contend is its author, who has been an influential commentator on his own work. Students can easily be prompted to do a little basic research on this influence. Beginning with my second day of teaching James in Germany, I made a habit of assigning students at just about every level the task of digging up whatever they could find about how readers respond to the story, in any context and time frame. After giving a brief lecture on the premises of reception studies and on the types of material to look for (see Machor and Goldstein), I sent them to the library. In Germany, I stayed close to my host department's American studies curriculum, so I had them seek predominantly

Anglophone materials, although they did turn up a few interesting German reviews of James.

When I make this assignment, I can usually count on one or two intrepid researchers to turn up James's 1880 letter to Mrs. Lynn Linton, reprinted in William T. Stafford's excellent collection of documents related to the story (students in search of reception material for *Daisy Miller* are more likely to look at Stafford than at Leon Edel's *Henry James: Selected Letters*, which also contains this letter). Linton had written to ask James about his title character, declaring that an argument over Daisy's disposition had cost her at least one friendship (Edel 171). In his reply, James offers the opinion that "poor little Daisy Miller was, as I understand her, above all things *innocent*" (Stafford 115), a notion he repeats several times in the letter. He concludes:

> The whole idea of the story is the little tragedy of a light, thin, natural, unsuspecting creature being sacrificed as it were to a social rumpus that went on quite over her head. . . . She never had a thought of scandalising anybody. (115–16)

Thus, according to James, could the breach between friends be healed. All controversy about Daisy is neatly contained by his broad disavowal of any effective agency in her actions.

James offers a similar reading in his 1909 preface to the story in the heavily revised New York edition. More than a few students will fulfill the assignment by bringing in this preface, which, given its inclusion in the Penguin Classics edition of the story, is not hard to find. James observes, "my little exhibition is made to no degree whatever in critical but, quite inordinately and extravagantly, in poetical terms" (42). Similarly, in recounting a conversation he once had in Italy with a friend who tried to identify a nearby group of young women as "Daisy Millers," James reports that he "bristled" and, again, affirmed that his "supposedly typical little figure was of course pure poetry, and had never been anything else" (43). In both the Linton letter and the preface, he attempts to close off any speculation about his character's motives: she was "innocent," unaware, and above all more literary artifice than realistic. Many a classroom discussion of *Daisy Miller* has begun and ended on the question of Daisy's innocence. Indeed, lacking alternatives, students will be quick to judge the book solely on James's terms, a tendency that we would be wise to resist. His readings are best taken as one reader's impressions; a measure of how a wider culture understood and embraced the text, they are hardly authoritative or definitive.

Reception study involves the examination not of what an author meant to write but of how a particular text—misprints, typos, and all—fared with its historical readers. That is, one looks not at what was written but at what was read (Machor and Goldstein ix–x). This key methodological move proves quite useful for *Daisy Miller*, because the version of the story that readers have responded to over the years was not always the one that James favored (see Horne, "Henry James at Work" 63–72). Even such small details as the changes he made in supervising the tale's publication in book form bear significantly on interpretation. How, for example, do readers respond to a story divided into two parts (the 1878 *Cornhill Magazine* serialization titled "Daisy Miller: A Study") instead of into four chapters (the 1879 book version published in Britain by Macmillan and reproduced by Penguin)? How does the addition of a subtitle, apparently unintended by James but nevertheless a key feature of the novella's initial serial and book publication, affect the understanding and production of meaning? In his New York edition preface, James disavows the *Cornhill* subtitle, writing that his story

> qualified itself in that publication and afterwards as "a Study"; for reasons which I confess I fail to recapture unless they may have taken account simply of a certain flatness in my poor little heroine's literal denomination. Flatness indeed, one must have felt, was the very sum of her story; so that perhaps after all the attached epithet was meant but as a deprecation, addressed to the reader, of any great critical hope of stirring scenes. (41)

He laments that, as a title, "Daisy Miller: A Study" put readers in a critical frame of mind, whereas, as noted above, he claims to have intended not criticism but "pure poetry" (43). But a careful reader will consider what manner of cultural or textual work the story performed for the many readers who did—and still do—encounter it with this subtitle. What meanings might "a study" communicate to those who read *Daisy Miller: A Study* in the *Norton Anthology of American Literature* (not a small, isolated group) or those who read the four-part text of the 1879 Macmillan version, complete with subtitle (curiously, Penguin reproduces the text of the original book version but not the full title). At the very least, the subtitle highlights not only the moments where Winterbourne is said to be "studying" women (48, 116) but also the several related instances where he picks Daisy apart in his mind, piece by piece (e.g., 53, 57–58, 111). These representations of a gendered gaze qualify as much more than textual matters thinly hung on questions of poetry and innocence.

Contemporaneous materials such as book reviews, letters, and otherwise recorded commentary often provide the fullest and most telling index of a book's initial reception. Aided by such resources as Daniel Mark Fogel's immeasurably useful chapter on reception in Daisy Miller: *A Dark Comedy of Manners* (12–22) and Kevin J. Hayes's collection of published reviews (67–78), students working on an assignment to gather reception materials will discover a good deal of chatter about the social scandal generated by *Daisy Miller*'s publication. As Fogel points out, the story "occasioned intense debate and some outrage in polite American society" (14). W. D. Howells, James's friend and editor at the *Atlantic Monthly*, famously commented to James Russell Lowell that soon after the novella's publication, "society almost divided itself into Daisy Millerites and anti–Daisy Millerites" (271). A review of Fanny Kemble's *Record of a Girlhood* published in the May 1879 issue of *Scribner's* alludes briefly to the "petty and provincial spirit . . . which in America rails against the warning truth of Mr. Henry James's 'Daisy Miller' " (Penn 157; this reference I recently found by conducting a keyword search for "Daisy Miller" in the *Making of America* archive of nineteenth-century periodicals [cdl.library.cornell.edu/moa/index.html]). Finally, the *New York Times* commented in June 1879 that "[t]here are many ladies in and around New York today . . . who feel very indignant with Mr. James for his portrait of *Daisy Miller*, and declare that it is shameful to give foreigners so untrue a portrait of an American girl" (Fogel, Daisy Miller 14).

Arthur Penn's mention of James's text in his review of Kemble's memoir, taken together with the concern for a truer "portrait" of American girlhood noted in the *New York Times* editorial, indicates the speed with which the name "Daisy Miller" was becoming a crucial signifier of class, nationality, and gender in late-nineteenth-century American culture. For a time, everybody talked about this woman and about what she represented. This phenomenon was perhaps most notable in the use of her name in advice and etiquette guides for young women (Hoxie; on American "girl culture," see Wardley; Tarbox 33–52; Dunlop 153–99). According to the guardians of manners and social decorum, to be a Daisy Miller was to be the unwitting bearer of a "crude and unmanageable prosperity," that is, a young American woman desperately in need of taming and educating (Hoxie 478). James's companion in Italy was hardly alone in wanting to identify, and thus deprecate, someone as a Daisy Miller.

Another method for measuring the extent to which a text has entered the critical lexicon of a culture is to examine adaptations (textual as well as visual), copies, and rewrites. As the catalog of *Daisy Miller*–inspired texts found in chapter 10 of Adeline R. Tintner's *Henry James's Legacy* clearly testifies, Daisy's appeal has cut deeply across the years (see 297–327). James's own 1882 stage adaptation of the story, complete with a revised happy ending in which nobody dies, shows how much audiences had come to cherish Daisy. The ultimate union of Daisy and Winterbourne in the stage version signals James's acknowledgment that his title character may have been worth more to him alive than dead. This play was never staged, only published in the *Atlantic*, so it offers only a tempting glimpse of what James thought audiences wanted to see of his heroine. Tintner provides an impressive record of more than a dozen illuminating examples of creative reinterpretation, including Peter Bogdanovich's controversial 1974 film adaptation based on James's New York edition text and starring Cybill Shepherd. Not surprisingly, students respond well to this film; it engages them on the now more familiar level of the visual and also provides further access to issues central to the original story. As Peggy McCormack's reception study of the film argues, Bogdanovich's direction compels viewers to gaze sympathetically at James's title character. At the same time, the studio's advertising, conducted when everyone knew that Shepherd was the director's mistress, invites a more critical gaze at Daisy/ Cybill (55, 45–46). Paired with the details of the film's reception, the film's compelling interpretation of the story's central concern for how Daisy is seen thus becomes a meditation on how cinematic form continues to hold women's behavior to the excruciating standards encountered by James's "typical little figure" (43).

The issue of *Daisy Miller*'s representation of the gaze brings matters back to my German classroom and to the text of 1878. In the first few lines of his second paragraph, James uses the words "looking" and "looked" (48), which I have always pointed out to my students as an indicator of Winterbourne's dissecting, studious approach to Daisy. My students in Germany, however, were the first (in my experience) to connect this double use of "look" with James's parallel repetition of the word "tourist" in the opening lines of the first paragraph (47). This connection qualifies Winterbourne's relationship not only with Daisy but also with the locale in which he finds her, namely, Europe. In short, "looking" as a form of "study" is a tourist activity practiced equally on unsuspecting women and nationalities, with ramifications of potentially equal severity. The initial moment of dissonance between me and my German students and, more important, the exercises in reception study that we developed as a consequence brought us to a broader understanding both of the text and of its work as a piece of American culture. By reading *Daisy Miller* with self-identified Europeans, I, equally self-identified as an American, began to see how attention to reception and response can contribute productively to an interrogation of the labels of nationalism. Together we developed a reading that recognizes that the line distinguishing tourist from native is often negotiated at one's figurative, if not literal, peril.

Perhaps James had some of this peril in mind in writing the novella as he did, and then again perhaps he did not. At the end of his preface, addressing the question of whether any hint lingers of the social controversy generated by his story, he refers once more to the conversation he had with his companion in Italy: "As for the original grossness of readers, I dare say I added, that was another matter—but one which at any rate had then quite ceased to signify" (43). To say the least, readers of the story continue to find that it signifies quite remarkably. An attentiveness to questions of both historical and ongoing reading brings to life not only those issues raised by the text but also many issues of equal significance that are found only in what readers have had to say about it.

"Dramatise, Dramatise, Dramatise!"

Greg W. Zacharias

Henry James's fiction, including *Daisy Miller* and *The Turn of the Screw*, is fundamentally dramatic. The earlier fiction depends on the drama of realism, which presents character and plot in a fictive version of stage performance. In fact, James rewrote *Daisy Miller* for the stage as both *Daisy Miller: A Comedy* (1882) and *Daisy Miller: A Comedy in Three Acts* (1883). The dramatic model is essentially the one that he offers in "The Art of Fiction" (1887); through it the artist presents to readers "a concrete image and produce[s] a reality" ([*Literary Criticism*] 53). He recalls in his New York edition preface that *Daisy Miller* was the product of his reminder to himself to "dramatise, dramatise, dramatise!" (*Art* 267).

James developed the later fiction from a dramatic model as well. In the preface to *The Awkward Age* (1908), he remembers composing that novel as if he were a "dramatist" (*Art* 109). He continues, describing his idea for *The Awkward Age* (1899), which he published six months after *The Turn of the Screw* (1898):

> The beauty of the conception was in this approximation of the respective divisions of my form to the successive Acts of a Play—as to which it was more than ever a case for charmed capitals. The divine distinction of the act of a play—and a greater than any other it easily succeeds in arriving at—was, I reasoned, in its special, its guarded objectivity.
> (110–11)

After the publication of *The Awkward Age* preface, in his notes for what would become *The Ivory Tower*, James thus conceives his plan for that work: "I mean I come back, I come back yet again and again, to my only seeing it in the dramatic way—as I can only see everything and anything now" (*Complete Notebooks* 260). And as Leon Edel writes of James's fiction that followed his disaster in the theater with *Guy Domville*, "Henry James now brought to fiction the very mechanics he had invoked for the writing of his plays. He talks of his fiction as if it were drama" ("Henry James: The Dramatic Years" 63). Thus James's characters act, and we readers watch their actions. Narrative intrusion is kept to a minimum, ideally, and characters present themselves, as it were. We readers are left to ourselves to understand them, their plots, and their meanings. To witness the imaginative drama is to understand Jamesian fiction "really and completely [as] a scenic thing" (*Art* 110).

The relation between dramatizing and performing on the one hand and fiction on the other was present for James through much of his life. In his autobiographical volume, *A Small Boy and Others*, he recalls his theatergoing habit (103–27) and remembers that productions based on Charles Dickens's fiction, as well as the dramatic power of Dickens's fiction itself, impressed him deeply (113–20). He remembers vividly one reading of *David Copperfield* by his cousin, to which he listened from beneath the dining room table. He hid there because he was supposed to be in bed but did not want to miss the introduction to his home of the new installment of the serialized novel. He was discovered only after he "broke into sobs of sympathy that disclosed [his] subterfuge" (118–19). Clearly James knew and felt the power of the dramatized reading deeply enough to recall it some sixty years later. Nevertheless, though public readings of fiction were frequent during his lifetime, he neither remarks on his attendance nor seems to have read from any of his own work. Instead, he comments on the fascination the book and the bookstore held for him (65–66, 75–76, 77–78, 80–82; *Notes* 4). He did, however, give a lecture series late in his life, in 1905: "The Question of Our Speech" and "The Lesson of Balzac." Contemporary reports commend the competence of his subject and his delivery (Edel, *Master* 280–82). His dramatic sense is a power that teachers may use today.

James's dramatic method has important consequences for reading and teaching. Given the degree of visual and aural specificity of his fiction, it makes sense to find ways to make that drama present and available for students. In addition, helping students see and hear the fiction counters the charge that it is too difficult to understand or relate to. James's fiction *is* difficult if one tries to read it as one reads the newspaper. But if one takes James on his own terms and thinks about what one has taken, then the difficulty diminishes and the pleasure of reading and talking about it increases. Teachers can use a range of strategies for modeling a dramatic reading of the fiction.

For example, one reads James slowly to "hear" the characters speak, as if one were listening to actors in the theater or on film. But one sees and hears the dramatic nature of the fiction not only in the dialogue, as one would in a stage play, but also in the narration, since James's narrators are highly dramatic, holding their own as quasi characters. So in James's work what can be explored about a character in dramatic and performative terms can also be explored about a narrator. More careful reading (the central aim of this strategy) in order to experience what words do to establish and develop meaning in terms of character and place encourages thinking, discussing, and writing about some of the elements of the fiction—narrative voice, characterization, details of scene—taken either alone or in relation to one another.

Such a strategy for reading, thinking, and talking about James's fiction as dramatic in nature also engages instructors with students, students with one another, and instructors and students alike with the text, which becomes the focus of dynamic work in the classroom. Attention to crucial passages, either alone or in the context of other passages, encourages extra attention to those texts. Students enact character and narrative attitudes, trying on a range of perspectives and provisionally advancing a range of meanings. The methods of teaching drama may be adapted easily to teaching James's fiction. Edward L. Rocklin speaks of "the performance approach" (50), in which the text becomes a "*performing text*":

> The term *performing text* denotes the intersection of a performing art with literary interpretation, as well as emphasizes that the double existence of drama is irreducible. . . . Because the performance approach works by focusing on the design of a text and the choices embodied in that design, the approach also invites students to think about themselves as writers. (53, 60; see also Shand)

James dictated his later fiction, including *The Turn of the Screw*. A way of reading that recognizes the speaking pace of prose encourages students to pay closer attention to the text and thus to details of character, plot, and figurative language. What is more, James structures *The Turn of the Screw* as a layered oral performance, emphasizing the orality of this text first through the introductory first-person narrator, then through Douglas's implied reading, and then through the governess's first-person narrative. In addition, James's way of presenting *Daisy Miller* as a kind of literary stage piece (it was, we recall, adapted for the stage) suggests reading aloud.

Instructors should model a way of reading that emphasizes character voices and also considers the voice of the main narrator. (This strategy, as all those offered here, works well for all of James's fiction.) The instructor might ask students if they hear characters in the same way and to discuss how and why they hear them differently. Students could be encouraged to read key passages aloud while trying to represent character and meaning, stressing what for them are important words and phrases. The reading itself, either by an instructor or a student, becomes a performed interpretation available for discussion. Through discussion of that reading-performance, students and their instructors both find new ways to discuss James's texts and their meanings.

In *Daisy Miller* such scenes for combined reading, performance, analysis, and interpretation might include Daisy's first long speech to Winterbourne (" 'Yes,' said Miss Miller, without examining this analogy; 'it always made me wish I was here. But I needn't have done that for dresses' " [56]). Or later, in Rome, as Daisy speaks to Winterbourne, James's narrator directs our attention: "The young girl looked at him more gravely, but with eyes that were prettier than ever. 'I have never allowed a gentleman to dictate to me, or to interfere with anything I do' " (88). How one interprets these speeches says much about how one interprets Daisy and thus *Daisy Miller*. Instructors can ask questions such as, "Is Daisy flirting?" "Is she manipulating?" "Is she ignorant and innocent?" They should always make sure that students address the question, "How would one hear that in her voice?," when they answer.

Such a strategy can encourage students to ask such questions themselves, eventually taking over the role of the instructor altogether.

Winterbourne's exchange with Mrs. Costello following his first meeting with Daisy, as he plans to take Daisy to the Château de Chillon (beginning with "He had, however, engaged to do more than proved feasible, in promising to present his aunt, Mrs Costello, to Miss Daisy Miller" [61]) is another long passage whose reading may yield different, and thus interesting, interpretations from students. What is Winterbourne's motive, toward the end of the conversation, for "smiling and curling his mustache" (64)? How do students hear that description, so nearly a stage direction? What would it mean to emphasize either "smiling" or "curling"? Or should each receive the same emphasis? And what is Mrs. Costello's reason for warning Winterbourne, just before he strokes his mustache, "You have lived too long out of the country. You will be sure to make some great mistake. You are too innocent" (64)?

Reading Randolph Miller aloud can be fun and prompt a closer reading of all the characters in *Daisy Miller*. Whether a student—or an instructor, for that matter—reads Randolph's "We've got a bigger place than this. . . . It's all gold on the walls" (81) with pride, boastfulness, whining, or some other way reveals how that reader explicitly or implicitly understands James's parody or satire of American children like Randolph. It will all be in the voice of the reader.

The Turn of the Screw's narrator may be studied similarly. How a reader/auditor/performer delivers a sentence shapes how one understands the narrator at that point in the tale. The meaning of even a sentence as easily overlooked as "I was lifted aloft on a great wave of infatuation and pity" (37) turns on how one reads and hears the narrator's voice. The governess's ego is emphasized if one hears an emphasis on "I was lifted aloft." But her attention to and concern with Miles gain significance if "infatuation and pity" are emphasized. The degree of vocal tension or relaxation one reads/hears when, after confronting Flora at the beginning of chapter 10, the governess recalls, "At that moment, in the state of my nerves, I absolutely believed she lied" (69), affects how one interprets the governess then. So too does the tension in "How can I retrace today the strange steps of my obsession?" (80) demonstrate both the reader's and speaker's understanding of her rationality. Of course, the hearing/reading of two of the most dramatic sentences in *The Turn of the Screw*, Miles's "Peter Quint—you devil!" and the governess's last line, "We were alone with the quiet day, and his little heart, dispossessed, had stopped" (120), determines much about how we understand the entire story. But for almost any passage, a dramatic reading reveals the reader's interpretation and, by inviting counterreadings, opens discussion.

In James, local color and scene often function as accompaniments or supplements to character. Gilbert Osmond's homes in *The Portrait of a Lady*, Venice in *The Wings of the Dove*, Paris in *The Ambassadors*, Rome in *Daisy*

Miller, and Bly in *The Turn of the Screw* are only a few examples. Details of scene carry meaning. Here, too, reading aloud and thinking about how to read the text provide a strategy for students to approach James's style and meaning.

The opening paragraphs of *Daisy Miller* are intensely visual. With the cue of James's original subtitle, *A Study*, they gain significance. One could discuss the representation of Vevey's attractiveness, especially the Trois Couronnes, to American tourists like the Millers in terms of its comfort, "entertainment," and "business" (47). Good details are the flags flying from the new fashionable hotel, the "neat German waiters," "Russian princesses," "little Polish boys," "the Dent du Midi," and "the picturesque towers of the Castle of Chillon" (48). Scenes in Rome, both exterior and interior, bear similar examination. As with characterization, the investigation of setting should begin with discussion of how a reading ought to be or was performed in order to stress the meaning of the details of a scene.

James's narrative voice is one of the most difficult aspects of the text for many students to account for confidently. Part of the difficulty may rest in the narrative persona James assumes; in the narrative irony; or in the deployment of a character as narrator, as in *The Turn of the Screw*. But discussion of the narrator and of narrative description may bring students to a new understanding of the text and of some of James's basic tactics, such as the use of irony and indirect discourse.

An example of ironic narration in *Daisy Miller* is the narrator's comment concerning Winterbourne, that "when his friends spoke of him, they usually said that he was at Geneva, 'studying.' When his enemies spoke of him, they said—but, after all, he had no enemies; he was an extremely amiable fellow, and universally liked" (48). At the end of the story, after Winterboune's remark that "I have lived too long in foreign parts," the narrator says, "Nevertheless, [Winterbourne] went back to live at Geneva, whence there continue to come the most contradictory accounts of his motives of sojourn: a report that he is 'studying' hard—an intimation that he is much interested in a very clever foreign lady" (116). To consider the narrator as an active player in the fictive drama rather than a passive reporter of action encourages students to apply the same strategies of reading to James's narrator that they apply to James's characters.

Discussion of indirect discourse, a device by which the narrator reports the thoughts or feelings of a character without quotation marks—either with the words that the character would use (indirect discourse) or with the narrator's own words (free indirect discourse)—is a useful way of talking about how the narrator affects our understanding of a character. When the narrative persona moves away from quotation of a character (direct discourse) and toward free indirect discourse and, further, speculates about a character's thoughts, feelings, and motives, the report becomes less objective, and its fictive reality merges with aspects of the narrator's subjectivity. Investigating this process leads to an exploration of James's point-of-view technique—but with a difference. Attention to narrative discursive strategies raises questions about whose point of view—the character's or the narrator's?—is being deployed and how such a deployment affects meaning. This consideration is important in both *Daisy Miller*, whose subtitle points to the implications of studying, and *The Turn of the Screw*, where interpretation of facts and motives is as much an interest for the governess-narrator as it is for the reader, who must rely on the governess for almost all the information. In both texts, examining the narrator leads to discussions of James's narrative logic and thus to strategies of reading and meaning.

In Winterbourne's first conversation with Daisy, as Winterbourne listens to her talk about tutors for Randolph, the narrator describes his perceptions indirectly:

> He found it very pleasant. It was many years since he had heard a young girl talk so much. It might have been said of this unknown young lady, who had come and sat down beside him upon a bench, that she chattered. She was very quiet, she sat in a charming tranquil attitude; but her lips and her eyes were constantly moving. She had a soft, slender, agreeable voice, and her tone was decidedly sociable. (56)

The challenge for readers of this passage—like so many others—is to work out which descriptions and emphases ought to be attributed to the narrator and which to Winterbourne and how either attribution affects meaning.

Later, in the pivotal scene when Daisy and Mrs. Walker confront each other, Mrs. Walker in her carriage and Daisy in the street, the text reads, " 'Gracious me!' exclaimed Daisy. She looked again at Mr Giovanelli, then she turned to Winterbourne. There was a little pink flush in her cheek; she was tremendously pretty" (92). The reader must decide to whom Daisy is "tremendously pretty"—the narrator or Winterbourne—in this use of indirect discourse.

The narrative logic of *The Turn of the Screw* is more complex and possibly more interesting. There are only first-person narrators—the conventional narrator who opens the tale, Douglas, and the governess—and each operates as both narrator and character. The inherent ambiguity of the novella, so much of which is the consequence of narrators who tell their own stories—invites such experimentation with reading and meaning. How, for example, should the concluding lines, all given in the past tense, of chapter 1 be read? With innocence? sarcasm? cynicism?

> Was n't it just a story-book over which I had fallen a-doze and a-dream? No; it was a big ugly antique but convenient house, embodying a few features of a building still older, half-displaced and half-utilised, in which I had the fancy of our being almost as lost as a handful of passengers in a great drifting ship. Well, I was strangely at the helm! (32–33)

Finally, it should be said that this approach, like any other, isn't for everyone. It is useful for the teacher who structures a student-centered class, since it foregrounds what students bring to the classroom community and nurtures their respect for and trust in each member of that community.

Teaching Theory through *Daisy Miller*

Pericles Lewis

Readers of David Lodge's novel *Changing Places* will recall the character Morris Zapp, whose ambition was to write a series of critical commentaries on Jane Austen:

> . . . to be utterly exhaustive, to examine the novels from every conceivable angle, historical, biographical, rhetorical, mythical, Freudian, Jungian, existentialist, Marxist, structuralist, Christian-allegorical, ethical, exponential, linguistic, phenomenological, archetypal, you name it; so that when each commentary was written there would be simply *nothing further to say* about the novel in question. (44)

At the end of each semester, I tell Zapp's story to my students in Introduction to Literary Theory, overwhelmed as they sometimes are by the array of theories, from the New Criticism through deconstruction to cultural studies, to which the course introduces them.

Students often crave demonstrations or examples of how to apply theory. Throughout the semester, I bring in short poems or prose passages for discussion, and I refer to novels that many will have read. However, I keep my main demonstration for the last day of class. Students are required to read *Daisy Miller* over spring break and encouraged to talk about it in relation to literary theory in their sections as well as to write their final paper as an application of a particular theory to the story (or to another story of their choosing). Teaching assistants (for whose excellent work in this difficult course

I am most grateful) report that the weakest and the strongest students tend to write on *Daisy Miller*, while those in the middling group are more inclined to choose a favorite text of their own. On the final day of class, I sketch a series of potential readings of *Daisy Miller*, seen from various theoretical angles.

After my students read challenging articles by Cleanth Brooks, Hans-Georg Gadamer, Stanley Fish, Roman Jakobson, Jacques Derrida, Paul de Man, Barbara Johnson, Jacques Lacan, Michel Foucault, Edward Said, Henry Louis Gates, Jr., Stephen Greenblatt, Catherine Gallagher, and Judith Butler, they often want to see how these theories apply to a work of literature. Drawing on philosophy, linguistics, anthropology, and other disciplines, theory does not always resemble what one typically thinks of as criticism. Yet each theoretical movement we discuss in the course has spawned its own type of literary criticism. Too often, alas, critics merely take the theory of their favorite theorist and apply it wholesale to a literary text. Offering theoretical readings of *Daisy Miller* inevitably involves a certain violence toward a rather delicate text. It also has a tendency to devolve into parody, but I hope that a little bit of parody gives the students some sense of the various schools of critics. My demonstration suggests to the students how literary theory can sometimes go over the top. It shows both the power and limitations of theory. In *S/Z*, Roland Barthes took apart a classic or "readerly" text (Balzac's "Sarrasine") to show it to be modern or "writerly" (3–28). Like "Sarrasine," *Daisy Miller* is a story about interpretation and the social codes associated with gender. Following Barthes's example (and that of Frederick Crews in *Postmodern Pooh*), I argue that the apparently straightforward text of *Daisy Miller* is susceptible of a variety of interpretations. I treat some schools in detail and others only in passing. I do not aim to give thorough readings of the text, since students are doing so, and I treat least thoroughly the theories on which they are expected to write their final papers. In my representations of various critical schools, no similarity to actual critics, living or dead, is intended.

The course begins by looking at three older types of criticism, each of which was attacked by the New Critics: the mimetic (old-historicist), the expressive (biographical), and the affective or pragmatic (moralizing). All three are described by M. H. Abrams in *The Mirror and the Lamp* (3–29). The New Critics, reacting against these types of criticism, proposed something that we could call formal criticism, or objective criticism, which is concerned with the text as object rather than with its relations to nature, an author, or an audience. The mimetic model of literature inspired older historical critics, who might look to *Daisy Miller* as a portrait or study of young American womanhood during the Gilded Age (James uses the word "study" in the subtitle of the story and the word "portrait" of course in *The Portrait of a Lady*). For mimetic critics who demand realism of a work of art, James might well score points for how he describes a young woman of middle-brow education but significant wealth on the European tour. Critics of his later work often complained that he fell away from the standards of realism attained by such stories as *Daisy Miller*.

The expressive critic, concerned with the greatness of James's mind (T. S. Eliot called that "mind so fine that no idea could violate it" [*Selected Prose* 151]) might look to James's biography to see possible sources of inspiration for *Daisy Miller*. Here, the biographical critic would probably be interested in James's adolescent fascination with his cousin Minny Temple, who died young and who inspired such characters as Isabel Archer in *The Portrait of a Lady* and Milly Theale in *The Wings of the Dove*. The biographical critic might also look at Winterbourne as a sort of self-portrait, a theme I delve into later in the lecture when I get to queer studies. At any rate, the expressivist is likely to praise James's fine description of a certain type of sensibility in Winterbourne.

The affective critic naturally asks, What is the moral of this story? The most obvious moral concerns Daisy's behavior: Don't go around with strange Italian men. The stern, puritanical moralist may be happy enough with Daisy's fate, but some moral critics will remind us that the code to which Daisy Miller is held is an old-fashioned one and that malaria is carried by mosquitoes, not by strange Italian men. Another, more troubling moral lies in Winterbourne's final judgment about Daisy, which I explore later in the lecture.

Against all this moralizing, biographizing, and realizing, the formalist critic or New Critic objects, asking us to return to the text itself. There are all sorts of interesting formal patterns in the text, but I examine an obvious one, the series of flower metaphors. Annie P. Miller's nickname is Daisy, and a daisy is a short-lived flower. It represents innocence. The formalist calls our attention to James's use of words associated with flowers to describe Daisy, as when Winterbourne thinks that her glance is "perfectly direct and unshrinking" (she is more a daisy than a shrinking violet) and also that her eyes are "singularly honest and fresh" (53). Daisy unfortunately meets up with Giovanelli, who has a penchant for plucking flowers and putting them in his buttonholes (108), just as he enjoys practicing his fine English on American heiresses. When Daisy dies in the spring, she winds up in the Protestant cemetery beneath the cypresses and the "thick spring flowers" (115). This tracing of metaphors is of course fairly simplistic. A New Critic would be alive to the ironies of James's text and undoubtedly notice the central tension that animates it: the tension between Winterbourne's desire for Daisy and his fear of her recklessness. The New Critic would note that Daisy displays "no irony" (53), which suggests immediately that she is innocent, and finally the New Critic would note the central irony of the story, namely, that Winterbourne in a sense makes Daisy guilty by failing to believe in her. This central irony is what I referred to earlier when I said that there were messages in this story that the moralist critic might object to; I further explore the problem of this irony below.

After an introductory unit on formalism and the New Criticism, the course turns to hermeneutics and reader-response theory. The reader-response critic might be interested in how the narrator of *Daisy Miller*, who acts like a third-person narrator with access to Winterbourne's thoughts but nonetheless refers to himself in the first person, sets up a sort of dialogue with us, the readers, by addressing us as "you" (47). He then corrects his interpretation of events and claims to lack knowledge of Winterbourne's character, as in the expressions "I hardly know whether . . ." and "What I should say is . . ." (48). The reader-response critic might note how the narrator forces us to experience Winterbourne as a mystery: it is difficult for us to know his thoughts, just as it is difficult for him to know Daisy's.

A good portion of the course is devoted to structuralism and deconstruction. The structuralist sets up for us a neat set of oppositions that define the text:

male	female	innocent	coquette
Protestant	Catholic	Winterbourne	Eugenio
America	Europe	Winterbourne	Giovanelli
Geneva	Rome	cultivated	wild
reason	instinct	exclusive	common

In this context, we might note Winterbourne's name: his bourne or harbor is wintery Geneva; and he can be opposed to the Italian Eugenio, whose name means "well-born" and who was born in the south of Italy. The structuralist does not fail to note that all the oppositions center on the problem of sex.

There are several tacks that the deconstructive critic could take, but let us begin with the word *flirt*. The deconstructor will note that each binary opposition described by the structuralist breaks down. What is the agency of this breakdown? It is Daisy, the flirt. The deconstructionist turns to the *American Heritage Dictionary* and reads that the verb *to flirt* is defined as follows:

> *intr.* 1. To make playfully romantic or sexual overtures. 2. To act so as to attract or provoke: *The bullfighter flirted with death*. 3. To move abruptly or jerkily. —*tr*. 1. To toss or flip suddenly. 2. To move quickly.

The first intransitive definition includes precisely the problem that Winterbourne faces, whether to view Daisy's overtures as romantic or sexual. He decides that Daisy is a flirt—"a pretty American flirt" (57)—but this category does not make it easy for him to place her on one side or the other of the binary oppositions offered to us by the structuralists. Rather, her tendency as a flirt is to flirt from side to side. James even uses the verb in sense 3 when he writes that Daisy "flirted back with a pretty little cry and a shudder from the edge of the *oubliettes*" (76). Whereas women are supposed to stick strictly to the private sphere, Daisy enjoys being seen in public (on the Pincian hill, in the lobby of her hotel, out on the lake, in the Château de Chillon, in the

Colosseum). As her mother says, "She goes round everywhere" (83). Daisy moves abruptly or jerkily from apparent innocence to apparent guilt.

She also moves up and down the social scale at will, as her intimacy with servants indicates. As James writes, "She seemed to [Winterbourne], in all this, an extraordinary mixture of innocence and crudity" or again "an inscrutable combination of audacity and innocence" (78, 90). The word "flirt" sets up a chain of signifiers—a daisy chain?—that can never find its transcendental signified. The other signifiers associated with it are: "wild," "respectability," "nice," "dreadful" (63); "innocent," "uncultivated," "guilty" (64); "exclusive" (66); "natural" (68); "common," "delicate," "grace" (68); "freedom" (75); "ignorant," "vulgar," "bad" (80); "indelicate" (94); "the Golden Age" (103); "pretty," "undefended" (105). The deconstructionist would note how both "delicate" and "indelicate," as well as the opposites "innocent" and "guilty," appear in this list. Flirtation is the free play of the signifier detached from the signified. The flirt seems to occupy both sides of the opposition and to be unwilling to settle into one side. In this, Daisy displays the logic of the supplement that students have encountered in Derrida's "Structure, Sign, and Play in the Discourse of the Human Sciences" (Richter 878–89). She suggests to us that innocence always already contains in it the seed of its opposite, experience, and that innocence can be defined only by its opposition with experience. We see this dynamic of innocence and experience in Winterbourne himself, of whom his aunt says, "You are too innocent," then, "You are too guilty" (64).

A more de Manian mode of deconstructive inquiry might note how Winterbourne tries to read Daisy as if she were a text. This desire to read her is forever frustrated. We see an early formulation of this problem in relation to Daisy's Italian friend, Mr. Giovanelli. Winterbourne tells Daisy, "He is not a gentleman, . . . he is only a clever imitation of one," then inwardly complains about her inability to distinguish a spurious gentleman from a real one. Immediately afterward, though, he perceives that such a distinction is indeed difficult to make, for "It was true that if he was an imitation the imitation was very skilful" (89). The problem of how to read Mr. Giovanelli is small compared with the problem of how to read Daisy. A crucial moment occurs in the Colosseum when, seeing Daisy there at night with Giovanelli,

> Winterbourne stopped, with a sort of horror; and, it must be added, with a sort of relief. It was as if a sudden illumination had been flashed upon the ambiguity of Daisy's behaviour and the riddle had become easy to read. She was a young lady whom a gentleman need no longer be at pains to respect. (111)

Winterbourne thus gives her up, but as he learns later on, when she sends him the message that she never was engaged to Giovanelli, he may have misread her. The passage about reading in James continues, and it deconstructs itself: "He stood there looking at her—looking at her companion, and not reflecting that though he saw them vaguely, he himself must have been more brightly visible" (111). Remember that he thinks he sees Daisy "as if a sudden illumination had been flashed upon the ambiguity" of her behavior. In fact, as the passage tells us, Daisy and Giovanelli remain in the dark; it is Winterbourne who becomes visible. Similarly, whereas Winterbourne thinks he is seeing Daisy as she really is, we realize that we are seeing him in a new light, the light of one who no longer believes in Daisy's innocence, the light of a cynical gentleman of the world. The text that seems to tell us how easy Daisy is to read, then, really tells us about her unreadability and about its own unreadability. The text reminds us that the question of her innocence is ultimately, in a favorite expression of deconstruction, undecidable.

Closely related to this rhetorical reading would be a narratological account of Winterbourne's status as what James called a "centre" or "reflector" (*Wings* 45). Because of James's use of a sort of free indirect discourse, we see most of the story as if through Winterbourne's eyes. This device, whereby the author speaks as if from the perspective of a given character, involves a collapsing of the distinction between narrative and discourse that is central to the narratology of such theorists as Gérard Genette (Richter 844–53). Most of the observations made about Daisy seem to fall somewhere between the third-person perspective of an omniscient narrator and a first-person perspective that we might associate with Winterbourne's point of view. Winterbourne thus becomes what some narratologists have called a "focalizer" for the story (Bal 146–49). This mode of criticism—or other, ethical modes, which we do not discuss much in the theory course—might concern itself with the problem of justice in the narrative, raised on page 111, when Winterbourne denies the fear that he is doing an injustice to Daisy; then again on page 113, when the narrator speaks of doing justice to Winterbourne; and finally on page 116, when Winterbourne confesses to his aunt that he may have done Daisy an injustice.

We next turn from deconstruction to psychoanalysis. The theme of Winterbourne's decentering may tap into a Freudian reading of the story, which would return to some of the concerns of the affective or moralizing critics by way of the observation that all the flower metaphors that the New Critic identified for us are connected to the reproductive function of flowers. Winterbourne both wants to deflower Daisy and fears deflowering her. (The figure of his dominating aunt may represent a phallic mother.) A Freudian critic might make a great deal of Winterbourne's death drive (he steers toward his winter's bourne, though it is Daisy who winds up pushing up the daisies). Here, like the occasionally intrusive editor of our Penguin edition, the Freudian critic would note the passages in which Daisy seems to foresee her doom. She says, "I'm not afraid!" (66). Later, she comments to Winterbourne, "You look as if you were taking me to a funeral" (75). Eventually she announces,

"We are going to stay [in Rome] all winter—if we don't die of the fever" (87). The psychoanalyst would note also how eager Winterbourne is, on page 90, to think lightly of Daisy, since that view makes his task of seducing her that much easier. The Lacanian, of course, would emphasize the radical excentricity of Winterbourne in relation to his self, caused by his unfulfillable desire for Daisy.

Our imagined moralist drew attention to James's concern with justice. A rather less interesting form of a concern with justice might be that of a traditional Marxist, who would view Daisy's story as the result of the conflict between a rising bourgeoisie with its mores of open intercourse between the sexes and an aristocratic code of morality that is becoming outdated. Here, much would be made of the fact that Daisy's father, Ezra B. Miller, has, according to his son, "got a big business" in Schenectady (54). A more subtle Marxist interpretation might follow up on Walter Benjamin's claim that "the birthplace of the novel is the solitary individual" (87) or on Theodor W. Adorno's notion of art as "giv[ing] voice to what ideology hides" (39; students have taken me up on the second suggestion).

On the level of ideology, there are a number of interesting readings of *Daisy Miller*, most of which I touch on only briefly, since my students often write about them in their papers. What might occur last to many of them but first to many current James critics is the idea that *Daisy Miller* is a story about a closeted gay man. James had many passions for young men, and there is much debate about whether he acted on them (which demonstrates how queer studies tends to lead us back to biographical criticism). Winterbourne fears Daisy because he does not understand his own sexuality. In this regard, a particularly interesting figure is Randolph, Daisy's younger brother. In one of James's better-known memoirs he remembers himself as "a small boy" (*Small Boy*), and Randolph may be an image of James's childhood as well as Winterbourne's. When Winterbourne first encounters Randolph, James writes, "At last he finished his coffee and lit a cigarette." (Note the cigarette as a symbol and source of oral pleasure.)

> Presently a small boy came walking along the path—an urchin of nine or ten. The child, who was diminutive for his years, had an aged expression of countenance, a pale complexion, and sharp little features. He was dressed in knickerbockers, with red stockings, which displayed his poor little spindleshanks; he also wore a brilliant red cravat. He carried in his hand a long alpenstock, the sharp point of which he thrust into everything that he approached—the flowerbeds, the garden-benches, the trains of the ladies' dresses. (49)

I remark to my students on the phallic nature of the alpenstock and the way that Randolph thrusts it, first to the metaphor for women's sexual organs (flowerbeds) and then to a metonymy for them (ladies' dresses). But if

Randolph is always sticking his alpenstock where it doesn't belong, his true pleasures, like Winterbourne's, are oral: when he gets three fragments of sugar from Winterbourne, he thrusts two in the pocket of his knickerbockers and one in "another place" (49), his mouth, an example of James's wonderfully periphrastic style, which recalls for the reader of Dante the prominence of the mouth in the canto of Paolo and Francesca. Note that the boy has lost several teeth (50).

Why see Randolph as an image of Winterbourne? He looks prematurely aged, and Winterbourne wonders "if he himself had been like this in his infancy, for he had been brought to Europe at about this age," as indeed James had (50). The interest aroused by the small boy is displaced onto Daisy, but Winterbourne's failure to respond actively to her can be traced to his fundamentally oral form of sexuality. The older woman in Geneva is essentially a front (no one, after all, has ever seen her). His attitude to sex with women can be compared to Randolph's attitude to the ship, *The City of Richmond*, that brought the Millers to Europe: "it was turned the wrong way" (83). In directing himself toward women, Winterbourne is pointing himself in the wrong direction. A sexual interest in Giovanelli might even be made out, on the theory of triangular desire: Winterbourne's desire for Daisy seems to grow once Winterbourne realizes that Giovanelli is courting her. He comments repeatedly (though apparently in anger) on Giovanelli's "very pretty face" (89).

The question of performativity raised by Judith Butler would be crucial for understanding the nature of the judgments Winterbourne passes on Daisy. For example, at a party, Daisy says, performatively, "If this is improper, Mrs Walker, . . . then I am all improper, and you must give me up" (93). Her declaration makes her improper. On page 109 comes a particularly important series of performative statements: from Daisy, "I *am* engaged"; from Winterbourne, "Yes, I believe it!"; then from Daisy again, "Oh, no, you don't, . . . Well, then—I am not!" I recommend to my students J. L. Austin's *How to Do Things with Words* as the background to Butler's article, "Imitation and Gender Insubordination" (Richter 1514–25).

I conclude our tour of critical schools with a comment on new historicism. The most easily anticipated new-historicist approach would probably involve exploring the discourse of women's innocence in the late nineteenth century—perhaps finding a girl or young woman who actually died in Rome on vacation and comparing her story with Daisy Miller's and preferably associating both with the history of the Italian risorgimento or urban sanitation in papal Rome. Closely related to the new-historicist interpretation would be the possibility of a Foucauldian treatment of the problem of discipline by way of the statement that Mrs. Miller was "apparently constantly of the opinion that discretion is the better part of surveillance" (101). The story tells of the consequences of Daisy's failure to internalize the norms of young womanhood.

Another quasi new-historicist or cultural studies reading would focus on the representation of Protestantism in the story. We might look at Winterbourne in relation to the fate of the Protestant ethic, which was most famously theorized by Max Weber but which was also studied by Henry James's brother William in his *Varieties of Religious Experience*. We might note Winterbourne's attachment to Geneva, which the narrator refers to as "the little metropolis of Calvinism" (48). Winterbourne leaves Geneva for Rome at the halfway point of the story (the beginning of chapter 3), and Daisy lies buried in the Protestant cemetery in Rome (along with the poets Keats and Shelley). He compares Randolph to the infant Hannibal, who grew up to be the Carthaginian general who invaded Italy and nearly took Rome (82). We might even think of the Christian martyrs in the Colosseum and imagine that Daisy winds up a martyr to Christian morality. We would pay particular attention to Winterbourne's observation, "I suspect, Mrs Walker, that you and I have lived too long at Geneva" (94). We would explore further the fact mentioned in endnote 11 that many early Protestant reformers were locked up in the Château de Chillon, which Winterbourne visits with Daisy. Henry James presents Winterbourne and most of the story's Protestants as behaving with what Weber would call worldly asceticism, the tendency to live in the world but deny oneself the pleasures of that world, an example of taking monastic morality out of the monasteries and applying it to the population at large. We would then see in the fate of Daisy Miller and of Winterbourne the power of the "iron cage" of modernity that the Protestant ethic and the spirit of capitalism have created for us (123). This Protestant ethic turns out to be too inflexible to deal with the complexities of a place like Rome. It maintains the purity of Winterbourne's wintry soul only at the cost of losing the world represented by Daisy's brief flowering.

I close my lecture by suggesting that various themes reappear from one group of imagined critics to another: the psychoanalyst shares something with the moralist, the new historicist with the old historicist, the queer theorist with the old expressive critic, the deconstructor with the New Critic. When the British protagonist of Lodge's novel, Phillip Swallow, meets up with Morris Zapp again in the sequel, *Small World*, set ten years later (in 1979), Zapp has rethought his project of producing exhaustive commentary on all Jane Austen's work. As he explains in a lecture at a poorly attended conference:

> Of course, I never finished [that project]. The project was not so much Utopian as self-defeating. By that I don't just mean that if successful it would have eventually put us all out of business. I mean that it couldn't succeed because it isn't possible, and it isn't possible because of the nature of language itself, in which meaning is constantly being transferred from one signifier to another and can never be absolutely possessed. To understand a message is to decode it. Language is a code. *But every decoding is another encoding.* (25)

I hope that by giving a tour of potential theoretical readings of *Daisy Miller*, I suggest to my students how much each theoretical decoding offers another possible encoding.

The students themselves find ways to read the story that I never anticipated. In their papers for the class, they have taken up some of my suggestions and found applications of their own. They have written about the text's deconstruction of its own binary oppositions, the performative definition of innocence, the Marxist categories of reification and alienation in respect to the capital off which Daisy and her family live, the construction of Daisy as an object of exchange in a homosocial paradigm, Winterbourne as psychoanalyst, and the problem of objectivity in interpretation. One student, drawing on the work of Wolfgang Iser, argued that "Daisy's charm for Winterbourne is the very fact that she eludes his understanding" (Fishbach 8). Some of the most interesting papers explore the limits of the theories that they set out to apply. At semester's end, I leave the students with a reminder of Hans-Georg Gadamer's "hermeneutic circle" (Richter 671) and the thought that any encounter with a text, especially one as rich as a James story, should not simply reinforce our existing theoretical presuppositions but should challenge them. As Gadamer writes, the challenge of interpretation is to "distinguish the true prejudices, by which we understand, from the false ones, by which we misunderstand" (683).

Teaching *The Turn of the Screw* and/as Literary Theory

Sheila Teahan

I am sometimes asked, especially by colleagues at my institution, whether and how I attempt to teach Henry James to undergraduates. I teach at a large land-grant state university, and the students I encounter at every level, from the introduction to the major through advanced upper-division courses, vary dramatically in their academic preparedness and motivation. This mix would seem unpromising, given James's reputation for being difficult. Happily, students have few preconceptions about James. If they haven't been forewarned that he is too hard to read or that they shouldn't like him because of his alleged class or gender politics, they respond to his work in ways that are lively, intelligent, and heuristically productive. Among the many James novels I have taught with some success and considerable benefit to my students, *The Turn of the Screw* especially lends itself to multiple pedagogical agendas. Although a late James work, it does not present the formidable linguistic and epistemological barriers of the triad of novels *The Ambassadors*, *The Wings of the Dove*, and *The Golden Bowl*. Its style and length make it accessible to literature students at every level. Best of all, students find it intriguing: *The Turn of the Screw* will kindle controversy and spirited debate even in the quietest and most passive group.

Although much of what follows would apply to teaching *The Turn of the Screw* in a variety of courses, I focus on the challenges and benefits of teaching it in the context of literary theory. Anyone who has taught theory to undergraduates knows that their responses to it range from exhilaration to indignation. Not without reason, they tend to perceive theory as technical, abstract, and laden with scary-sounding terminology such as "hermeneutics" and "hegemony." When teaching our semester-long course Modern Critical Theory, but even when including a modest unit of theory in a course that introduces the major, I have found that the best strategy is to teach a number of "literary works" alongside the assigned "theoretical texts." I put these terms in quotation marks to register the ultimate instability of the ontological distinction between literature and theory, since all literary works are demonstrably theoretical and theoretical texts are nothing if not narratives. Students may initially be disconcerted to hear their instructor call into question the distinction on which the conceptualization of theory seems to depend, but they find it reassuring to realize that literary theory is always an attempt to tell a story of some kind about the nature of representation, the status of beginnings and endings, the text's relation to its historical moment, and the like. (It may be less reassuring for them to realize that poems and novels are at least covertly theoretical, but I try to accentuate the positive.) Because it so insistently dramatizes questions of reading and interpretation, *The Turn of the Screw* is ideally suited to a course on theory. The inclusion of one or more novels in a theory course helps make theory more accessible, even as it raises the stakes of reading literature.

Modern Critical Theory is less a survey of schools or methodologies than a problem-oriented investigation of how different writers have thought through recurring questions that have animated theory at least since Plato: questions of rhetoric, poetics, narrative, history, sexual and racial difference, and so on. Jonathan Culler's brief and readable *Literary Theory: A Very Short Introduction*, which takes a similar problem-centered approach and contains a useful appendix of theoretical schools and movements, offers an accessible way into the major issues; even teachers who choose not to assign such a text will find in Culler many pedagogically useful suggestions and insights. Though I prefer to assign the entire text, the first two chapters, "What Is Theory?" and "What Is Literature and Does It Matter?," could stand alone as a course-pack assignment. We return throughout the semester to Culler's useful opening observation that theory is

> interdisciplinary—discourse with effects outside an original discipline. . . . analytical and speculative—an attempt to work out what is involved in what we call sex or language or writing or meaning or the subject. . . . a critique of common sense, of concepts taken as natural. . . . reflexive, thinking about thinking, enquiry into the categories we use in making sense of things, in literature and in other discursive practices. (15)

Especially at this early stage, it is important to make concrete for students some of the implications and applications of these ideas, preferably using examples from popular culture. When asked to think about the Aretha Franklin song line "You make me feel like a natural woman," students are quick to recognize that some troublesome gender constructions are at play. What is a natural woman? Who decides what is natural? Is it possible to be an unnatural woman? What does it mean that the speaker, addressing an apparently male addressee (assuming the song takes for granted a heterosexist plot), says that he makes her feel like a natural woman? She can only approximate the condition of being a natural woman, it would seem, and she depends on a man even for that. Simple examples of this kind (I ask students to bring in others from TV and magazine ads) help students see that appeals to the idea of the natural, like appeals to common sense, are always ideological constructions. It is critical for students to see that, far from being an arcane subject that has no relation to daily life, theory can and will make them savvier readers and consumers of their own culture.

The other text I have found indispensable to teaching theory to undergraduates is Andrew Bennett and Nicholas Royle's *Introduction to Literature, Crit-*

icism, and Theory, an imaginative and innovative collection of twenty-eight brief essays on such theoretical topoi as the author, the tragic, figures and tropes, ideology, desire, and the postmodern. A number of the essays—notably "The Uncanny," "Ghosts," "Suspense," and "Secrets"—are of particular interest to *The Turn of the Screw*, and Bennett and Royle refer to James's tale repeatedly, along with myriad other literary examples. Part of what makes Bennett and Royle so effective in the classroom is their insistent illustration of theory at work in literary as well as in contemporary and classic theoretical texts. I assign one essay from *Introduction to Literature, Criticism, and Theory* per class, and students find this a manageable supplement to the main assigned readings (in recent years, I have used Rivkin and Ryan's excellent *Literary Theory: An Anthology*). I introduce *The Turn of the Screw* itself about midway through the semester, by which point students have acquired a degree of confidence and competence in reading theoreticians as different as Bahktin, Freud, Derrida, and Foucault. They are also more than ready for a text that they perceive as entertaining fiction rather than as opaque and demanding literary theory.

The students have two class periods in which to read *The Turn of the Screw*. During this first week, I make no explicit connections to the material we have been reading thus far. They are free to take the discussion in any direction, although some of the issues that inevitably come up (the question of the governess's sanity, the implications of the open-ended narrative frame) have theoretical implications to which we later return. Controversy is welcome, and part of what makes *The Turn of the Screw* so teachable is that everyone has an opinion about it. One year a student in my theory course who had appeared fairly disengaged and resistant until that point in the semester reported to the class that she had stayed up all night reading it, unable to put it down, and that she intended to reread it until she had "figured it out." It is useful (and entertaining) at this early stage to ask students to take a vote about whether they think the governess actually sees the ghosts or is mad. This move is, of course, reductive, but students love to register their opinions, and those who resist this simplifying either-or dichotomy help prepare for our later discussions.

After this first week, we try to identify some of the tale's overt or covert theoretical concerns. The question of the governess's reliability as a reader of the events at Bly provides a perfect opening, and I inform students that it has been the source of much critical controversy. What kind of reader is the governess? Is it possible to argue that she hallucinates the ghosts of Quint and Jessel? What evidence does James provide both for and against such an argument? In the governess's favor, students cite the apparent accuracy of her description of Quint; against her, they cite her prompting of Mrs. Grose in certain exchanges and her seeming determination to discover that the children have been corrupted by the ghosts. Who else in *The Turn of the Screw* is a reader? Students are quick to see that the tale's narrative frame has a series of nested listener-readers: the unnamed frame narrator; Douglas, to whom the governess's narrative is transmitted; and the governess herself. Douglas identifies the frame narrator as an ideal reader ("You'll easily judge," he repeated: "*you* will," [24]), but that he supplies a title for a narrative he has not yet heard should give us pause (when asked by one of the listeners, "What's your title?," Douglas responds, "I have n't one," and the frame narrator interjects, "Oh *I* have!" [29]). Douglas's comment that the "story *won't* tell . . . not in any literal vulgar way" is another important metatextual moment; in it, James warns his reader the story will "tell" in ways that may be counterintuitive, figurative, or allegorical (25). I foreground as much as possible, in my classes, the counterintuitive character of literary critical reading, and *The Turn of the Screw* provides an excellent opportunity to do this. I point out that a literary text, unlike a bumper sticker, does not equal a message. "Have a nice day" is a message, "Go Spartans!" is a message, "Jesus loves you" is a message. Poems, plays, and works of fiction, instead, refuse to tell in any literal, vulgar way.

As with other challenging texts, one can help students get a handle on James's tale simply by asking them what makes it difficult to read. This query elicits comments that lead to important interpretive cruxes: How can we know whether or not to believe the governess? Why does James use a nested narrative structure and leave it open-ended? It is empowering for students to realize that identifying difficulties encountered in their reading can provide them with useful interpretive tools, and it is easy to get them to see that *The Turn of the Screw* is a highly theoretical text that dramatizes and thematizes questions of narrative voice, repetition, undecidability, authority, and mastery.

When teaching any novel in the context of a course on theory, one should assign students to read five or six critical essays representing a range of methodologies and theoretical positions. There are several excellent extant collections of essays on *The Turn of the Screw* (see Beidler's Bedford editions of the novella; Cornwell and Malone; Esch and Warren's Norton edition). Or, of course, one can assemble a course pack. The point is to expose students to a range of readings of the story that reflect identifiable vocabularies and interpretive procedures they have encountered in their readings of theory. I want the methodologies represented to include, at minimum, feminism, Marxism, psychoanalysis, and deconstruction. Drawing connections among a half dozen critical essays and our previous readings in theory helps ground discussion—which some students have at times found dizzyingly abstract—in a work of fiction that everyone in the class has read. Ideally, students by now have a sense of where these methodologies come from, both historically and philosophically. The specific choice of essays, as long as they are reasonably accessible to bright undergraduates, seems to me less important than a diversity of viewpoints that helps students formulate some generalizations about the kinds of questions they can expect the different theoretical orientations to ask about the same text—about what blindnesses and insights each orientation brings.

An argument might illuminate *The Turn of the Screw* as a psychological case study of its narrator while ignoring issues of class—or vice versa. One essay that I find consistently useful with students is Wayne Booth's piece in the Bedford editions of *The Turn of the Screw*. Like the other texts in the Bedford series Case Studies in Contemporary Criticism (the Schwarz edition of Conrad's "The Secret Sharer" also works beautifully in a theory course), this edition provides half a dozen critical essays in the same volume as the primary work. Booth's essay helpfully classifies previous readings of the tale under the three categories of "straight," "ironic," and "mazed": the straight reader believes that the ghosts do indeed threaten the children and that the governess attempts to save them, the ironic reader believes that the governess's narrative is delusional or untrustworthy, and the mazed reader believes that the story is an ironic and undecidable "maze with many intentionally deceptive false turns and dead ends" (173). Students find Booth's threefold classification accessible and useful, and it can be fruitful to ask them where or whether each additional critical essay we read fits in this categorization.

Shoshana Felman's influential essay on *The Turn of the Screw*, which is nearly as long as the tale itself, would go over the heads of all but the brightest and most advanced undergraduates, but I find it useful to summarize in class her thesis about the hermeneutic trap James creates for his reader. Felman points out that the critical history of *The Turn of the Screw* is divided over the question of the governess's sanity: readings tend to fall either into the

> "psychoanalytical" camp, which sees the governess as a clinical neurotic deceived by her own fantasies and destructive of her charges; and the "metaphysical," religious, or moral camp, which sees the governess as a sane, noble saviour engaged in a heroic moral struggle for the salvation of a world threatened by supernatural Evil. ("Turning" [1977] 98)

She demonstrates that whichever camp one chooses to support, one is merely repeating a dynamic that is already dramatized in James's text. If one believes that the ghosts exist and that the governess is engaged in an earnest quest to save the children, one is adopting the position embodied by Mrs. Grose. If one believes that the governess is insane, one is adopting the position embodied by the governess herself, who at several points questions her own sanity (as who would not in her circumstances?). In Felman's view, James both forces us to make a judgment about the governess's sanity and makes it impossible for us to do so, because whichever position we take, we have been preempted by the text. Perhaps, Felman suggests, this hermeneutic trap is what James has in mind when he refers in his preface to the tale as "an *amusette* to catch those not easily caught . . ." (*Turn* [Beidler (2nd ed.)] 182).

When discussing with students a deconstructively inflected reading such as Felman's, it is important to spend some time on the concept of undecidability. Undecidability does not refer to a situation in which one simply throws up one's hands in frustration, unable to decide what a text means. On the contrary, from a deconstructive perspective, one can always define with some precision in what specific ways the text is undecidable and what the implications of that undecidability are. A useful connection can also be made between undecidability and the related concept of ambiguity. Unlike unintentional ambiguity, as in the sentence "He helped the lady across the street," which could mean either that he helped her cross the street or that he helped the lady who lived across the street, literary ambiguity is always purposeful and meaningful. When we encounter ambiguity in a literary text, our job is not to try to get rid of it by explaining it away but to identify its effects and implications as precisely as we can. Bennett and Royle's chapter "Readers and Reading," which develops a close reading of Shelley's "Ozymandias" (a sonnet that is itself about reading), offers an invaluable indirect commentary on these issues as they relate to *The Turn of the Screw*. Like James's story, the sonnet involves a series of nested readings and dramatizes explicitly the question of "how [we can] tell if a particular reading or interpretation is valid" (10). Although Bennett and Royle use the term "equivocality" rather than *undecidability*, their comments about equivocality, irony, and ambiguity can be easily mapped onto a discussion of the arguable undecidability of James's tale.

What is *The Turn of the Screw* about if not the problematics of reading—and specifically, the dangers of imposing a totalizing theory on evidence that fails to conform to that theory? Felman's essay investigates the fatal consequences of the governess's willful catching and grasping of the putative clues dropped by Miles and Flora. At the novella's conclusion, the governess's comprehension of Miles—an etymological grabbing hold—has literally fatal consequences. In this view, James has created a cautionary tale of reading. I suggest to students that *The Turn of the Screw* can be seen in part as a critique of the coercive power of metaphor, since the governess is guided by governing metaphors (such as the nautical trope of clutching the helm [33]) that shape her reading of the events at Bly and of her own actions. I believe that James problematizes her interpretation of virtually everything; but teaching is not about consensus, and I not only encourage dissent but go to pains to lay out different ways of approaching the text. It is entirely legitimate, for example, to embrace what Booth calls a "straight" reading of *The Turn of the Screw* as a tale about menacing ghosts. (When I taught the novella in a graduate seminar recently, two doctoral-level students reported to me that they found the story so disturbing that they lost several nights of sleep.) As James makes clear in his 1908 preface, he intended in part to create a frightening tale about ghosts, and for some readers it is exactly that. Students should be told that hundreds of ghost narratives were elicited and published by institutions like the Society for Psychical Research, with which James's father, Henry, and James's brother William were significantly involved. (On this topic, see Beidler, "Introduction" and *Ghosts*.)

Finally, James's retrospective preface is of critical interest in the context of a course on theory. Students should know that James wrote a series of eighteen critical prefaces that have proved enormously influential in Anglo-American literary theory; he was also one of the first great novelists to assert the formal value and philosophical seriousness of fiction. I try to show that the tale's self-reflexive commentary, which both models and preempts the reader's interpretive activity, is mirrored in James's 1908 preface. I encourage students to think about the preface not as an objective account of authorial intention or achievement but as another piece of rhetoric (in the double sense of argumentation and of figurative language) that demands to be read alongside and against the text of the story. Our discussion of the preface enables us to question the distinction between so-called fictional and nonfictional prose, and James's prefaces are ideal for teaching students about the literariness of nonfictional prose. What do we make of the fact that the preface is as heavily metaphoric as *The Turn of the Screw*? Is the preface theoretical, fictional, or both? To what extent does it engage in a strategics of mastery that is critiqued in the tale? After all, a preface patently aspires to shape our reading of the text that follows it. Finally, I use Beidler's "Critical History" in the Bedford first edition to illustrate that all readings of this text (or any text) are theoretical, whether self-consciously or not. I ask students to identify the theoretical assumptions that underlie the numerous readings of Miles's death that Beidler usefully juxtaposes (141–44). Have the questions critics asked of this text changed? Why do certain questions, such as that of the governess's sanity, resist closure? Why is the absent figure of the master so important? Is the governess attempting to master something in her narrative and, if so, what? If a definitive statement can be made about *The Turn of the Screw*, it is that James's brilliant tale, which both elicits and resists any number of readings, will continue to elude our attempts to master it.

Teaching *The Turn of the Screw* Metatextually

Diane Long Hoeveler

The methods of cultural studies have been influencing teachers of literature for more than thirty years, and teachers of James, luckily, have a rich storehouse of materials from which to select in planning their course. Adeline R. Tintner's *Henry James's Legacy: The Afterlife of His Figure and Fiction* (1998) provides a treasure trove of ideas for pairing and juxtaposing James's works against a variety of literary works by other artists who were compelled to rewrite him from a number of different angles. Tintner suggests that *The Turn of the Screw* can be usefully read in conjunction with Frances Hodgson Burnett's *The Secret Garden* (1911), Rumer Godden's *The Peacock Spring* (1975), Elizabeth Taylor's "Poor Girl" (1951), Peter Straub's *Ghost Story* (1979), Hilary Bailey's *Miles and Flora* (1997), and Joyce Carol Oates's "Accursed Inhabitants of the House of Bly" (1992). This essay focuses on only the last story, although teachers should be encouraged to plan a course that groups all these works in a metatextual dialogue that studies James's work as the urtext of one particular genre: the class-based ghost story.

Students who read James's classic gothic conundrum, *The Turn of the Screw*, have been asking themselves essentially the same questions since the tale appeared in 1898. That is, the central puzzle has been to understand the psyche of the governess. If she is insane, as the reader increasingly suspects, then how does one read a text that is quite possibly occluded, implicated in her self-serving strategies of deception and paranoia? Certainly critical opinion inside the classroom and out of it has focused on the governess, or the children, or Douglas and the narrator—the living, in other words—in order to comprehend the meaning and significance of the events in the story. But focusing on the living alone has led these same instructors to the proverbial dead end of interpretation: how can one interpret a text that is riddled with suppressed hysteria, perhaps insanity so profound that it appears as a manifestation of normative behavior? How does one understand a narrative voice that is so clear that it is actually impenetrable? And so we are back at the beginning: we cannot understand what happens in this story if we attend only to the living. There is an entire layer of meaning to the tale that is buried in the dead lives whose ghostly presence continues to motivate the actions of the living. Students are able to understand this layer by reading Joyce Carol Oates's rewrite of the story alongside James.

In 1992, Oates published a rewrite of *The Turn of the Screw* from the point of view of its dead, "Accursed Inhabitants of the House of Bly." This story attempts to answer the questions that have plagued critics for generations: Is the governess insane and imagining the ghosts? What happened between the children and their dead governess and valet? What force is so strong that it can draw the dead back to the living? What haunts the living and the dead?

My essay places the James text and the Oates text in a metatextual juxtaposition that mimics the strategy I take in the classroom when teaching a course on the gothic. By using the Oates story, I force students to adapt another point of view, one that they usually do not see in reading James's text.

As any instructor knows, James's tale is notoriously subtle on one level, hopelessly transparent on another. That is, the governess is either insane or not. The only major character who is unnamed in the story, she is either hysterical, sexually perverse and repressed in her attraction to the uncle and the children, or not. The ghosts must be manifestations of her madness, her sexuality writ large for only her to see, because there are no such things as ghosts—no one else sees them, after all. But she has written her story and given it to a family friend, Douglas, who in turn regales a group of men and women with the events as a Christmastime fireside chat. Unlike most people who insist that they have seen ghosts or who are believed to be responsible for the death of a child in their care, she has lived out her life in respectability and credibility. If the governess is indeed mad, then somehow the patriarchal system that has propped her up and placed her in charge of innocent lives is also perverse and corrupt. Somehow that aloof "master," living in splendid isolation in London and untouched by the tragedies occurring in his family, stands finally as a representative of empire; or a clockmaker God; or, most damning of all, the omniscient author who sees all but fails to intervene with a moral or a lesson.

If the governess is not mad, if ghosts have appeared to her, then what exactly is the story about? Are the ghosts evil and seeking to claim the children? Or are they themselves victims and doomed for some reason to haunt the environs of their crimes? And what exactly were those crimes? In other words, whose story is it? These questions are the starting point for Oates's rewrite of the story, for Oates provides answers to what James's reader cannot resolve. Her answers are not comfortable or pleasant, but she is deeply honest about the dark and unspoken urges in James's text. I speak about pedophilia and the kind of frustrated, infinite erotic suffering, the kind of loss and pain that is so intense, it exists even after we die, the kind of insatiable longing that would constitute hell should there be such a place.

I lead students through the two texts simultaneously by focusing our discussion first on three major sightings of the ghosts that occur in James's text. Each sighting is carefully recrafted—turned over and over again in Oates's hands—and finally and slyly commented on by Oates. The first sighting happens only a few weeks after the governess's arrival at Bly to take up her duties to two orphaned siblings, the eight-year-old Flora and the ten-year-old Miles. The Jamesian reader recognizes that the smugness and the self-deception of this young woman will be her undoing, but the reader also participates in the story on more than this first level, that of character critique. The postmodern position that Oates provides us in her story places the governess in a fictitious universe of literary intertextuality that is implicit in James, explicit in Oates.

In the ironic and twisting perversion of a young governess's fantasies, both James and Oates reveal the persistent power of Victorian master narratives to turn our heads not simply once, in the initial reading of them, but twice, in our futile attempts to apply those fantasies to our own lives.

Students immersed in the other gothic texts we have read in class recognize quickly the self-referentiality of the governess fantasy operating in James, for the governess is in the grip of the *Jane Eyre* narrative of the well-meaning, scrupulously diligent, oh-so-good and deserving young woman who wins the master (and his estate and income) away from the evil and dark woman (read: mother substitute). The root of the fantasy is oedipal, and the power and persistence of the narrative bespeak its hold over the female imagination. On one of her meditative nocturnal rambles, Jane encounters Rochester, the master, and the unexpected sight of her throws him from his horse. James rewrites Charlotte Brontë's novel much more darkly: the male figure who suddenly appears to the governess is not the longed-for master but the ghost of his servant, Quint, a randy and promiscuous valet who chooses as the locale for his first haunting the towers of the old house.

Oates's postmodern spin on this scene is revealing for the explanatory context given. In her more cynical rendering, the first and doomed governess is a woman who allowed her head to be fatally turned by the governess fantasy. Succumbing to it, Miss Jessel became easy pickings for Quint, who was merely a poor substitute for his master. Jessel expected, according to the structure of her well-studied narrative, the sudden appearance of the master, his love, marriage, and an instant family of children that she would not have to soil her body to bear. Instead, she was easily seduced and impregnated by the master's valet, Quint, and destroyed. According to Oates, the fantasy of marrying the master leads not to the happy ending that Brontë provided but to a much more ordinary and typical narrative closure, the suicide of the pregnant and disgraced young woman.

The second appearance of Quint to the governess occurs with the medium of glass between them, as in the biblical sense: we see through a glass darkly now. The mirrored intensities of both James's and Oates's tales lie not simply in the three ghostly appearances but in the way these performances are also manifestations of the frustrated and diverted erotic impulse of the dead. In James's version of this second haunting, the governess comes upon Quint one late Sunday afternoon; he is staring at her from outside the dining-room window. The description of him again focuses on his body, but this time in an even more displaced manner:

> He was the same—he was the same, and seen, this time, as he had been seen before, from the waist up, . . . His face was close to the glass, yet the effect of this better view was, strangely, just to show me how intense the former had been. He remained but a few seconds—long enough to

> convince me he also saw and recognised; but it was as if I had been looking at him for years and had known him always. (44)

How, we might ask, could the governess have known the man "always"? The standard critical explanation is that the man in the window is a manifestation of her oedipal fixation on her whimsical curate father (shades of Brontë's father). She sees, that is, her frustrated oedipal longings diverted first from her father, then from the master, then Quint, then fixed murderously on Miles as the final substitute. This interpretation has led many critics to see the hauntings as a form of self-haunting, a descent into insanity. But the face in the window can also be read as an image of one form that narcissism can take. In her construction of Quint the governess sees herself, because she reads in him her own interest in the children. Experiencing this interest as unnatural, she projects onto Quint her anxious evasions and fear of perversion. Despite her best efforts, however, some instructors and students sense in the unnamed governess a perverse sexual interest in the children, in their activities, in their secrets.

But Oates brings us face-to-face with the dark and hidden acts that bind Jessel and Quint to the children: group sex. We are confronted with this scene not directly but filtered as a particularly delicious memory of Quint. It is sex, the need to touch and fondle both children's bodies as the two adults engaged in sex themselves, that holds Jessel and Quint to the children. While Quint amuses himself with his startling appearances to the new governess, Jessel is revealing herself to Flora across the lake, compelled to make herself known to the little girl: the girl is, she says, "my soul, I will not give her up" ("Accursed Inhabitants" 258). In James this incident is muted, with the governess only vaguely aware that there is "a third person" present in her dyadic rambles with Flora (54). Later the governess tells Mrs. Grose that the woman appeared to them as "a figure of quite as unmistakable horror and evil: a woman in black, pale and dreadful—with such an air also, and such a face!" (56).

In Oates, Jessel's face is explained by her desperation to get at Flora, and equally explicit is Flora's longing to be reunited with her dead governess: "Jessel appears to little Flora in emboldened daylight, daring to 'materialize' on the farther shore of the placid Sea of Azof. . . . Is not little Flora in her innocence, as in her need, necessary to the vision?" (275). For Oates, Flora and Jessel feed each other in their excessive and mutual need for each other, just as Miles and Quint do. But where does that leave the governess? She is the third wheel in every configuration, the screen onto which both frustrated pairs project their longings. As the term that signifies excess as well as lack, the governess must be eliminated for the two pairs to reunite, and yet she will not go quietly. She refuses to erase herself, because in James's text, at least, this story is hers.

In both tales, by now Quint recognizes that he is connected with Miles in the same intense manner. In Oates's story, he remembers Miles as a "child starved for affection," a child who hugged and kissed Quint, "seiz[ing] him around the hips, burrowing his flushed little face into the elder man as a kitten or puppy might, blindly seeking its mother's teats" (262). It is her mother that Flora seeks in her infatuation with Jessel: "Flora must have seen, yes, here was her lost young mother restored to her, at last!" (259). The visual dimensions of seeing and being seen form the dominant motif in both tales, but in Oates the visual is blatantly intertwined with the question of sex and power.

It has to be made clear to students that in both tales there are two levels of ghosts haunting: Jessel and Quint are substitute love objects as well as substitutes for the parents, who were abruptly swept away by disease in India two years before the story begins. The originating wound for the children is the death of their parents, but they are traumatized again by the sudden and violent deaths of their parent substitutes. The unnamed governess steps into a morass of unresolved mourning, of grief so intense that it swerves away from thanatos to eros in a desperate bid to deny the power and existence of death.

Voyeurism, exhibitionism, as well as oedipal desire and mourning are operating in both tales, but Oates spells out what James implies, whispers: the narcissistic basis of all human affection. We love in others what we project onto them—hence the heavy use in the stories of glass, mirrors, eyes, lake surfaces, and polished wood, in which we see only ourselves. When Oates's Miss Jessel says that Flora is her "soul," that she cannot live without possession of the girl, she is actually saying that she sees in Flora her younger, pure self. She loves herself as an unspoiled beautiful girl, hence her love for Flora is simply a manifestation of her narcissism. The same can be said of Quint's attraction to Miles, in his eyes ultimately a younger and innocent version of himself. So when Jessel and Quint involve the two children in their sexual acts, they are not so much seducing others as making love to split-off manifestations of themselves. That they had easy access to these orphaned and unprotected children constitutes the horror of their crime, a perversion of the trust that was placed in them by the uninvolved master.

Students see that in James's tale they are being teased, as it were, with hints and innuendos. When the governess tells Mrs. Grose that she is certain the apparition came with the purpose of finding Miles, she is told by Mrs. Grose that yes, the two were "great friends": "It was Quint's own fancy. To play with him, I mean—to spoil him. . . . Quint was much too free" (51). The governess does not need to hear any more; sufficiently disgusted, she is determined at that moment to function as a "screen—I was to stand before them. The more I saw the less they would" (53). So while appearing to position herself as a sacrifice, the one who will take the suffering on herself in lieu of the children, she actually positions herself at the keyhole, peeping, peering, blocking the views of others so that she can see it all. A visual mania, a scopophilia possesses this woman, who ultimately represents every reader who has wanted to see the unseeable, who has wanted to invade the primal scene of textuality/sexuality.

We move to this scene in Oates's version of the tale, the scene that we have been forming vaguely, fearfully, perversely in our minds. What we are afraid to put into words even mentally, Oates presents in stark terms:

> It had been Miles's habit, charming, and touching, perhaps a bit pitiful, to seek out the lovers Quint and Miss Jessel in just such trysting places, if he could find them; then, silky hair disheveled and eyes dilated as with an opiate, he would hug, burrow, twist, groan with yearning and delight—who could resist him, who could send him away? And little Flora, too. (273)

We learn from this description that the children are active participants with their parent substitutes in sexual acts. They do not simply fantasize the primal scene, they live it. Eyes enlarged and reflecting their desire, they "burrow" into the adults, as if to return to the womb. The description is sad as well as horrible, yet the reader of Oates who has also read James's cryptic story now has the sensation that, yes, the crime has finally been uncovered. There surely could be nothing worse. What the unnamed governess wanted so much to uncover and have confessed is here, in these acts of desperate erotic grief.

As the memories of shared intimacies increase and actually haunt the dead, Jessel is ever more anxious to claim Flora, who she sees now as not simply her soul but as "her own little girl, the babe cruelly drowned in her womb, hers and Quint's, in this very pond" (275). As she silently communes with Flora, drawing her closer and into the world of death, the new governess, called "St. Ottery" in mockery by Jessel and Quint, suddenly leaps up and saves Flora, snatching her from the imploring arms of what she sees as a ghoul: "My God, what a—horror! Hide your eyes, child! Shield yourself! . . . Don't look at her, Flora! The horrid, obscene thing! You're safe now" (276). Death and insatiable longing have turned Jessel into a craven thing with "hard-shelled beetles" infesting her pubic hair. Salvation for her can arrive only through her capture of Flora, because in seducing the child and gaining her love, Jessel redeems herself, returns symbolically to her "virginal" and pure self, and her flower of femininity is restored to what it was before she was deflowered by Quint (276).

The love Jessel has for Flora has held her to the catacombs of the dead that encircle the house of Bly. Jessel cannot claim Flora as her own because of the vigilant and obsessive surveillance of St. Ottery, a "terrier" of a woman (276), as dogged in her pursuit of the ghosts as the ghosts are determined in their pursuit of the children. One is tempted to label this contest a life-or-death struggle; someone has to lose. Unfortunately, it is the weakest who cracks "when a bubble bursts at last in Flora's brain" (278). Driven by St.

Ottery to confess about the ghostly appearances of the woman at the lake, Flora disintegrates and is removed to London. According to Oates, she is accompanied there by Jessel, who no longer needs to haunt the house of Bly. Jessel's disappearance allows Quint to come to terms with his prey, Miles. The story of Quint and Miles is not shrouded in any soothing mother-daughter imagery. Nor is it presented as the quest of one soul for another. The tie between the two is much more sexual and physical, making it especially dangerous for Miles.

The connection between Quint and Miles is the core of both James's and Oates's texts. We have in this relationship the association between an older servant and a young, upper-class boy who is desperate for a father, whose love and acceptance are crucial for the boy's identity. In James we learn that "for a period of several months Quint and the boy had been perpetually together" (61). Hints are dropped in James about the exact relationship between Quint and Miles, but in Oates we are given the full spectacle, the evidence that Quint has engaged with the boy in oral sex and that Miles has bragged about the acts to his closest friends at school, hence his immediate and disgraced expulsion. In Oates, the final scene, the struggle for Miles, is a confrontation that neither side can avoid. St. Ottery has been called "Fate" by Jessel (275), and, to capture the moral ambiguity of the situation, Oates places us inside Quint's mind, not the governess's:

> Quint, with trembling fingers, readies himself for the final confrontation. He perceives himself as a figure in a drama, or it may be an equation, there is Good, there is Evil, there is deception, there must be deception, for otherwise there would be no direction in which to move. Squinting at his sallow reflection in a shard of mirror, plucking at his graying beard to restore, or to suggest, its old virility; recalling with a swoon in the loins, poor Miles hugging him about the knees, mashing his heated face against him. How is it evil, to give, as to receive, love's comforts?
> (279–80)

Why, I ask students, is the word "deception" used twice? All the moral categories we construct in order to explain our lives' events are for Oates necessarily built on self-deception. No one, in other words, thinks that he or she is evil. We are all capable of vast amounts of rationalization, of deception, without which we would not be able to function. For Oates, it is not evil to give or receive any of love's comforts; it is only human. All the inhabitants of Bly—living and dead—are accursed by their longings and their persistent need for "love's comforts" (280). In the catacombs of the dead, where Jessel and Quint rattle around, plucking beetles from their bodies and preening before shards of broken mirrors, the same emotions play out. They are just as jealous, needy, narcissistic, and perverse as are the living. There is, in other words, no peace in death, only a continuation in a higher key of the same psychology, the same deceptive emotions.

In Oates's tale the climatic scene and third sighting occurs in the family library, where Miles has curled up one evening to read a particularly appropriate volume, the *Directorium Inquisitorum*, an inventory in Latin of sins that are unforgivable in the eyes of the church. St. Ottery confronts him, demanding a confession, and Miles denies all. St. Ottery goes so far as to point to Quint, who is pressing his "yearning face" against the glass, but Miles claims that he cannot see Quint. " 'There, I say—*there*!' In a fury, the governess taps against the glass, as if to break it. Quint shrinks away." As Miles flees the room, St. Ottery and Quint are left to "regard each other through the window, passionless now, spent as lovers who have been tortured to ecstasy in each other's arms" (282).

Oates concludes her tale by suggesting that Miles commits suicide in the lake and with the eerie rationalization: "We must have imagined that, if Evil could be made to exist, Good might exist as rightfully" (282). The postmodern morality of Oates positions both the living and the dead as victims. Her conclusion—a variation on the just-world ideology—goes something like this: in James's moral universe, the unnamed governess needed to believe that those who had died were evil, so she created manifestations of evil to convince herself that she inhabited a wholly different world, the world of the living that was by nature just and good. A tremendous anxiety about death motivates James's work, as well as an almost pathological fear of sex in any of its forms. Oates makes plain the forces driving *The Turn of the Screw*, and she puts forward an alternative morality: there is no sharp demarcation between good and evil. They exist, if they exist at all, on a continuum where we will all at some time in our lives find ourselves. Oates does not mystify, nor does she coddle her readers. She slaps us in the face with the realization that at some point we all may be prey to obsession, to an erotic mania and nostalgia so intense and irrational in their choice of object that we will wish ourselves dead.

James's tale has famously persisted to enthrall and puzzle. Students are drawn to its glossy surface and its unspoken depths. Oates begins her story in those depths. She forces her readers to confront the polymorphous perversity that is implicit in human relationships, and she portrays a world that has no neat boundaries either in morality or mortality. In an essay that attempts to define the short story, Oates observes that years earlier she "believed that art was rational, at bottom, that it could be seen to 'make sense,' that it had a definite relationship with philosophical inquiry, though its aim was not necessarily to resolve philosophical doubt." But now she thinks otherwise:

> The short story is a dream verbalized, arranged in space and presented to the world, imagined as a sympathetic audience . . . the dream is said

> to be some kind of manifestation of desire, so the short story must also represent a desire, perhaps only partly expressed, but the most interesting thing about it is its mystery. ("Short Story" 214)

As an instructor who believes in pushing the envelope in the classroom, I would claim that students who come to accept and appreciate fiction as the "dream verbalized" are the better for the experience.

Teaching Ambiguity: *The Turn of the Screw* and Shoshana Felman's "Turning the Screw of Interpretation"

Michelle E. Moore

My students often tell me *The Turn of the Screw* is boring. When I ask what, specifically, is boring, they point to the long, convoluted sentences. By the time they finish a single paragraph, they are unsure of its beginning. After further questioning, I find that their difficulties stem from the assumptions that the narrator conveys a fully formed story and that the governess states exactly what she means. The point most students miss is that the story's ambiguity goes beyond basic literary concepts like the unreliable narrator. We know something has happened to someone, but we can't determine what it is. Consequently, a character's behavior appears uncaused, unattached, and uncanny. Each word, statement, or action may provide a clue, but ultimately the crime or violence that determines the behavior never reveals itself. Shoshana Felman's often anthologized essay "Turning the Screw of Interpretation" aligns this reading pattern with the method of a detective or analyst. The professional reader hunts for clues to solve a mystery. Felman notes that the different critical perspectives readers assume are reflected back from between the words of the governess's story. Just as the novella mirrors critical perspectives, so too does it mirror students' perceptions of novels and literature, which makes for an extremely frustrating reading and teaching experience.

When I show the students that this text becomes about what they choose it to be about, their confusion clears up completely. Felman's essay shifts the focus of readerly inquiry and guides my approach to teaching the novella. She says the "question underlying such a reading is thus not '*what* does the story mean?' but rather '*how* does the story mean?' " ([1977] 119). When we read, we must decide whether the governess is lying or truthful, sane or insane. These choices allow us to participate in the making of the novella's meaning and its scandals. Felman observes that "the scandal is not simply *in* the text, it resides in *our relation to the text*, in the text's *effect on us*." What bothers us, affects us, and gives us nightmares is that which in the text "speak[s] *to us*" (97). Each reader has made strikingly different choices when filling in the narrative gaps that appear on every page. Because the classroom turns textual analysis into a group activity, a discussion of *The Turn of the Screw* can show readers that they have made only one set of choices out of an endless array of possibilities. The classroom, therefore, presents a ready-made laboratory for studying the novella's effects and the ways in which they occur.

My essay provides strategies for teaching a text that slips out from under its readers at every point and threatens to dissolve classroom discussion. I approach the novella through Felman's analysis, because her study strives to preserve the ambiguity of the text without reenacting the reflective readings of earlier critics. She proposes a reading that tries

> not so much to *capture* the mystery's solution, but to follow, rather, the significant path of its flight; not so much to solve or *answer* the enigmatic question of the text, but to investigate its structure; not so much to name and make *explicit* the ambiguity of the text, but to understand the necessity and the rhetorical functioning of the textual ambiguity. (119)

Her theory has had a profound effect on Jamesian scholarship and provides an alternative method for teaching the text. An ideal classroom discussion of the novella preserves the ambiguity of the text by focusing not on master narratives but on the way potential narratives are generated.

I teach the text in the middle of the entry-level course American Gothic, which begins with Charles Brockden Brown's *Wieland* and ends with contemporary examples of the postmodern gothic. By the time we get to *The Turn of the Screw*, the students have become adept at finding overt uses of gothic convention. After reading Poe thoroughly, they will not be surprised by a narrator who murders. After reading *Wieland*, they recognize a masochistic heroine who turns out to have masculine ambitions. They also expect shocking plot twists: Poe's narrators wall up corpses in basements and Wieland kills his entire family because he may or may not have heard voices telling him to do so. On the first day I teach *The Turn of the Screw*, students able to follow the novella tell me "nothing much" happens. There are always a few who admit they don't know what happened, even though they read it, and a few who don't make it past the story's frame because they fall asleep.

It is absolutely true that with alarming frequency nothing happens in the novella. Felman observes:

> Nothing, nobody; no-thing, no-body: marked by the very sign of negation and denial, prefixed by a "no" which bars them in the very act of calling them up, the ghosts—like the letters—manifest themselves only to negate themselves, but through this self-negation, carry out their own self-affirmation; their mode of being and of self-manifestation is that of their own contradiction. (150)

Since the novella's ambiguity seems to arise from its tendency to negate itself, I ask students to find the repetition of "no" and "nothing" in the novel. They find the repetition on almost every page. I list the repetitions on the board, for them to see graphically that almost every element of the novella that may be called a plot point or moment of character development erases itself as soon as the narrator reveals it.

For the remainder of the first day, we investigate how the novella's frame contributes to the overall blurring effect. The frame blurs the lines among text, reader, and audience by performing a narrative twist. When Douglas reads the governess's story, our elusive narrator sits as an audience member and recognizes Douglas's voice as the master's voice. Our narrator tells the story to us from "an exact transcript of [his] own made much later" (26). He begins as an audience member and then becomes the transcriber who tells the tale. Now he occupies Douglas's position of mastery and is the constructor of the master narrative. The role change suggests that all audience members, like the narrator, will be drawn in and eventually create master narratives as well.

When we read the governess's strange tale, we are drawn into it and occupy both the position of audience member and that of reading master. As a new audience for the terrible tale, we are at the teller's mercy. But Douglas and the unnamed narrator show that our seat in the audience is neither static nor secure. Readers control the flow of the story. They may stop reading, read faster, or savor the most gruesome descriptions. Soon, we begin to horrify ourselves in the same way that Douglas horrified our narrator. We become master storytellers who repeat the actions we find to be most horrible.

When students see how the frame suggests that we all become tellers of the horrible tale, I assign a two-page paper. They must "ask a question of the text and then follow a line of inquiry to a thoughtful and analytic answer." The paper requires them to become Felman's detective-analysts who force a story to emerge from the ambiguity. The only way they will understand the novella's structure is to make the words mean something. I want them to become masters of the text who will fall into the very traps they think they can avoid.

On the second day, the students have written their papers and have consequently developed individual readings of the story. I divide the class into groups of three, tell students to open their books randomly, and instruct them to find the first complete paragraph on the page. The students then take turns explaining to their group how they filled in the narrative gaps in the chosen paragraph. Because each student has read the page slightly differently, some even skipping over it completely because it didn't fit into the narrative they were constructing, they begin to understand the text's ability to generate multiple meanings in a single, random paragraph. This exercise makes a strong impression on my students; they have written about it enthusiastically in their course evaluations.

After completing this activity, I let the class list the different events that might be transpiring at Bly. They enjoy discovering and reporting on the possibility of ghosts, insanity, trespassers, child molestation, and murder. I stay out of the discussion, acting only as mediator, because I don't want to seem as if I am embracing one position over the other.

For the third day, I assign Felman's and Edmund Wilson's essays out of the Norton edition (ed. Esch and Warren). I prefer using this edition because the excerpt from "Turning the Screw of Interpretation" retains most of the article's original content and is a reasonable two-day reading assignment. Because I teach James's text in an entry-level course, my expectations for reading comprehension are fairly low. I assign each group one of the essay's major terms—like "ambiguity," "ghost," "master," "trap," "madness," "truth," "suspicion," "literal reading," or "murder"—and expect them to bring a working definition to class out of their completed reading. I want them to search for definitions and, through them, approach an understanding of Felman's complex essay.

On the final day, we explore its implications. I ask the groups to share their definitions of the terms in the same sequence in which the terms appear in the essay. This exercise allows the class to piece together a general meaning of each with only a small amount of guidance and encouragement from me. Out of this discussion a new understanding emerges of how the story means. We conclude the class with an examination, in this new context, of the moment Wilson declares is "left open to a double interpretation" (171): Mrs. Grose's identification of the first ghost as Quint, the master's valet.

First, Mrs. Grose and the narrator make up Quint's identity through a series of conversations. It takes two appearances of the figure for the two women to debate and finally name the man as Quint. The governess recognizes the figure from the first appearance. Then, after she tells Mrs. Grose, the housekeeper recognizes the description as belonging to Quint. Information must always be transmitted twice before recognition occurs, and an identity forms from nothingness. The housekeeper is able to name the figure as Quint because she has seen Quint before; likewise, the governess has seen the figure before. Through the banter that signifies naming in the novella, the two women fuse the figure and Quint. The almost constant repetition of names between the two women linguistically shows the importance of repetition to form identity.

Second, the two women debate the intricate meaning of the figure exactly as they previously debated the relation of Miles's expulsion to Quint's identity:

> She thought a minute. "Was he a gentleman?"
> I found I had no need to think. "No." She gazed in deeper wonder. "No."
> "Then nobody about the place? Nobody from the village?"
> "Nobody—nobody. I did n't tell you, but I made sure."
> She breathed a vague relief: this was, oddly, so much to the good. It only went indeed a little way. "But if he is n't a gentleman—"
> "What *is* he? He's a horror."
> "A horror?"
> "He's—God help me if I know *what* he is!" (46–47)

At this point, Mrs. Grose has identified the figure as Quint, who was not a gentleman and did not wear a hat. The conversation between the two women consists of questions and answers in rapid succession and provides the method by which the women give concrete identities to ambiguous figures. Declaring he's like "nobody," the governess renders him completely devoid of identity-forming characteristics. He is indescribable and therefore a nobody who has no body to describe. Then, he quickly takes a shape, because the two women cannot live with the horror of the ambiguity that results from not knowing the evil's proper name.

If the figure is a gentleman, he could be considered at all times mannerly and therefore above laws of state. Redeemed by the title *gentleman*, he would act by definition for the good of his society. His name prescribes his actions and therefore his meaning for the two women. The debate about the figure is a debate over his identity. Just as Miles was good or bad in the debate about the contents of the letter sent from the school, this figure is categorized in similar but more adult terms. If he isn't a gentleman, then "he's a horror," and the word "horror" aligns itself with the bad nature of Miles. No conclusion may be drawn, however, as to whether the figure belongs or doesn't belong on the estate, whether he is or is not actually a trespasser. Because it is unknown whether he commits this crime or any crime, the women's debate perfectly replicates the confusion over the meaning of Miles's expulsion. Similarly, the two women cannot decide what to call the figure who stands on the tower and peers into the dining-room window. He becomes marked as a horror because he commits unmannerly actions, because he cannot be fixed as good or bad. Like Miles, his inability to be properly named is in itself horrible. We don't know "what he is," just as we don't know what Miles is.

Third, the governess remarks after seeing the shadowy figure on the tower, "So I saw him as I see the letters I form on this page; then, exactly, after a minute, as if to add to the spectacle, he slowly changed his place—passed, looking at me hard all the while, to the opposite corner of the platform" (41). Felman uses the first half of the sentence to draw her now famous equation: "*to see ghosts = to see letters*." From the formulation she asks the question, "But what is 'seeing letters,' if not, precisely, *reading*?" (151). Seeing ghosts becomes a form of reading, and the governess's liberal use of interpretative strategies to explain the ghosts' presence solidifies the connection. The "visitor" moves across the platform, unable to be fixed to one spot for too long (42). The "figure" stands in for all letters and texts that cannot be deciphered or cannot have their meanings determined or fixed (41). The lack of identity, not knowing who the man is or what he means, causes great horror and distress for the governess, Mrs. Grose, and the reader.

Mrs. Grose's method of naming Quint mirrors our move as readers, critics, students, and teachers. We want to name Quint and name the text, so we can escape the horror of its signifying nothing. This idea always generates a lot of debate among the students.

My approach, then, embraces the ambiguities that make the novella so difficult for students to understand. They leave class with a palpable sense of what textuality is and an understanding of the labyrinthine structure of *The Turn of the Screw*.

GENDER AND SEXUALITY

The Jamesian Turn: A Primer on Queer Formalism

Eric Savoy

"The story *won't* tell, . . . not in any literal vulgar way."
—James, *The Turn of the Screw*

Because *The Turn of the Screw* is usually offered to students as an object lesson in unreliable first-person narrative, pedagogical approaches to this inordinately difficult tale tend to be framed, and short-circuited, by the controversy that critics have protracted over the decades: students are invited to decide whether the ghosts of Peter Quint and Miss Jessel are "real," or whether a hysterical governess is merely "seeing things." While teachers who encourage this debate might accrue immediate profit in terms of lively classroom discussion, it is ultimately a costly move, not least because the exclusionary logics of the argument require a certain suppression of reading. It seems to be pedagogically axiomatic that the impulse to choose strong, even vehement positions is directly proportional to the obscurity of narrative. This strategy is understandable, because it provides relief: one moves from the irritating overstimulation of a complex fiction to the comfort zone of interpretive conviction. However, the pedagogical value of *The Turn of the Screw* lies in its invitation to the troubled pleasures of complexity: the novella comprehends the interpretive desire to make coherent sense out of obscure historical happenings in the field of its narrative (for all readers are cast as students as we trace the governess's lesson in reading) even as it refuses to fulfill, to authorize, or even to countenance that desire. To put this another way, *The Turn of the Screw* provides teachers with an opportunity to ask their students to discern both the desires and expectations that they bring to narrative and the particular ways in which James's tale subjects that contract to renegotiation.

If students respond—as they likely will—by claiming that they want literature to be meaningful, then teachers might particularize this term by locating it in the task at hand—that is, by orienting it along an axis that is congruent with James's narrative trajectory. Rather than take up the pointlessly abstract matter of what students mean by *meaning*, teachers might inquire where meaning lies. Is it situated in the prehistory of the governess's narrative—that is, in the events that actually happened between Miles and Flora and their caretakers before the governess's arrival at Bly? Is it comprehended, paradoxically, by the very incomprehensions that the governess registers in her manuscript? Is it suggested obliquely, or in symbolic fashion (students love the term *symbolic*), by the things represented by the ghosts? If so, then what are those things? The point of this perseverated spinning of initial—and initiatory—interrogation is, of course, to demonstrate that any question about the situation of meaning will be referred to and interlined with others. Such a preliminary exercise ought to encourage students to accomplish three things in their critical grappling with *The Turn of the Screw*.

Bewilderment and Its Forms

The first is to take up the implications of the titular metaphor: in the real world of tangible things, a screw functions to increase pressure in order to fix an object in an immovable place; its physics requires a reiterated turning, or returning, in a line that is also a spiral. By figurative extension, the tale might be understood as the governess's process of writing the history of strange happenings at Bly, a process that anxiously, and obsessively, returns the question of things happening to an obscure past in the attempt to laminate the one to the other.

The second project, which is concerned with the overall narrative structuring of meaning, can be articulated as arising from the implications of the screw's spiral. If students are invited to consider how the story unfolds in time, then it is but a short step to recognize the tension between the prospective and retrospective orientations of the governess's curiosity. Each puzzle the governess encounters in the unfolding of the story—the mysterious letter of expulsion from Miles's school; her encounters with the ghosts; the oddly empty things the children say; her inconclusive conversations with Mrs. Grose, her companion in probing Bly's mysteries—entails a further, and more panicked, speculation about the past. The intensity of tension in the tale is, clearly, a function of its narrative temporality, which can be summarized as a dialogics of tense: what is is a function of what was. More precisely, the present is dissolved into the imperfect because what is happening is both clarified and obscured by its referral to what was happening in the temporality of the unfinished and the unresolved. The governess's mission is to locate a point in historical time that offers an explanatory plenitude—a kind of primal scene in the case history of Miles and Flora that would clarify the link between what happened and what is happening. The basic conjugation of narrative time, however, permits no such arrival, at least not in a linear sense. Rather, the persistent spiraling of an obscure past around an incalculable present—which is the basic temporal unfolding of the governess's reconstructive endeavor—obviates the linearity of narrative arrival and consequently fractures interpretive certainty. Thus, in figurative terms, the screw turns, but it does not go anywhere.

It is useful to present this model of narrative time to students in diagrammatic form: they respond enthusiastically to geometric precision, indeed to any kind of mathematical configuration. One might begin by conceptualizing time as the horizontal axis of meaning in *The Turn of the Screw*, then demonstrate visually the undecidability of where the present and the imperfect meet. Subsequently, one might overscore this line with a spiral, then fold the diagram into something approaching a circle. By this point in the pedagogical encounter, *meaning* should be articulable as something that, far from being static or fixed at a point in the text, is a function of time, of particular processes governed by time. It is therefore hard-won, contingent, provisional—perhaps best understood not as a thing but as a certain potential that conjoins unpleasant historical happenings with the narrator's suspension between a determination to know them and a fear of such knowledge.

The third mode of exploration that attentive pedagogy might encourage is a reconceptualization of meaning from the macrostructural, horizontal axis of narrative interpretation in time to a localized or vertical axis of meanings that arise—in highly tentative but nonetheless traceable ways—at the pointed level of the paragraph or sentence. It is highly effective, I have found, to employ the idea of horizontal and vertical axes to represent to students simply the distinction as well as the diacritical relation between close reading and what we might call reading for the plot. I term this movement a reconceptualization of where meaning lies—which it is not, really—in order to emphasize that students' readings will persuade to the extent that students present fine, and finely tuned, evidence. The pedagogical foray into the larger organization of the tale's repeated returns will have demonstrated that, far from permitting a reductive or even coherent reading (if by "coherence" one means a smooth certainty with all the ducks lined up in a row), *The Turn of the Screw* is a profoundly recessive tale. Just as the unhappy history of Bly recedes from the governess's grasp even as she encounters more and more evidence in its reality in the present, her tale generates not a certainty that accrues but a hypothetical thing that coalesces, in fits and starts. In order to trace these things, these glimpses, these fits and starts—both in their individual articulation and in their collective resonance—it is imperative to encourage students to read slowly, to reread passages that provoke (in several senses of the word) their interest, and—the greatest challenge for a contemporary audience—to attune both the ear to the grain of the narrative voice and the eye to the image and its attendant hazardous course of development.

The approach I have been outlining here is broadly deconstructive. Indeed, to trace the subversion of coherent meaning in *The Turn of the Screw*—which is to say, to read attentively—is necessarily to follow the text's problematization of hermeneutic desire. Certainly there are moments in the pedagogical framing of the tale in which an explicit deconstruction can focalize the parameters of engagement. To reinvoke the conventional choices assigned to students with which I took issue at the outset of this essay, it is helpful to present the critical legacy of hysteria versus real ghosts not as binarized and mutually exclusive alternatives but as entirely continuous, that is, not as an either-or choice but as a both-and continuum. This approach can be an effective way of inviting students to situate themselves in a long history of readers; of distinguishing among earlier and contemporary critical practices (while noting, I hope, their deep continuities); and, most important, of fostering interest in the tale's episodic structure, in which the occluded meaning of ghostly visitation arises from and confirms the governess's own occluding hesitations before these shadows emanating from Bly's unquiet history.

Yet, deconstruction *tout court* seems too narrow and limiting a pedagogical agenda, even if, given the contours of James's writing, it necessarily underlines and informs every conceivable analytic engagement. To consider the ghosts as signs, generated by the governess's writing, is inevitably to take up their dark import as symptom. The psychoanalytic resonance of the ghosts ought to be traced not to neurosis or hysteria but (in a decidedly less misogynist manner) to the gothic's perennial interest in spectrality as the return of the repressed. Freud's succinct essay "The Uncanny" is an excellent companion text to *The Turn of the Screw*; particularly apt and applicable is his theory that "the uncanny is something which is secretly familiar, which has undergone repression and then returned from it" (368). This simple and straightforward model of the gothic effect can be brought to bear on the governess's primary exercise in interpretation. In her reading of the letter from Miles's school, which reports his expulsion but "go[es] into no particulars" (34), she may be said to know the one necessary thing. The evasive letter, she claims, can "have but one meaning . . . [t]hat he's an injury to the others"; she proceeds immediately to speculate that Miles's presence at school was "to contaminate" and "to corrupt" (34, 35). In the context of the 1890s—the era of the Oscar Wilde trials, the consequent policing of aberrant sexualities, and the cultural fetishization of childhood innocence—the governess's verbs cannot fail to register her moral panic at the irruption of sex in public-school homosociality. From this moment forward, her speculations are thoroughly conjoined to the spectral in the spiraling, oblique circuits of repression and its insistent return.

In the Jamesian turn of narrative, the governess disavows what she initially intuits, taking refuge in "the real rose-flush of [Miles's] innocence," the sign that he "was only too fine and fair for the little horrid unclean school-world" (43). This turn, however, is interrupted—between the acts, as it were, of the governess's intuition and her refusal of its implications—by the troubling counterturn of Peter Quint's first appearance. If Quint isn't exactly who she was hoping "would appear there at the turn of a path," his presence nonetheless suggests that "[her] imagination had, in a flash, turned real," for "the figure [she] had so often invoked seemed most in place." She concedes her "bewilderment of vision" (39), as well she might, for the "imagination" that Quint "figure[s]" persists as the symptom, the gothic revenant, whose function is to conjoin the recesses of pederastic history with the very sexualized present that the governess both knows and refuses to know. In other words, *The Turn of the Screw*'s spiral from speculation to spectrality, the oblique legibility of horrible history, is the return of the repressed par excellence.

If deconstruction requires the supplement of psychoanalysis in order to locate the field of meaning in the tale, a meaning that is bound up with the generic imperatives of the gothic, then psychoanalysis itself benefits from the particularization of the homosexual panic that generates repression and is, it would seem, the thing that lies at the unspeakable heart of this narrative's darknesses. By particularization I mean discourse formation or, more simply, rhetoric: image, trope, syntax. How, students wonder, can this thing be simultaneously there and not there? Is this thing, wherein meaning may be said to lie, a ghost effect of storytelling, as insubstantial as the ghosts themselves? If so, what is the value, the point, of tracking it? To respond to these questions and myriad others, I like to set up, in the classroom, a chain of connections around the term *queer* and tease out its assorted implications. The queerness of the tale inheres, most immediately, in its particular exploration of horror. The ghosts appear with some sort of diabolical intent; we learn that in life they had relations with the children that were somehow inappropriate. The governess returns repeatedly to confront the ghosts' meaning but invariably retreats from an interpretation that she has already instigated: that is, she is suspended between her fear and her desire to know. Consequently, her narrative cannot chart a straight path to disclosure; her anxiety about the "thing" continually subverts her narrative.

This thing has something to do with sexual relations between adults and children, although we do not know whether this something is an embodied sexual practice or another kind of inappropriate initiation. In contemporary queer-theoretical practice, *queer* can signify an overt gay and lesbian cultural property, or—more usefully for our purposes—it can signify an obliquity, a suspension of homosexual meaning, in textual production. To articulate these related dimensions, these mutually implicated quandaries, of *The Turn of the Screw*, my critical and pedagogical practice is best described as queer formalism: certainly a neoformalism—that is, the practice of close reading unencumbered by the humanistic, moral imperatives of the New Criticism—is deployed in the matrices of deconstructive, psychoanalytic, and queer-theoretical protocols. Queer formalism is not only a means of illuminating the complexity of James's characteristic form, it also provides a concrete way of moving from textual example to an initiation into these contemporary theoretical protocols. Queer formalism is fundamentally about style—that is, style's relation both to historical moments when meaning, in the modern sense, could exist without expository clarity and to texts in which to read "between the lines," as our students like to call it, requires absolutely a reading of the lines. It is a dilation of poetics, a poetics of the attenuated. In practice, it requires very precise field methods, and to those I now turn.

Field Methods

As a student and teacher of French, Alice Kaplan observes that "*explication de texte* gets more precious to me as I grow older with literature." Her distinctly American Francophilia inheres in "the history and sense of ritual that gives [this] activity its charm and power. In French class we bend over the language, we caress it and we question it, and we come to understand" (211). I find myself drawn to Kaplan's tactile metaphors; they illuminate a "ritual" whose protocols locate the pedagogical I in the classroom's we, in the shared enterprise of a certain textual erotics. The most effective strategy in fostering a collaborative reading is to assign one's students a deceptively simple task—to come to class with a very short passage, even a single sentence, from *The Turn of the Screw* that piques their curiosity, regardless of whether it strikes them as ripe with explanatory potential or irritates by thwarting their desire to read conclusively. Paul de Man's memoir of his experience as a teaching assistant at Harvard in the 1950s focalizes the goal of this initiatory assignment:

> students were to start out from the *bafflement* that such singular turns of tone, phrase and figure were bound to produce in readers attentive enough to notice them and honest enough not to hide their non-understanding behind the screen of received ideas that often passes, in literary instruction, for humanistic knowledge. (23; my emphasis)

The teacher's role in this exercise is to attend to students' bafflement rather than to speak around or contain it, to follow Kaplan's example of bending over the language and caressing it, to explain the occasions of bafflement without explaining them away.

Such explanation will necessarily have recourse to the anthology of tropes and to the broad question of how meaning is provisionally generated. It is especially pertinent to remind students that the English word *trope* derives from the Greek verb "to turn." In the light of this interesting bit of etymology, students are often quite enthusiastic about approaching *The Turn of the Screw* as an exercise in turns of language. Most, of course, come to this exercise already versed in the matter of figurative language and rhetoric: the teacher's opportunity is to consolidate this knowledge, to cultivate its confidence and expertise, and to provide new terms for the students' critical lexicon and analytic toolbox. What follows is a catalog of analytic moments derived from my experience of the queer turns of *The Turn of the Screw*. It is by no means exhaustive: I do not address metaphor or personification, for example. Nonetheless, this sampling might provide opportunities for teachers to field questions of engagement and bafflement.

Fragmentation

The entire structure of the governess's attempt to produce a history of the odd happenings at Bly—its frustration and spiraling circularity—is beautifully condensed in four scant lines of dialogue that occur late in the tale, when the governess confronts Miles about what lies behind "this queer business of ours" (92):

> I waited a minute. "What happened before?"
> He gazed up at me again. "Before what?"
> "Before you came back. And before you went away."
> For some time he was silent, but he continued to meet my eyes. "What happened?" (94)

Miles's strategy of response—driven by evasion, incomprehension, or both—is not simply to answer a question with questions but to fragment the governess's question and return it to her in pieces. Parody generates a grammatically perfect hermeneutic circle, an imprisonment of interpretation, because the opening and concluding questions are virtually identical. Paradoxically, emptiness resonates. In this circle, the governess attempts to particularize the two obscure historical befores—the scandalous events at school that occasioned Miles's return to Bly and his prior, obscure relations with Quint—in order to relate one to the other and thereby construct a temporal continuity of explanation. We have in this scene a reiteration of the governess's thwarted attempt to "go behind" symptoms to grasp causes; once again, Miles "had given exactly the account of himself that permitted least [her] going behind it" (75). The circular spiral of the passage itself is implicated in, and in turn determines, the macrostructural pattern of spiral and return. The governess's interrogation seeks to put before—before her ears and eyes, in linguistic presence—an absent behind. But Miles is a recalcitrant subject: he keeps his back to the wall; he is a boy without a behind.

Simile

There is something tentative, tenuous, and attenuated about simile: as a performative speech act, it follows the trajectory of metaphor's will to comparison but, implicitly acknowledging its inaptness, shrinks from the exactitude of identification. In the governess's discourse, simile is one of the surest signs of her simultaneous impulses to know and to repress. The epistemological occlusions of her similes might be referred to a situational chiasmus: she tells more than she knows, and she knows more than she tells. A tracing of simile might supplement the vexed matter of Miles's behind that I analyzed above. The governess's pedagogy takes certain liberties with the boy's body; her interest in his behind is, once again, configured as a function of the historically prior. Consider the retreats and disclosures in the following:

> [The children] were like those cherubs of the anecdote who had—morally at any rate—nothing to whack! I remember feeling with Miles in especial as if he had had, as it were, nothing to call even an infinitesimal history. . . . If he had been wicked he would have "caught" it, and I should have caught it by the rebound—I should have found the trace, should have felt the wound and the dishonour. I could reconstitute nothing at all, and he was therefore an angel. (43)

Like the previous passage, this textual moment dilates the governess's illusory conviction that she is "reconstitut[ing] nothing at all," but unlike that passage's fragmentation, she demonstrates a poetic process by which a metaphor gradually accrues through the progression of simile's attenuations. Note the escalation of comparative predication: "were like," "as if," "as it were," "was." Miles enters this representation as "like" a "cherub" and leaves it with the history of an "angel." The circularity of this figurative process is comforting to the governess for reasons other than the coherence of tropic induction. A supplementary metaphoric chain, however—a figurative counterturn—deftly destabilizes her hard-won security and riddles her repression of history with anxiety. Her calculus reasons that because Miles has no posterior "to whack," he has no anterior history of "dishonour." Troubling her negation is the conditional mood of the sentence that links wickedness to "wound." By the logic of the conditional, historical wickedness, the matter of "what happened before," is located in a wound that the governess understands as psychic trauma but that cannot fail to have a somatic resonance. As Cathy Caruth points out, the origin of the English word *trauma* is the Greek word for wound, "referring to an injury inflicted on a body" (3); in psychoanalysis, it accrues a certain personification as "a voice that is paradoxically released through the wound" (2). It is fairly safe to assume that James intends his reader to resist the governess's disavowals here, as elsewhere. The path of resistance is to juxtapose the textual itinerary of the cherubic simile against the metaphoric return of the wound, legible in this context as the anus. Beginning with the erasure of the body, we return ironically to the body. Perhaps Miles has a behind after all.

Connotation

To tease out the implications of the wound—laminated as it is by the sequence of the governess's appositives to the more literal, denotative meaning of "dishonour" in her syntactic field—is already to have broached the critical uses of connotation. As the dominant signifying practice of homophobic or homosexually panicked texts, connotation extends a discreet invitation to recognize or to "know what *that* means"; at the same time, as a discourse overdetermined by the closet, it is careful to cover its tracks. It is liberating for students to be asked to address connotation: they can begin with a fairly free association, which the teacher can then particularize along the lines of historically specific usage. The relation of gay historicity or thematics to this eminently queer inflection is sustained, paradoxically, by what D. A. Miller calls its "semiotic insufficiency." For connotation displays an aptitude for "allowing homosexual meaning to be elided even as it is also being elaborated" (124). From the perspective of the closet's logistics, connotation "has the advantage of constructing an essentially insubstantial homosexuality"; but from the perspective of the assiduous reader, "it has the corresponding inconvenience of tending to raise this ghost all over the place" (125). Miller's metaphor of reading as a process of raising ghosts suggests the congruity between lexical connotation and the exquisite paranoia of the gothic; connotation induces, he suggests, that "prolonged state of expectation we call suspense" (131). A pedagogical caressing of connotation in approaching *The Turn of the Screw* can serve a larger formal agenda, as narrative suspense is located more firmly in the governess's reiterated acts of suspending, in the trajectory of her sentences, the calling of things by their proper names. Nowhere is this apparitional mystification more apparent than in her detective work on the life, times, and death of Peter Quint. Here is the end point of her research:

> The icy slope, the turn mistaken at night and in liquor, accounted for much—practically, in the end and after the inquest and boundless chatter, for everything; but there had been matters in his life, strange passages and perils, secret disorders, vices more than suspected, that would have accounted for a good deal more. (53)

The Turn of the Screw is replete with wrong turns. As Ned Lukacher observes, "the task of reading James is one of remembering that although there is a right track, we are not going to be on it" (123). Quint's sudden death literalizes the wrong turn, but it also ironizes it in ways beyond the obvious. The slippery slope and the wrong turn "account," even after "boundless chatter," for everything. But what is everything? As James frequently points out in his late fiction, everything's nothing—that is, nothing in particular. As we have seen before, irony attaches to the tense of the governess's speculative turn, to the conditional mood: other matters, she suggests, *would* have accounted for a great deal more—that is, a great deal more than everything—if. . . . Narratively, if not grammatically, her sentence remains unfinished; the condition is left tacit: if what? The undermining and revision of "everything" with "a good deal more" is one dimension of queerly ironic contestation; another accrues in the ways in which the unspecified if of the conditional mood coalesces in her sequence of connotative appositives, in the various things that "would have accounted [if]." It is of crucial importance to note the way in which the governess dilates, item by item, her arrival at the verb: if such perseveration is a form of deferral of naming the thing itself, it is also, ironically, an escalation of the particular, for each sign in the chain accrues greater specificity, a narrower register of meaning. It is through the gestural, indexical logic of connotation—the truth of its pointing—that we are led from vague "matters" to obscure "passages and perils" and from there to "secret disorders," which turn out, literally, to be "vices more than suspected." More than suspected but not known: abominable but not nameable. We have not quit connotation, yet we know. And we know that she knows. And we know that she knows that we know.

Paradox

The Turn of the Screw is organized—if such rampant incoherence may be said to have an organization—around contradiction: the history of pederastic abuse at Bly emerges and recedes, the governess knows and doesn't know, she recognizes and represses, the children are angels and fiends. Paradox might well be articulated as the master trope of the narrative; in any case, its location and elaboration bring into a certain relief the competing impulses that govern the governess and, to the extent that she is our interpretant, our reading. When she is told by Mrs. Grose that the segregation of genders at Bly, concealed and prevaricated about by the children, "suited them all," she concludes with a nonconclusion: "It suited me too, I felt, only too well; by which I mean that it suited exactly the particular deadly view I was in the very act of forbidding myself to entertain" (63). This passage might work equally well in the classroom as a moment of departure or arrival: in both situations, it represents succinctly the narrative tension between recognition and repression in its syntactic balance. If paradox is a kind of grammatical and rhetorical equilibrium, an assertion counterpoised with a negation, it is not necessarily a zero-sum game. It leaves a residue, and the trick is to locate the residual effect of the debit and credit, the plus and minus, in the tiniest surfaces, which, like Poe's purloined letter, are fully open and visible. We can entertain the text most hospitably by particularizing its explicit "particular deadly view" (this spiral might be quite delightful to students who wish to play) that the governess won't entertain. If teachers arrive at this passage after a lengthy foray, then such particularization can be interpretive, building on other evidence gleaned from reading. If it is a point of departure, then teachers might confine their gaze to the definite article and its fine balance: "the particular deadly view" (whatever that means) is arrested by "the very act" of interdiction. Charting the precise economy of paradox in this fashion might lead—or lead afresh—to a teasing out of what is deadly about the dead.

Paradoxically, *The Turn of the Screw* speaks to our cultural concerns and those of our students, despite and because of its sheer difficulty. It has an astonishing relevance, not to say urgency. It troubles our easy certainties and renews our contemplation of what is perhaps the greatest social panic of our time: the inappropriate sexual initiation of children. It legitimates this issue even as it interrogates the contours of our anxiety by its interlinearity with paranoia and monster making. It should generate lively cultural and political debate in the classroom: does this text elide the difference between homosexuality and pederasty? If so, was this elision determined by the tale's 1890s context, when the distinctions among perversions were in the early stages of a pathologizing taxonomy? To the extent that this narrative underwrites its culture's pathologizing of sexuality, does it locate the problems in homosexuality or a homophobic paranoia? To put it another way, are the ghosts real or is the governess seeing things?

I have come full circle to my opening gambit, but I hope I have demonstrated that students and teachers cannot assume any argument outside the text's queer formalisms or any certainty, ever, even if (or particularly if) James's tortuous rhetorical paths are carefully followed. Meanings, like the arguments they should generate, are best offered as provisional. *The Turn of the Screw* is a perverse tale, a scandalous supposition, and its ultimate point is lost if queer formalism does not generate a certain queer political critique. Let me conclude, then, with an exam question: If you were Miles, would you rather hang out with the governess or with Peter Quint?

Mothers and Others: Anxieties over Substitute Mothers in *The Turn of the Screw*

Dawn Keetley

This essay introduces an approach to teaching Henry James's *The Turn of the Screw* that emerged from a lower-level undergraduate course called Bad Mothers, a semester-long exploration of discourses of motherhood circulating in England and the United States from the early nineteenth century to the present. We read the novella in a section of the course about the nineteenth-century emergence of the mandate that the mother-child bond be exclusive—that is, that small children should be raised mostly if not entirely by their mother. One point of the section was that this ideal came to wield such power that those others who intruded on the mother-child dyad became invested with all the attributes of the culturally taboo, among them perverse sexuality and almost supernatural malevolent powers. In this context, we contemplated James's tale as the story of a governess who creates herself as mother in large part to ward off the ambiguity and corrupting aspects of those others. (Both Curtis Hanson's 1992 film, *The Hand That Rocks the Cradle*, and a fascinating 2001 novel by Suzanne Berne, *A Perfect Arrangement*, continue this theme into the present, representing both the mother's and the culture's deep-seated anxieties about caregivers who trespass on the mandate of exclusive mothering.) But *The Turn of the Screw* does not only disclose the cultural pressure that young children be mothered. It also dramatizes the dangers of exclusive mothering.

Although I pursued this particular approach to *The Turn of the Screw* in an interdisciplinary course that focused not on the literary tradition but on an enduring and provocative social and cultural issue, it can work either in an introductory literature course or in an upper-level course that pays more attention to both the fiction and the life of James. Such an upper-level course could consider, for instance, *The Turn of the Screw* alongside *What Maisie Knew* and the lesser-known "The Author of Beltraffio," which is discussed below. (For an intriguing discussion of how James's fictional representations of motherhood are rooted in his own relationship with his mother, see Graham.) The distinct interpretation of *The Turn of the Screw* proffered here is of course not the only possible reading; in the classroom, we move toward and often against it through a series of questions that raise conflicting answers. In the end, I frame my reading as a hypothesis to consider and to challenge, not as inviolable.

The first important question I raise is, What is the governess's understanding of her role as she arrives at Bly? How does she apprehend her position as governess—as educator? The students will at some point need help from contextual material, but at first the class can compile references to her teaching practices and, more generally, to her daily activities and her attitude toward Miles and Flora. There is, of course, some evidence that the governess does instruct her children: just before she sees Miss Jessel for the first time, she and Flora are by the lake and, since they "had lately begun geography," the child pretends the lake is the Sea of Azof. Flora's imaginative construal of her geography lesson, however, should be understood in the light of the governess's prefacing of it with one of her many disclaimers that she did not direct what the children did: "I walked in a world of their invention—they had no occasion whatever to draw upon mine," she concludes, after having admitted that all her attention went strictly to "seeing them amuse themselves immensely without me" (54). Thus the most direct reference to the governess's teaching (the geography lesson by the lake) is dramatically qualified by her prior admission that she simply watches Flora engage in self-generated imaginative play. The governess's pedagogical abilities are more seriously eroded if we remember that the one lesson we know the governess generates for the precocious Flora is to copy some "nice 'round O's' "—a duty that Flora promptly (but nicely, of course) rejects, perhaps as an insult to her intelligence (34). Aside from these few references, the governess's instruction appears in the negative—the things the governess couldn't or didn't do for the children. We never hear what Miles and Flora learned from her. We hear that "for weeks the lessons must have been rather my own"—as the governess learns to "be amused" (38). We learn that Miles was "too clever for a bad governess . . . to spoil" (65); that in arithmetic both children went "soaring quite out of *my* feeble range" (95); and that, at the end, she is finally relieved when they renounce the "pretension" that she is actually Miles's teacher (111). The novella itself, then, places in serious doubt the governess's role as governess.

Understanding the place of the nineteenth-century governess suggests at least one reason why, her pedagogical abilities aside, the governess may not have wanted to be Miles and Flora's governess. M. Jeanne Peterson's "The Victorian Governess: Status Incongruence in Family and Society" and selections from Mary Poovey's chapter on the governess and *Jane Eyre* in her *Uneven Developments: The Ideological Work of Gender in Mid-Victorian England* remain the two best historical and theoretical discussions of the place of the nineteenth-century governess. Both illuminate the governess's fundamentally ambiguous position, particularly in terms of class and sexuality: typically a middle-class lady (though poor), the governess nonetheless must sell her labor—an activity antithetical to the middle-class ideal. She is also, as a paid employee, sexually suspect, as were all servants in the Victorian household. Yet she was employed precisely to protect her charges from the always potentially problematic sexual activity of servants. Peterson's essay is especially useful in its focus on the contradictions and conflicts raised by the liminal position of the governess, who is neither fully middle-class woman nor fully servant.

After discussing the ambiguous status of the nineteenth-century governess, I turn back to James's novella and ask how the governess responds to her inherently conflicted location in the household and how, more generally, she responds to ambiguity. Two important points to raise are her extreme self-consciousness about class position and her absolute intolerance of ambiguity. Together, these traits predict her rejection of the role of governess.

While acutely and persistently aware of both her lower-class status and the uncertain in-betweenness of her position at Bly, the governess mostly represses her disquietude. Instead, she projects both debased class qualities and a frightening class precariousness onto Quint and Miss Jessel and then attempts to distance herself from them. In eliciting student responses to the governess's class anxieties, a useful strategy is to ask why the governess is so terrified of the ghosts. A close examination of some of her sightings reveals that the ghosts terrify her in large part because they mirror her (see Robbins). Quint and Miss Jessel represent her unwanted status as "base menial," as she calls Quint at one point (62). Her status uncertainty is reflected in the way Quint aspires to climb the social scale (wearing the master's clothes and pretending to be a "grand tutor") and in the way Miss Jessel falls (her "abasement" with Quint) (48–49, 62, 58). As moments that embody fears about her equivocal position, the governess's sightings can be analyzed also in terms of their permeation by liminal qualities. The ghosts almost always appear at physical boundaries and thresholds: at twilight (38–39, 44), by a window (44), at the edge of a lake (54, 101), and on a staircase (67, 70). Indeed, James makes clear that they mirror the governess: she replicates Quint's second appearance at the window (44); she apprehends, in one of her many melodramatic conversations with Mrs. Grose, that Mrs. Grose might regard Miss Jessel's "awful eyes" as akin to those of the governess (57); she sees Miss Jessel sitting at her own table (88); and, finally, of course, the "white face of damnation" that she sees in the culminating scene with Miles could very well be her own (119).

The governess's categorization of Quint and Jessel as infamous not only serves to ward off her unconscious self-identification but also accords with her need, in general, to establish certain meaning. Discussion about how the governess interprets Quint and Jessel can therefore be linked with a broader deliberation of how she perceives the world—notably her inability to dwell in ambiguity. Students can explore her constant (and seemingly unwarranted) references to having achieved certainty (44–45, 50–51); her quick arrival at what she insists must be the "one meaning" of the tantalizingly unseen letter from Miles's school (34); her frequent conviction that the ghosts are present, at the same time that the text clearly undercuts the possibility of that conviction; and, most notoriously, her sudden arrival, in chapter 12, at the conclusion that Miles and Flora meet Quint and Miss Jessel regularly, that they are defrauding her, and that they are evil (76–77).

In response to all the conflicts that her position as governess entails, James's protagonist, I suggest, remakes herself as a mother. (For a quite different view, see Millicent Bell's "Class, Sex, and the Victorian Governess," which draws on the work of both Peterson and Poovey to argue that the governess sees herself as governess.) A first step in raising the notion, in the classroom, of the governess's maternal fantasy is to provide some background about the emergence of the nineteenth-century maternal ideal. Two essays that map the emergence of a particular kind of exclusive motherhood in the nineteenth century are Ruth Bloch's "American Feminine Ideals in Transition: The Rise of the Moral Mother, 1785–1815" and Jan Lewis's "Mother's Love: The Construction of an Emotion in Nineteenth-Century America." Bloch describes how until the late eighteenth century mothers were mostly ignored, or their role was linked with that of the father. Only between 1785 and 1815 did the notion arise that the mother's role was somehow unique. Writers from this period on, according to Bloch, pictured the fulfillment of mother and child joined in an exclusive and intense bond; they also described the particular job of mothers as guardians and educators of their children's moral and emotional life. Lewis's essay has particular relevance to *The Turn of the Screw* in the two claims Lewis makes that extend Bloch's argument. She explores how a mother's love obliterates "the distinctions between—the separateness of—mother and child," serving to create the child as a "moral and emotional replication" of the mother (216). She also describes the emergence in the nineteenth century of the "national civil religion" of motherhood—that is, the idea that through their loving self-sacrifice mothers could ensure salvation for their children and thus for themselves (220–21, 224). Significantly, James sets his novella some fifty years before its publication in 1898, thus locating the governess at precisely the moment when the ideas of motherhood that Bloch and Lewis describe were consolidated.

When the class turns back to *The Turn of the Screw*, the instructor can ask to what extent students think the governess fantasizes for herself the role of mother. What details of her feelings and activities seem incommensurate with her role as governess? What kind of mother is she? I try to get students to see that her mental state and reliability (two central issues in any discussion of the novella) are powerfully affected by immediate and intense emotional investment in the children and in her role as mother. This investment seems more powerful than her much-discussed romantic and sexual interest in their uncle, although at this point the class should certainly address the more obvious fact of the governess's seduction in Harley Street. She is fairly conscious of entertaining fantasies about the uncle, though, almost admitting to Mrs. Grose that she was "carried away" in London (31). It is precisely this self-awareness that erodes the argument that what the governess is so disturbed by at Bly are her romantic and sexual fantasies about the uncle. Instead, it seems to me that it is her maternal desires for Miles and Flora, desires that never completely surface, that preoccupy her, directing her responses to the children and the ghosts. A good counterpoint to my reading is an essay by Priscilla L. Walton. Walton sees Mrs. Grose as the mother figure and argues that the governess attempts to create herself outside this confining and fixed role, to find an "indeterminate" place in the narrative ("He Took" 314).

There are hints in the text that the governess begins her self-making as mother from the moment she arrives at Bly and is seduced not by a man but by Flora—"the most beautiful child I had ever seen." In one complex sentence, James links "the wonderful appeal of my small charge" with particulars about the governess's bedroom: the "great state bed," the "figured full draperies," and the long mirrors "in which, for the first time, I could see myself from head to foot" (30). This imagery suggests that the governess sees herself for the first time as a mother, the "figured full" drapes and the large bed evoking pregnancy and childbirth. Indeed, her arrival at Bly sets off extreme emotional swings—"a succession of flights and drops"—that, conjoined with a chronic sleeplessness, suggest postpartum symptoms (29). She also hears "faint and far, the cry of a child" during her first night at Bly, which hints not only at her immersion in Romantic and gothic literature (the standard interpretation) but also at her unconscious conviction of her maternity (30).

That the governess is not Miles and Flora's mother, that they have no mother, just serves to heighten the governess's maternal fantasy, and indeed her culture's maternal fantasy. From her first night, her relationship with the children is characterized by a possessive and hyperbolic emotion, with the desire for exclusivity, that partakes of unreality and thus unmasks the ideology of motherhood. As she persistently refers to Miles and Flora as her children (30, 44, 51), with equal persistence she describes her feelings for them in the language of inflated emotion, such as her "passion of tenderness" for Miles (37). She details what students easily see as a disconcerting propensity to grab the children and hug them: "There were moments when I knew myself to catch them up by an irresistible impulse and press them to my heart" (64). She willfully constructs the three of them as all alone, dependent only on each other: "They had nothing but me, and I—well, I had *them*" (53). Together, these qualities of her imagined relationship with the children suggest the love of a mother rather than the affection of a teacher. The governess is certainly clear in her construal of her role at Bly as one of pleasure and enjoyment, not one of work and paid employment. As she writes at one point: "My charming work was just my life with Miles and Flora" (42). It is exactly this transposing of work into "life"—of labor into joy and even passion—that marks her rejection of the role of governess.

The entire turn of the plot of *The Turn of the Screw*, as the governess becomes convinced of the children's possession by evil and of her role as redeemer, is understandable through the "national civil religion" of motherhood that Lewis describes as dominant from the mid-nineteenth century on (224). The governess creates herself not just as the children's protector and defender but also, increasingly, and especially with Miles, as their only chance of salvation. Still more specifically and conforming to the ideology of maternal redemption described by Lewis, she feels that *her* only chance of salvation lies in her ability to save Miles. Their identities intertwine as he becomes the sign of her ability to be a good mother, one who can secure for him, and thus for herself, eternal life. The governess says near the end, in a conversation with Mrs. Grose, "If he confesses he's saved. And if he's saved—," and Mrs. Grose responds, "Then *you* are?" (110). When the governess grasps Miles for the last time, exclaiming, "What does he matter now, my own?—what will he *ever* matter? *I* have you," she has fully internalized a maternal role that is founded on the necessity of a possessive and exclusive mother-child bond, a bond that is inextricable from moral, even religious salvation (120).

That the governess is bound up in this mother complex explains further her vilification of Quint and Miss Jessel, who are not just repositories for her anxiety about her class status but who are also in competition with her, in her mind at least, for her children. Quint and Miss Jessel are those others who threaten the exclusivity of the mother-child bond. At the end of *The Turn of the Screw*, when Miles qualifies his statement that they are alone by saying, "Of course we've the others," and then voices what he clearly sees as the governess's view of those others, "they don't much count, do they?," he articulates both her anxiety (about the others) and desire (that they not count) (113). Those who threaten to attenuate or dissolve the mother-child bond, Quint and Miss Jessel, inhabit a debased class status and engage in sexual practices that include not only a taboo heterosexuality (their affair) but also, implicitly, homosexuality and pedophilia. Underlying the governess's calling Quint a devil at the culmination of the novella is that she is saving Miles from an otherworldly evil and also from a homoerotic love that is very much of the world. (For readings of Quint and Miles's relationship as homosexual, see Ellmann; Schrero; McWhirter, "In the 'Other House' "; and Person.)

A last major point for discussion is, of course, the ending. How can we read Miles's death in light of the governess's maternal fantasy—of her self-creation as the redemptive good mother? A reader might at first think that her role as mother would preclude her culpability in Miles's death. However, it is precisely the fact that she is implicated that allows the class to interrogate the consequences of the purported redemptive power of exclusive mothering. Henry James was one of the first writers to offer fictional representations, in both *The Turn of the Screw* and his 1884 story "The Author of Beltraffio," of what psychologists now call altruistic homicide. This term designates the killing by a parent, usually a mother, of one or more of the parent's children to ensure their salvation or in the belief that they would be better off dead. In their comprehensive survey of studies about why mothers kill their children, all of which include the category of altruistic homicide, Cheryl Meyer and Michelle Oberman show how the very notion of an altruistic killing is made thinkable by the exclusive, symbiotic mother-child bond and by the overidentification of the mother with the child that this bond encourages: such a mother simply cannot imagine her child's surviving without her (21–31). The exclusive mother-child bond is implicated in harm to the children in another way: psychologists and anthropologists alike have consistently found that women who mother alone are much more likely than mothers with a network of other caregivers to respond to their children in unstable emotional ways—to inflict pain on and to abandon and kill their children (see Hrdy 58; Bernard 9).

The dangers of mothering in isolation are explored in Sarah Blaffer Hrdy's fascinating essay "Mothers and Others." In its confirming that mothers actually mother better with the help of others, Hrdy's essay can be used in the classroom as a counterweight to the scholarship by Bloch and by Lewis on the historical construction of the exclusive mother. Hrdy argues (as other anthropologists have done before her) that mother-centered models of child care, along with their corollary gendered division of labor, are unique to certain Western cultures and to a relatively recent time period. The care of children by mothers and others, called cooperative breeding, is much more common through history and across cultures, and it is also strongly adaptive. Hrdy's argument suggests, in terms of *The Turn of the Screw*, that while the cult of exclusive mothering led the governess to fear and even demonize the others in Miles and Flora's life, they might in fact have been beneficent influences—something Miles and Flora themselves seem to believe. When Miles objects to the life the governess forces him to lead with her—one that is "so unnatural for a boy"—as well as to the "queer business" of the way she brings him up, he could be voicing an objection to the cult of exclusive mothering. James brings that objection to tragic fruition in Miles's death in the grasp of his "mother" (86, 92).

"The Author of Beltraffio" anticipates *The Turn of the Screw* in its representation of the danger of the maternal grasp. The story is told by a man who is visiting the home of a writer he reveres, Mark Ambient. Ambient's wife, Beatrice, believes that both her husband and his art (ostensibly a commitment to aestheticism) are immoral. The narrator-visitor, during the course of his stay, witnesses the struggle of husband and wife, which gets enacted over their son, Dolcino. Just as James would do later in *The Turn of the Screw*, the reiterated language of touching, holding, and grasping serves to define the mother's possessiveness of her son, her desire to deny separation and to be the exclusive source of an intertwined love and redemption. According to Mark's sister, Gwendolyn, Beatrice Ambient considers her husband's character and ideals to be so poisonous that "she'd prevent Mark from even so much as touching him" (53). In one scene, Mark calls his son to come to him, but the son, though he "struggled in the maternal embrace," was "too tightly held" (34). In another instance, the narrator remarks that Dolcino does not move around and play much, and the boy responds that "mamma's holding me close!" (66). In the climactic scene, Dolcino becomes seriously ill; Beatrice refuses to send for the doctor until it is too late, and the boy dies. Gwendolyn declares, of Dolcino's death, that her husband's book "gave [Beatrice] a horror; she determined to rescue [Dolcino]—to prevent him from being touched"

(76). Beatrice does seem to have accomplished what she promised, to see her son in heaven rather than corrupted by his father: she permitted his death in order to save him. In this story, as in *The Turn of the Screw*, the perfect mother turns deadly. Ambient's sister points this out directly, for while she claims that "Beatrice is perfect as a mother," she recognizes that Beatrice is capable of causing her son's death (49). It is precisely this deadliness of the fantasy of the perfect mother that both "The Author of Beltraffio" and *The Turn of the Screw* unveil—and the unveiling is a lesson not only for James's time but for our own.

Making Masculinity Visible: Teaching *Daisy Miller* at an All-Male College

Warren Rosenberg

The institutional context in which I teach James's *Daisy Miller* structures how I present the text. Wabash College is one of the three remaining all-male liberal arts colleges in the country. With thirty-five male students in my American literature survey course, I anticipate that James's narrative technique of telling the story through Winterbourne's limited perspective will lure them into making the same mistake Winterbourne makes in his study of Daisy. Because of James's genius and the tunnel vision that a seemingly gender-neutral reading encourages, this is exactly what happens for most of them. The way I use this initial misreading leads to a higher degree of engagement with James's emotionally nuanced text than I would have expected from my students who are primarily midwestern and from eighteen to twenty-one years old.

The realization, after class discussion, that James's narrative strategy has tricked them leads them to reread the story more closely. The rereading often results in a change in how they view Daisy and Winterbourne. In focusing on the process of my students reading as a distinctively constituted group, I am illustrating Barbara G. Pace's recent work on how "shared community standards" in the literature class can hinder our attempts to undercut stereotypical thinking. As Pace notes, "students often became so ensnared in their own perspectives that they did not fully read or carefully engage in the work of understanding texts" (411).

Certainly my all-male classes often confirm Pace's view, but teaching *Daisy Miller* in a way that allows my students to become conscious of their reading as men can begin the process of diversifying the reading. After discussing the story and reading one another's responses, they realize, and sometimes accept, that their misreading of Daisy was based on an invisible and unacknowledged gendered perspective, that stereotypical views of men and women limited their ability to look beneath the surface of character and incident. Of course, that all the students are men contributes to the uniformity of responses, but by using online discussion, they can begin to see that uniformity and challenge their classmates. As I note below, when certain monolithic views go unchallenged, I take a more active role. I am certain that this gender-sensitive, reader-response approach would be equally useful in a diverse college classroom, although the specific prompts I use would need to be modified.

To prepare students for class discussion, I ask them to read the story and post a paragraph response on the Web to the following three questions: "Would you date Daisy? Would you marry her? Who is responsible for what happens to Daisy?" (The first two questions assume a heterosexual orientation, but I acknowledge that when I give the assignment. At Wabash, a not particularly supportive environment for gay students, just raising the possibility that some students in the class may not be heterosexual creates a stir. Given the complications of James's own sexuality, one could read the story with a different take on the narrator's identifications, but in my survey class we have not reached that level.) The first two questions obviously elicit immediate emotional responses, but students are asked to give specifics from the story to support their answers. The purpose of the third question is to get students to think about the story as a whole and to see if their interpretation follows from the gendered perspective implicit in the first two questions. The third question also generates a discussion of the complex causation that is at the core of distinguishing realism from Romanticism, a key issue at this stage of the survey.

Since I began asking these questions, the responses have been, as one might expect, heavily weighted against dating Daisy and almost universally against marrying her. The slight difference in the 2002 responses resulted from students' reading one another's answers. They were still overwhelmingly critical of her. The following statement is typical of a more measured attitude:

> I think that I would try to date Daisy, but I would never marry her. She plays too many games and needs too much attention. I would grow tired of her flirting and playing me against other men. It seems that Daisy likes putting Winterbourne in a bad mood. Daisy says, "That's all I want—a little fuss!" and later she says, "I hope you are disappointed, or disgusted, or something!" The previous three lines are why I would not marry Daisy. (CJ 2000).[1]

Another student calls Daisy "conniving and controlling" (KC 2002). A third goes a bit further: "One might immediately argue that she is depicted as a crude, rude, American. The word 'slut' shamefully comes to mind when she discloses suggestively that she has had many male friends" (JB 2000).

At least this student puts "slut" in quotation marks and acknowledges that applying the label might be shameful. In every initial class discussion, one student, with the supposed protection of the all-male classroom and with a sidelong, challenging look at me, will call Daisy a "bitch." There is some embarrassment at this, some looks at me, and then a tirade of stories about women who lead one on, who play games. Hostility toward Daisy as the symbol of every woman who ever rejected my students fills the room. At this point, in some years, one student will buck the crowd. He will defend Daisy, raise the issue of the double standard, or question Winterbourne's reliability. This dissent usually is enough to begin the cooldown and initiate a closer look at the text and Daisy. If no student stands up, I will ask if in fact males too do not play games during dating. I mention a film, *Swingers* (dir. Doug Liman, 1996), that I know most of them have seen, in which the male characters discuss how long one should wait to call a woman whom one has just met and likes, so as not to appear too eager. (Some giggles.) I ask whether Winterbourne might not be playing such a game by refusing to call on Daisy as he promised, when she arrives in Rome after very straightforwardly asking him, back in Switzerland, to come to Rome for her sake and not for his aunt's (78).

The discussion of male game playing is an important step toward making masculinity visible. As students talk about their own dating practices, they begin to appreciate the reciprocity in dating and return to the story to look more closely at Winterbourne's behavior as well as at Daisy's. One possible misreading that we examine is the widely held view that Daisy, "besides her beauty, seems to be shallow and pushes away the people who try to help her (Winterbourne) . . . I personally want a relationship with someone that doesn't beat around the bush about their feelings and play mind games with me" (JH 2002). We focus on the visit to Chillon in the story, and I ask the students to read aloud Daisy and Winterbourne's conversation to evaluate her intelligence and directness as well as his observational powers. After Daisy asks Winterbourne why he looks so grave, he responds, "Am I grave? . . . I had an idea I was grinning from ear to ear." She quickly and wittily replies, "If that's a grin, your ears are very near together." "Should you like me to dance a hornpipe on the deck?" he continues. "Pray do," she says, "and I'll carry round your hat. It will pay the expenses of our journey" (75). The students agree that such repartee reveals an agile mind. Those who felt she is uneducated, is not interested in learning about the site, and rambles on incoherently now realize that she is intent on gaining personal information about Winterbourne. As for the complaint that she beats around the bush, she directly asks him to travel with them as a teacher for her brother. Winterbourne is in fact the one shying away, saying he has "other occupations" and "engagements" (77), which she immediately realizes involve not his business (he has none) but another woman. The game player is clearly Winterbourne in this scene, not Daisy.

Another critical moment in the text is of course Mrs. Walker's carriage scene. I must admit it is great fun to watch a class of young men debating whether Daisy should or should not have abandoned Giovanelli and entered Mrs. Walker's carriage to save her reputation. Interestingly—but predictably, given their male perspective—they need to be pushed to see the importance of Winterbourne's role in the scene and the narrator's subtle critique of his actions. We look closely at the distancing of phrases like "the truth, for Winterbourne," was that the gallant thing to do was tell Daisy to get into the carriage (93). That "for Winterbourne" throws his view of Daisy and her situation into question. We note what actually happens: Winterbourne is the one, succumbing to the entreaties of Mrs. Walker, to get into the carriage, leaving Daisy alone with Giovanelli. Was this a gallant thing to do? Students begin to wonder. They also debate whether Daisy's refusal to get in is an act of foolish rebellion or courageous resistance to empty convention. Although we have just completed reading *Huckleberry Finn* before this class meeting, many students fail to evaluate Daisy's decision to accept being labeled improper in the same brave spirit that they took Huck's decision to go to hell. They know Huck made the decision because of his personal commitment to Jim but miss Daisy's similar reason for not abandoning Giovanelli. As she tells Winterbourne, the Italian gentleman had been looking forward to the walk for ten days and to disappoint him "would have been most unkind" (98).

As for the third question, about who is responsible for what happens to Daisy, after their first reading and before discussion my students see her as causing her own death. I am not sure if this response is gendered or comes from the American attitude that individual responsibility is a paramount virtue. Gender does play a role, though, in shaping their answers to this question. One student writes:

> Ultimately, it is her perception of life that leads to her death. Daisy is aware of the consequences of contracting the Roman fever by going to the Colosseum at night, but to her its a gamble she is willing to take. Anyway, she says: "Eugenio can give me pills." She believes nothing will happen to her because nothing has before, and if anything were to happen someone else would take care of her. Daisy never takes anything seriously, and it is this indiscretion, dependency on others, and frivolousness that kills her. Also Daisy does not care about anything—social norms, feelings of other men, her parents, and even herself. When Winterbourne sends her off from the Colosseum she shouted, "I don't care whether I have Roman fever or not!" This passage solidifies the claim that to Daisy life is a game, for she does not even care about her life. (JB 2002)

Certainly an initially hostile view of Daisy contributes to such a conclusion, nor is the conclusion completely off base. But to say she does not care about getting the fever because she is frivolous distorts the text. In Winterbourne and Daisy's final two conversations she attempts to move him out of his passivity (he will not go beyond verbally defending her against the attacks of the Americans in Europe) by telling him she is engaged to Giovanelli and then denying it. After Winterbourne finds her with Giovanelli in the Colosseum at night, he thinks he has finally grasped the truth about her character, so when she asks him if he believed that she was engaged, he responds, with a laugh, "I believe that it makes very little difference whether you are engaged or not!" This statement crushes her hope of getting him to make the leap to loving her, and only then does she say, "in a little strange tone," the narrator tells us, that she does not care about catching Roman fever (113). Students now see that her defiance is a direct response to his rejection, not a function of her lack of seriousness or her willfulness. At this point I ask students to think of Hawthorne's "Rappaccini's Daughter," studied earlier in the semester. We discuss the parallels between Winterbourne's and Giovanni's lack of faith in and their inability to love the women to whom they are attracted. When the students learn that James had written a study of Hawthorne, they see there is some outside evidence supporting the idea that James, like Hawthorne, was critical of his male protagonist.

In all the years I have taught this story at Wabash College, including the past six when I asked these three questions, only two students, after an initial reading, felt that Winterbourne was responsible for Daisy's death—although Winterbourne himself admits that he made a mistake. Other characters besides Daisy have been blamed, but not Winterbourne. I quote one of these students' remarks from the electronic discussion board to show that unprompted resistance to the gender script is possible. In response to the many student entries blaming Daisy, this student labeled his entry "So Wrong":

> I couldn't disagree more. Daisy is not to blame at all. All she does is not follow social conventions. So what? The social conventions she is being asked to follow are stupid. I think Winterbourne realizes this at the end of the story. His last line is "You were right . . . I was booked to make a mistake. I have lived too long in foreign parts." What he means is that he realizes he should have stood up for Daisy against the silliness of the European social hierarchy, but he has lived so long in Europe that he had come to accept it as correct. I really hated Winterbourne throughout the story; I thought he was an elitist misogynist. That he may have realized his mistake by the end seems to redeem him somewhat, but James goes on to say that he goes back to Geneva anyway, suggesting that maybe nothing has changed for him. Who is to blame? It is the "society" which Daisy wishes to join but does not fit into.
>
> (AP 2002)

If all students read the story with such perception, I would be out of a job. Not to say that this reading provided the answer I was looking for. For one thing, I do not believe the story supports the conclusion that "Daisy is not to blame at all." But this reader did something my other students could not: he was able to sidestep James's trick of making it appear that Winterbourne's view of Daisy is the only acceptable one. That is the level I hoped my students would reach after their online and class discussions.

To test whether they have in fact changed their views, this year, for the first time, I put a follow-up question on the Discussion Board and asked for voluntary responses: "How did the Discussion Board and class discussion affect your view of *Daisy Miller*?" The response rate was low—only eleven out of thirty-five—but there was a range of replies, from "it confirmed my negative [or positive] view of Daisy" to "it modified my view of her." One student wrote:

> the most significant influence of the discussion on my view of the story was that I realized the fault that lies with Winterbourne. . . . It is clear

> that Winterbourne must be aware of the European cultural norms, yet shrugs them off to chase Daisy. . . . The fact that he allows the gossip to continue behind her back shows that his feelings were not strong enough for him to "gallantly" defend her. (DS 2002)

Despite his change in view of Winterbourne, this student ended his comments by reconfirming his negative view of Daisy. Another student made a more general comment about the value of the discussion:

> When I left class and we had argued and re-hashed the argument for some time only then did I truly understand that nothing in life is really black and white. It is good to always have an open mind and acknowledge the opinions and views of others because if we don't then we have just cut ourselves off from ever finding what may be the real purpose an author is attempting to present in his/her works. (CJ 2002)

While I hope James's "real purpose" will always be somewhat up for grabs, I appreciate that this student came away from class with a more complex view of the story.

This approach to teaching *Daisy Miller* leads to exciting, sometimes contentious discussions in which students have a stake in the outcome. Potential problems like the difficulty of James's prose style or the perception by my male students that this story is a soap opera seem to melt away. They come to appreciate the richness of James's art, how carefully he crafts his story, how realistically he portrays his characters, how perceptively he presents his psychological and societal vision. But the overriding purpose of this approach to teaching *Daisy Miller* at an all-male college is to demonstrate how powerfully gender shapes and often distorts the way we see the world—sometimes, as in this story, with tragic results.

NOTE

[1]All student quotations are used with permission. Initials indicate student names; the year given is the year of the class.

An Analytic Turn: Teaching *The Turn of the Screw* in the Writing Classroom

Marian Kelly

After a couple of decades of insisting on the rigid distinction between writing and literature courses, more and more writing teachers are returning to the use of literature as a way to teach the fundamentals of critical thinking and writing. Their motivation in doing so does not spring wholly from the fact that many teachers of writing are also lovers of literature; rather, these teachers recognize that literature is useful in teaching the analytic and interpretive skills that are required to produce any good piece of writing. However, integrating literature into the writing classroom poses many challenges, and it can be difficult to maintain a strong focus on the goals of a writing course in the face of the many distractions that teaching literature brings. Finding a text that lends itself to the development of writing skills can alleviate some of the problems teachers encounter in trying to align content and method; in this respect, Henry James's *The Turn of the Screw* proves an excellent choice.

Although I focus primarily here on strategies for teaching this novella in a typical first-year writing class, these strategies would also work well in a course on writing about literature. Teaching *The Turn of the Screw* is especially useful toward the beginning of either course because it allows students unfamiliar with literary analysis to begin in a highly structured framework. This essay models several specific questions about the text that give students the comfort of a clear direction in their analysis of James's tale as well as a sense of the goals of analysis in general.

The Turn of the Screw is attractive for a writing classroom because first-year students find it relatively accessible. The story is fairly short, and although the text is not exactly straightforward, it does not require too much explanation at the basic level of the plot. James's text, however, has enough complexity and enough potential for conflicting interpretations to lend itself to the kinds of debates that predominate in a writing classroom. Indeed, because *The Turn of the Screw* fosters two distinct and oppositional interpretations without finally endorsing either one, it is particularly well suited for courses that emphasize debate-style argument. Students can argue with equal plausibility either that the ghosts are real or that the governess is insane. Because James develops both possibilities over the course of the text and leaves both open at the end, this debate can easily be inserted into a class in place of the more usually encountered arguments on such topics as abortion and racial profiling, which similarly have two sides yet remain open.

The Turn of the Screw has distinct advantages over these more typical examples of the content of a writing classroom. First, because students do not have much personal investment in one interpretation of James's text over the other, as they might in a political or moral issue, it is easier to teach them rhetorical skills such as concession and counterargument. Second, writing on James makes it obvious, as it is not always in debate-style scenarios, that there is a need for interpretation. James prevents the reader from making untroubled assumptions about what his text means; thus, *The Turn of the Screw* can help make students aware of what they are bringing into any argument they create.

Despite the attractions of teaching James in a class focused on argumentative debate, I prefer to use *The Turn of the Screw* to teach a slightly different form of writing. I follow David Rosenwasser and Jill Stephen in designating the kind of writing that I teach as analytic. In Rosenwasser and Stephen's view, writing functions primarily as a tool through which students reach a better understanding of a text. Because analytic writing prioritizes understanding, it removes some of the pressures that truncate student thinking by causing students to look at evidence exclusively in terms of whether or not it backs their argument and will convince the reader. In analytic writing, the thesis is devoted to examining how something works rather than to lobbying for a particular reading of the text. The evidence functions as a means to focus and refine the thesis, so that evidence and claim exist in a more symbiotic relation. The relationship between writer and reader improves as well, since the writer is not required to bludgeon the reader into accepting the thesis; instead, the writer's goal is simply to convince the reader to entertain a different possibility about the text.

To illustrate the difference between a debate-style argument and an analytic argument, I begin my unit on *The Turn of the Screw* by encouraging students to engage in exactly the kind of debate one would find in a typical writing classroom. First I have them read and summarize the text on their own. The summary not only gives them some early practice in prioritizing details and finding organizing patterns in a text, it also allows me to see how they understand the text and provides a foundation on which they are able to expand that understanding. The class begins with students reading their summaries out loud. It usually transpires that some have read the text as a straightforward ghost story, some as a story of insanity, and some have grasped the point that James doesn't commit to either one. Once these possibilities have all become apparent, we move on to a discussion of the two primary interpretations of the text.

To do this most expediently, I divide the class into what I call the "pro-ghost" and "anti-ghost" groups and give them twenty to thirty minutes to marshal the evidence in support of their positions before a full-out class debate on whether the ghosts exist. Once the discussion gets started, it generally carries an impressive amount of momentum, typically leaving me with little to do other than insert occasional comments on good etiquette in debating. This discussion has two advantages: first, it gets all the major scenes on the table; second, it allows students who either didn't see or didn't want to believe the opposing interpretation to get a clear picture of how both sides are valid. If I were teaching a debate-focused paper with this text, I would go on from here to outline other possible debates: If the ghosts do exist, are they evil? Does the introduction set the tone for a story about ghosts or about insanity?

But in this class, I now begin to distinguish for my students what an analytic argument looks like in contrast to a debate-style argument. I outline the different goals that the two kinds of arguments have, the difference in the motivation for writing the two kinds of papers, and the difference in what the reader is meant to get out of the papers. We begin moving toward an analytic reading by discussing the limitations imposed by the debate. Over the course of their discussion about whether the ghosts exist, my students begin to see that this debate has no resolution. I offer an analytic approach as a way to move beyond the deadlock.

I redirect their focus by changing the emphasis from whether or not the governess is mad to how James suggests that she might be. We agree as a group that there is no way for us to determine absolutely whether she is insane and instead begin to consider the elements that bring into question both her sanity and, more important, her credibility as a narrator. I pose this particular problem by giving them a paper assignment in which they must select and analyze one chain of details that undermines the governess's reliability as a narrator. I encourage them to look at the way she uses her evidence to draw her conclusions and to consider what her logical processes look like. I ask them about the kind of evidence she relies on and her attitude toward her reader. All this sets us up nicely for the primary emphasis of my unit on *The Turn of the Screw*: using evidence.

Not only does the governess give us a way to talk about the responsibility that my students have in their papers of treating their evidence and their reader fairly, the text also provides many opportunities for them to learn how to use evidence in their papers. Because of both the quantity and the ambiguity of the evidence in *The Turn of the Screw*, students have an opportunity to work on various skills: in engaging the text, they must select and prioritize evidence, argue what the evidence means and why it is relevant, and distinguish their inferences about the text from the evidence that the text provides.

This final point gets particular attention the following day when they read excerpts from Harold Goddard's article "A Pre-Freudian Reading of *The Turn of the Screw*," which is available in the Norton Critical Edition of *The Turn of the Screw* (Esch and Warren) and which I compress into just a few pages for them. Goddard's article is excellent for demonstrating what both effective and ineffective use of evidence looks like. Students have already read the chapter in their handbook, *Writing Analytically*, that covers how to incorporate evidence into a paper, including the necessity of telling the reader what the evidence means and how it relates to the thesis as well as how much analysis to give of that evidence. I get them looking at these issues in the Goddard article by dividing the article and my class into four sections and giving them an exercise adapted from their handbook in which they calculate the ratio of evidence to interpretation by labeling each sentence as either evidence or claim. With this analysis in hand we have a specific way to talk not only about the quantity of analysis that Goddard provides but also about his selection and use of evidence in general.

We begin simply, with the ratio of evidence to claim, or fact to interpretation. We discuss how a writer can err in two ways in regard to this ratio: by having too much evidence with too little interpretation or by having too little evidence to support the claims being made. Goddard's article is very useful here because in some sections Goddard does one, in some sections the other, yet in the final section he hits a fairly decent balance, so students get a model of each ratio.

Goddard also provides opportunities to talk about the different kinds of evidence that can be used with a literary text. He gives a lot of plot summary and description, so that we can discuss how these vague and general forms of evidence are much weaker than direct quotation. He also uses several block quotations. Here we discuss how difficult it is to integrate block quotes smoothly because they create such a sharp division between evidence and claims, leaving a paper with huge chunks of evidence followed by huge chunks of claims. But Goddard does give examples of quotations that are not cumbersome and that he has adequately responded to and integrated into his article, so that students get a positive model of how to use evidence efficiently and effectively.

There are also opportunities in this article to discuss the problems that result when fact and interpretation are not clearly distinguished. Goddard's sometimes indistinct alternation between the two highlights James's ambiguity and illustrates the difficulty that confronts all readers of James's tale. As several of my students' summaries will have already shown, students frequently interpret James where they think they are merely relaying details from the text. We talk about the necessity of careful reading to determine what is actually in the text and the necessity of careful writing to distinguish clearly between the evidence in the text and the writer's interpretation of it.

Finally, we discuss the strengths and weaknesses of Goddard's overall argument. One key area of the article that causes problems when looked at closely is the section in which Goddard examines the governess's description of Miss Jessel. Here he claims, as many critics have, that because Mrs. Grose, rather than the governess, provides the bulk of the description in this scene, the ghosts' existence is brought into question. Goddard goes on to argue that the same thing happens in the scene where the governess describes Quint, which Goddard does not examine. Since the Quint scene is one of the major scenes used in support of the ghosts' existence, this omission is striking.

Once my students have recognized and become suitably piqued about such evasion, I point out to them that Goddard set himself up for this problem by embarking on an all-or-nothing approach to his subject. Rather than simply suggest to his reader how the governess might be motivated by a hero complex, he falls into the trap of trying to prove that the ghosts do not exist. This point enables me to show my students how a bludgeoning attitude toward both subject matter and reader detracts from a paper's potential, for my students quite rightly see that Goddard's thesis, despite the flaws in the way he develops it, is nonetheless compelling in the perspective it provides on James's story. Moreover, his claim that the governess has a hero complex resonates with my students as they try to brainstorm ways in which the governess proves a less than reliable narrator. Thus Goddard's article nicely segues into my students' ideas about how to pursue their own arguments.

When my students bring in the patterns of evidence on which they plan to write, the governess's greatest contribution to the writing classroom becomes clear. As I write these patterns on the board, the class begins to look as much like a tutorial on how not to write a paper as it does like an overview of the governess's flaws as a narrator. As a class we come up with an impressive list of problems in her narration. Not only does the governess exhibit certain attitudes, such as the need to be right, that make her assertions problematic, she also allows her emotions to dictate her perceptions: she equates the internal with the external by taking her personal feelings as objective facts. These are problems that beginning writers often have, which result from their insecurity and subsequent refusal to move beyond their opinions to argumentative reasoning based on evidence. Seeing how such tendencies cause us to mistrust the governess allows students to recognize the problems that a writer's attitude alone can cause.

But most damaging to the governess are the mental processes that she considers logical. She not only jumps to conclusions, she also obstinately holds on to those conclusions once she makes them, and she will admit no other point of view, as is evident in her authoritarian handling of Mrs. Grose. Her conclusions based on little, underanalyzed evidence are an improvement over her assertions that are based on no evidence at all, a trend that suggests that the governess, like an untutored writer, is not fully aware of the distinction between evidence and interpretation. Nor is she free of out-and-out logical fallacies, her favorite being the either-or fallacy that is exemplified by her decisions about the children's innocence and the ghosts' malevolence.

As one problem piles on top of the next, my students not only gain much entertainment at the expense of the poor governess, they are also able to put names to the various frustrations that they felt from the start with James's text. Moreover, they gain a new awareness and appreciation for a reader's frustrated predicament when faced with a piece of writing that succumbs to such problems. This awareness is especially helpful to me as I begin working with them on their drafts. Indeed, during conferences I frequently say to them, in as many words, "You are doing here exactly what you accuse the governess of doing." Because they have seen their mistake demonstrated, they grasp the problem more quickly. Having themselves been placed in the position of frustrated reader, they are better able to look at their papers with a reader's as well as a writer's eye.

The figure of the governess thus makes James's tale especially appropriate to teach to beginning writers because she serves as such an excellent example of what not to do. She provides us with insight into what makes both a bad reader and a bad writer. Her narrow-minded assertion "[t]hat can have but one meaning" (*Turn* [Beidler (2nd ed.) 34]) epitomizes the attitude of writers who take their positions to be self-evident and unassailable or whose intense focus on their arguments prevents a thorough consideration of the evidence. At the other end of the spectrum, James himself contributes a useful illustration of a writer with too little, rather than too much, focus. Robert Bridges eloquently describes the difficulty that readers of *The Turn of the Screw* encounter when he writes, "seldom does [James] make a direct assertion, but qualifies and negatives and double negatives, and then throws in a handful of adverbs, until the image floats away upon a verbal smoke" (154). For every frustration that students have with James's ambiguous language and with his refusal to come down solidly on one side or the other about what is going on, there is an opportunity for a teacher to emphasize that students need to do the opposite of what James does: they need to make their prose lucid, distinguish between their facts and their interpretations, and present their arguments clearly. Caught between James and the governess, students will, one hopes, reject both in favor of a rational, thorough, and fair presentation of their ideas.

"Dishonoured and Tragic, She Was All before Me": Daisy and the Governess in First-Year Composition Courses

Sallie Duhling and Patricia Worrall

Gainesville College is a two-year, liberal arts college in the university system of Georgia. It offers core-curriculum courses at the freshman and sophomore levels. Along with other courses, students are required to take two freshman composition courses: English 1101 and English 1102. English 1101 primarily focuses on essay writing with such methods as comparison and contrast, description, and persuasion; it deals with writing a research essay. English 1102 is an introduction to literature. Students in this course develop their writing skills through reading and analyzing short stories, poetry, and drama. Both courses, however, require that students read a novel, and that is where Henry James's Daisy and governess come into the picture.

Sallie Duhling teaches *Daisy Miller* in English 1101, and Patricia Worrall teaches *The Turn of the Screw* in English 1102. Students of both teachers have a wide range of skills. Some are freshman entering college right after high school; others are nontraditional students who have been away from an academic environment for as much as five years and sometimes more. Thus, we have to adapt our pedagogical approaches to James's tales to address diverse needs and skills. Since both tales are only part of the two courses' content, we also have to condense our approaches to fit in a limited amount of class time. Taking into consideration students' needs and our time constraints, Sallie uses a formalist approach in her English 1101 classes and Patricia introduces her students to different critical approaches in her English 1102 classes.

Our discussion of *Daisy Miller* and *The Turn of the Screw* gives some of the pedagogical strategies that we use and provides examples and suggestions for incorporating these two James tales into composition courses.

Daisy Miller

English 1101 does not have the research focus that English 1102 does, so my approach to *Daisy Miller* involves a close analysis of the primary text, with assignments of a historical or critical nature. I do not require a specific text. Portraying the international theme, *Daisy Miller* does not have the heavy psychological component of *The Turn of the Screw*; it is lighter fare and can be approached as a tale of manners, a study of innocence abroad, or a tragedy of misunderstanding.

Although the plot is easy to grasp, James's language warrants some instruction. Students need to be warned that the lengthy phrases explore impressions and emotions that are the meat of this tale. Action is not the focus here. Today's students, used to action-packed video games and quick takes on MTV, need to be prepared to spend time on this reading assignment.

Students can be placed in groups, each exploring an aspect of the tale, or general class discussion can cover the assignments. Because the problem addressed in the story and the results of Daisy's stubbornness may seem inconsequential to today's audience, students need to know who the people in *Daisy Miller* are. Where do Daisy, Mrs. Costello, Winterbourne, and the other Americans in Vevey and Rome come from? On the first page of the story, James sets the scene and describes Daisy:

> Vevey assumes at this period some of the characteristics of an American watering-place. There are sights and sounds which evoke a vision, an echo, of Newport and Saratoga. There is a flitting hither and thither of "stylish" young girls, a rustling of muslin flounces, a rattle of dance-music in the morning hours, a sound of high-pitched voices at all times. (47)

One group of students can discover what was significant about Newport and Saratoga. What were those places like? Who went there? Did James know Newport and Saratoga intimately? Another aspect of American society of the middle 1800s (and somewhat later) for students to explore is the cult of rich Americans, such as the Vanderbilts and Astors, going to Europe to buy culture and titles. Students may also want to translate Daisy into the present. Since flirting does not offend many contemporary young people, what does? What behavior might cause a person to be ostracized?

Daisy Miller's problem is one of perception—how others perceive her and what she perceives as her social responsibilities. Students can decide what Mrs. Costello, Mrs. Walker, Winterbourne, and others expect of Daisy and what Daisy feels are her rights.

Daisy can easily be viewed as innocent, defiant, or just stupid. At the end of *Daisy Miller*, Giovanelli pronounces her innocent, but Daisy has clearly flouted the social conventions of her peers. She tells Winterbourne, who is trying to get her to abandon Giovanelli in a public place, "I have never allowed a gentleman to dictate to me, or to interfere with anything I do" (88). This comment does not sound very scandalous to the modern reader; indeed, it sounds quite sensible, but what would it have meant about Daisy to readers in the middle 1800s? A group of students may investigate how James's contemporaries received Daisy's character. William Dean Howells was an influential defender of Daisy, but there were many detractors who felt Daisy set a bad example or defamed the American girl.

Daisy's independent nature can also be seen in her relationship with her mother, a woman completely dominated and outfoxed by her children. Discussing what Daisy's family life is like back in Schenectady and why mother, daughter, and son are in Europe without Mr. Miller will shed light on Daisy's character.

Another aspect of Daisy is her loyalty to Giovanelli, to whom she owes no particular allegiance. Does her loyalty to him put her in a positive light? She is not using him to get Winterbourne's attention or to make Winterbourne jealous or to defy those who say she should not be seen with Giovanelli. Winterbourne's initial fascination with her indicates that there is something about her that cannot be clouded by the fact that she is "very common," as his aunt describes her (62).

Daisy's relationships with Giovanelli and Winterbourne are innocent by modern standards. What does the men's behavior tell us about the men? Giovanelli is clearly besotted with Daisy, knowing full well that there is no future in their relationship. Winterbourne, on the other hand, who is clearly the object of Daisy's affection, cannot see past the criticism of Mrs. Walker and others and gives her up. How does his behavior color him? Has he "lived too long in foreign parts" (116), as he says of himself, or is he just shallow?

Peter Bogdanovich's film version of *Daisy Miller*, with Cybill Shepherd, certainly should not be substituted for reading the tale, but it is helpful in understanding the story. Other films—Jane Campion's *The Portrait of a Lady*, Iain Softley's *The Wings of the Dove*, James Ivory's *The Golden Bowl*—show Jamesian heroines in Europe. An assignment for students to view (on their own) these films to compare Daisy's fate with that of Maggie Verver, Milly Theale, or Isabel Archer would be fruitful. What did Europe mean to each? What role does money play in their lives? What are their relationships with men? Students will see very quickly the trap that fabulous wealth lays for Isabel Archer, Milly Theale, and Maggie Verver. Another writing assignment could be to discuss whether Daisy is outrageous or outraged, whether she is a tragic heroine or a pathetic one.

Given the time constraints in this course, I count the essay double, since we spend so much time on *Daisy Miller*. It is also one of the last essays in the course, and I use it as a bridge to English 1102, where students will have a semester's worth of analyzing literature.

The Turn of the Screw

Before students can enroll in English 1102, they must pass English 1101. Thus, students in English 1102 have had experience writing different types of essays as well as experience writing about a novel. In English 1102, they work on refining their rhetorical and critical thinking skills by reading and writing about literature. A novel is required reading for the course, and I use *The Turn of the Screw*.

I begin by showing Ben Bolt's film *The Turn of the Screw*. I find that most students are not familiar with the story; the film helps them with the plot and with visualizing the characters and setting as they read the tale. Seeing the film also helps them maneuver their way through James's prose, which is often complex and difficult for students. After seeing the film and discussing their responses to the characters as portrayed in it and, of course, their responses to the ending, we move to the tale itself.

I use the Bedford second edition of *The Turn of the Screw*, which contains not only the text of the tale but also biographical and historical contexts as well as a number of articles using different critical approaches to the story. Before we begin reading the tale, I have students read Peter G. Beidler's "Introduction: Biographical and Historical Contexts." We take a class period to talk about this section. For the tale itself, I divide the readings up over three class periods: the prologue and chapters 1–8, chapters 9–17, and chapters 18–24. The division of the readings helps facilitate focused class discussion. I also use the essays included in Beidler's edition to introduce critical theory to my students and to incorporate theory into our discussions; as we read the chapters, we also discuss these essays. Students are assigned Wayne Booth's reader-response article " 'He Began to Read to Our Hushed Little Circle': Are We Blessed or Cursed by Our Life with *The Turn of the Screw*?," Bruce Robbins's Marxist article " 'They Don't Much Count, Do They?': The Unfinished History of *The Turn of the Screw*," and Priscilla L. Walton's gender-studies article " 'He Took No Notice of Her; He Looked at Me': Subjectivities and Sexualities in *The Turn of the Screw*." I find that reader-response, Marxist, and gender theories are accessible to my students, and with time constraints I can cover only a few critical approaches.

To help my students find their way through the labyrinth of events, narratives, and apparitions, I use Terry Heller's The Turn of the Screw: *Bewildered Vision*, which provides a number of useful lists, such as a sequence of events from the prologue to the last chapter (22), a chronology of who tells the governess's narrative and when the narrative is told (40), and the appearances of the ghosts (74). These lists provide students with ways to view aspects of the plot and the narrative style.

Class discussions are important, and one way that I have found to encourage participation in them is to divide the students into small reading groups of about four or five and give the groups a focus for their reading. I ask half the groups to read the tale and concentrate on aspects that indicate that the ghosts are real. I ask these groups to consider how the reality of the ghosts affects a reading of the governess and the children as well as the ending of the story. The other half of the groups read the tale focusing on aspects that indicate that the ghosts are not real. These groups consider how their unreality affects a reading of the governess and the children as well as the ending of the story. When we meet in class to discuss the assigned chapters, the groups meet and list evidence for whether the ghosts are real or not. We then discuss how either interpretation changes our view of the governess, the children, and the ending of the story.

I also use a student survey to gauge individual interpretations of the tale. The first questions that I ask are: "If the ghosts are real, then do they possess the children? Are the ghosts harmless, or are they after the children?" In a recent class, ten out of the seventeen students who took the survey said that the ghosts were real. Of those ten, four thought the children were possessed, three thought the ghosts were harmless, and three felt that the ghosts were after the children. The second question deals with the sanity of the governess. If students thought that the governess was insane, they had to give reasons why they came to that conclusion. Some of the reasons they gave were: "emotionally and mentally stressed," "worried and suspicious all the time," "living in a huge house and all of a sudden has kids," and "she sees the ghosts when she thinks hard about them." The third question concerns the children. Students are given the following options for characterizing them: innocent, possessed by the ghosts, playing tricks on the governess, or in league with the ghosts. Half the students said that the children were innocent. The fourth and final question concerns the death of Miles at the end of the story. The possible explanations for his death are that he was smothered by accident, possessed and died after confessing, died of fright or shock, was physically sick, or was murdered by the governess. Eleven out of seventeen students said that Miles's death was an accident. I share the results of the survey with the students, and going over the responses provides for interesting discussion and debate.

Another strategy that I use is electronic postings. For these we use the discussion area in WebCT, an online course tool. Students are asked to post a focused critical question about an aspect of a character, a setting, a scene, or a conversation. We go over their postings in class. The postings provide a way to start discussion and allow those students to participate who would not normally respond in class. An example of a posting was written by a student who posed the question "Who is the biggest villain in *The Turn of the Screw*?" and answered it with the following comments (used with permission):

> To me the biggest villain has to be Miles. Miles shows his evil intentions on several different incidents. The time that he schemed a plan with Flora to put the governess to sleep with playing music was mischievous. The plan worked, so Miles had his laugh at the discomfort of the governess. Miles sneaked outside to prove to the governess that he could do whatever he wanted, which showed a great deal of misconduct and sneakiness. . . . I can't totally blame Miles because he was taught well from Peter Quint. He was an evil man who did a perfect job of training his pupil. Quint and Miles have a lot of qualities in common. I see them both as instigators of trouble, and characters who stop at nothing to achieve total chaos for everyone.

Such postings provide an opportunity for students to share their interpretations and to apply critical thinking skills. They also provide an opportunity for class discussions that are student-driven rather than instructor-initiated, which are much more interesting for both the students and the instructor.

After discussing the tale, the electronic postings, and the critical essays, students must write an essay in which they use a critical theory and must incorporate at least two outside sources. I put resources on reserve in the library and encourage students to use interlibrary loan for requesting articles. For instance, I place on reserve Neil Cornwell and Maggie Malone's The Turn of the Screw *and* What Maisie Knew: *Contemporary Critical Essays*. Although we do not discuss these essays in class, I encourage students to use material from them in their papers. Overall, I have been pleased by the papers I have received. Students' use of critical theory and critical thinking skills has been admirable, considering they have only a cursory exposure to theory.

Using *The Turn of the Screw* in a composition course that introduces students to literature has many advantages. That the work is short helps when there is limited time to devote to it. The most beneficial advantages are the ambiguity inherent in the novella and the lack of consensus among critics. The ambiguity allows students to explore different approaches and hold different views without feeling that their opinions have no validity. The lack of consensus enables them to find critics who support their opinions, empowers them to express their interpretations. Students enjoy the debates more when there is no risk of being wrong. I, too, enjoy the debates, discussions, and insights that my students share with one another and with me.

Our essay's title, "Dishonoured and Tragic, She Was All before Me," reflects both Daisy and the governess, and dishonor and tragedy, among other aspects, capture the interest of our students. Because of these two women and their stories, we both have had success using *Daisy Miller* and *The Turn of the Screw* in freshman composition courses. Each tale and woman provide challenges that have been rewarding for our students and for us.

What the Freshman Knew: Jamesian Ambiguity in the International Composition Classroom

Anna Despotopoulou

A freshman composition course in an undergraduate program that grants an English degree in a non-English-speaking country is not remarkably different from its equivalent in the United States or the United Kingdom. The course's aim and structure are the same: through the study of essays, articles, and literary texts, students are taught how to compose at least four types of essays (one that summarizes, one that analyzes, one that compares, and one that synthesizes), and, in the process, to identify and correct their errors in grammar and style. It should be pointed out that at the University of Athens, in my native Greece, English academic writing courses are offered only to English department students, to whom all language and literature units are taught and examined in English. At other private higher education institutions in Athens, where instruction in all disciplines is conducted in English, freshman English is offered to students of all majors. I assume that a similar situation exists in most non-English-speaking countries.

Despite their similar aims and comparable methodology, teachers of English majors for whom English is not the mother tongue are faced with completely different errors and needs to those of native speakers. Having studied English as a foreign language (EFL), such students were trained very differently from native speakers to read, comprehend, and write. The basic rules of grammar and syntax have been meticulously studied rather than assimilated naturally, and as a result an advanced student of English at university level will seldom make subject-verb agreement errors or commit comma splices. Problems are generally found in the structuring of complex sentences and the usage of tenses and idiomatic expressions. These needs are usually addressed through repeated practice of set exercises that require EFL students to transform, build, and complete sentences in ways that teach them both basic and advanced functions of the English language. These types of exercises are rarely featured in the writing handbooks used in composition courses for native speakers. *The Turn of the Screw* can be used to help both native and EFL students sharpen reading comprehension skills and practice a variety of writing tasks. In an international classroom, however, it can be used only in advanced academic writing courses, where learners already speak and write the language fluently. Only then can they benefit from the ambiguity of the novel and the numerous writing possibilities that the text offers.

The Turn of the Screw is ideal for introducing immature learners to the task of critical reading. For this purpose, from the first session on, I drop hints about the ambiguity of the text and the disputable character of the governess.

Used to accepting literary narration at face value, students are encouraged, through this story, to consider the possible unreliability of the narrator, which opens up the text to a multitude of reader interpretations. At first they are shocked by the suggestion that the governess may not be omniscient as are narrators in other works of fiction they may have read. The notion of subjective point of view is too abstract for them to grasp. Why is the narration not objective, and what are the factors that make it so? Critical reading invites students to distinguish the elements of the governess's narrative that reveal its subjective nature. In order to convey this notion to my class, I resort to a visual depiction of James's "house of fiction" theory. While reading to them the relevant paragraph from James's preface to *The Portrait of a Lady* (45), I draw for them a house with many windows, windows of different shapes and at different levels, and surrounded by a garden. This elementary-school teaching aid seems humorous to students, draws their attention, and eventually makes them see that the garden (the story narrated by the governess) may look a particular way from one window (the governess) but quite different from another, higher up, or with a pair of binoculars. The window, I stress, stands for the limits of one's vision.

Next, the students are asked to distinguish and describe the governess's particular window: the personal background and character features that frame her viewpoint. Her restricted upbringing; her scant family home; and her limited self-knowledge, which is suggested by her observation that in Bly's long mirrors she could for the first time see herself from head to toe (30), are identified as elements that primarily narrow her vision, making her prone to exaggerate when placed in an environment socially more privileged than her own. Students are quick to observe that her infatuation with the uncle in Harley Street makes her less objective and that her judgment is bound to be influenced by the promise she made him. Strangely, they do not see straightaway that the narrative itself, being in the first person, contributes to the subjectivity. After reading in class the ship simile at the end of chapter 1, I point out that the governess is at the "helm" (33) not only of the ship she envisages, which stands for the household she has been assigned to take care of, but also of the story that she directs and controls. Once students notice the absence of another narrator and the nonintrusiveness of the author, they begin to realize that their reading of the story is influenced by the strictly personal viewpoint of the governess, marked by phrases like "I remember," "I wondered," "I felt," "I believed," "I fancied," and so on, all of which impose on the reader a biased view of events.

I then prompt the students to distinguish between reported facts and impressions. They astutely notice that even descriptions of setting lack objectivity, filtered as they are through the impressionable mind of the narrator. With hindsight the governess herself acknowledges that at her arrival she imaginatively transformed the "big ugly antique but convenient house" into a "castle of romance inhabited by a rosy sprite" (33, 32). Throughout the story, the rendering of events is tainted by her tendency to exaggerate. Students initially take it for granted that Miles was expelled from school because he was "an injury to the others" (34). On second reading, however, they realize that the governess's words have controlled their judgment and admit that an expulsion from school could be caused by a number of offenses. Her adamant assurance that the dismissal "can have but one meaning" (34), his corrupting influence over others, indicates a quick-to-judge nature and a tendency to think always the worst. At this point students usually interpret her actions—or rather her refusal to take action regarding Miles's schooling—as immature, a result of her inexperience as a governess. The arbitrariness of her conclusions is also suggested in the first lake scene, where she conjectures that "Flora *saw*" (55) although there is no evidence that the little girl did. Once alert to the ambiguity created by the fine line between reality and imagination, students start mistrusting most of the governess's speculations, pointing out that she lacks tangible proof for her allegations.

For nonnative speakers who have had little or no exposure to English literature before their arrival at the university, James's long, convoluted sentences mystify and often irritate. Even though I assign only about six chapters' reading for each session, I find that students tend to skip long, descriptive passages or ignore rambling sentences with baffling syntax. To avoid simple misunderstandings of the plot, I assign summaries, where each chapter has to be studied and condensed to about a hundred words by one or more students (depending on the size of the group) and presented in class. In the beginning I often get summaries like those in Cliffs Notes, which reduce the plot to an oversimplified sequence of events. A careful in-class rereading of pertinent passages, however, helps students focus on the movement of feelings rather than events. A second summary-like exercise that is particularly aimed at international students, one that is familiar to them from their language training, is the jumbled passage. For example, the second paragraph in chapter 1 can be divided into the following short sections: "I had no drop again till the next day . . . younger of my pupils," "The little girl. . . . the liberality with which I was treated," "The large impressive room . . . as so many things thrown in," "It was thrown in as well . . . I had rather brooded," "The one appearance . . . showing it too much," and "I wondered even then . . . have made me uneasy" (30). The sections are mixed up, and students are asked to put them in the right order. Even though they are supposed to have read the piece at home, they have trouble solving this puzzle, but gradually and with practice they begin to recognize how the Jamesian paragraph works and to appreciate the significance of certain long and seemingly boring sentences. At the same time they learn cohesion, coherence, text structure, and global meaning.

Alternatively, I may give them a similar or longer passage in its original sequence again divided into sections. Underneath the text I provide a list of summary phrases or sentences that need to be matched with the sections. In the list I include two or three misleading sentences (they might borrow words from the text) that need to be excluded. In a dense passage like the last paragraph of chapter 1, for instance, an instructor can work with the first and last sentences, which suggest the governess's feelings in words that contradict each other and which contain punctuation that confuses syntax and consecutive metaphors that mix the past with the present. Nonnative speakers usually have trouble telling whether the governess felt cheerful or oppressed on the second day of her arrival, as the first three sentences play with antithetical diction: "cheer" and "oppression," "slight" and "fuller," "scared" and "proud" (32). Similarly, the clash between past impressions and present beliefs, as the governess mixes Romanticism and realism in the "castle of romance" and "big ugly antique but convenient house" antithesis (32–33), can be summed up in two different sentences, only one providing the correct assessment of feelings.

To help students acquire a deeper understanding of the story and hone their reading comprehension skills, I devise questions that focus on detail and style and call for commentary in context. In chapter 9, which has no dialogue to facilitate understanding, I ask students to provide brief explanations of "brush of the sponge" (64) and "unnatural composure" (65), to comment on the choice of the words "sharper" and "queerness" at the end of the first paragraph and "protectress" in the second (64, 65), to give a synonym for "deliberation" (67), and to explain the difference in nuance between the two uses of the word "grossness" at the end of the third paragraph (66). I also ask them to find details of physical setting that accentuate the suspense of this haunting. All these tasks are designed to make the text less daunting and help students grasp the double meanings inherent in its intricate prose.

In an international classroom, a Jamesian text may also serve to improve students' understanding and use of vocabulary. In the teaching of *The Turn of the Screw*, whose theme is conveyed through recurrent images and words of related connotation, a semantic approach may be particularly conducive to literary analysis. This approach has been proposed by H. G. Widdowson as a way to transform a literary text into "a link between literature and language teaching," a link that is inevitably made in any classroom of nonnative English speakers. Widdowson proposes that the learner write down as many details pertaining to certain words as possible and then try grouping the words according to their semantic similarities (104). Such grouping reveals a convergence of meaning among the definitions of some of these words, a convergence that points to a theme (107).

In my teaching I give my students at least two groups of words for such stylistic analysis. In the first I include "watch," "form," "helm," "enclosed," "save," "screen," "stifled," "tower," "gaoler," "shut in," and "governess," all of which I first present out of context, asking students to provide explanations and contexts in which the words could appear. After establishing a common preoccupation with control, imposition, lack of freedom, and physical confinement, we examine the function of the words in the text to see how these meanings apply to the story and affect theme. Students may initially take the prison images to suggest Quint's restricting presence, but they end up acknowledging that the similar diction the governess employs to describe her job hints at her own obsession with control. The claustrophobic atmosphere of the last chapter, where Miles suffocates both figuratively and literally from the mental and physical pressure the governess inflicts on him, emphasizes the catastrophic impact she has had on the children with her passionate resolve to "form," "screen," "enclose," and "save" them. At this point, some students, puzzled by my inclusion of the word "governess" on the list, ask me why we never learn her name. One plausible answer consistent with the literary analysis we have followed is that her namelessness serves to emphasize her occupation, and the etymology of *governess* suggests her obsession with authority and discipline.

A second word group I sometimes use aims at identifying more figurative patterns. It includes words that describe the physical setting, the weather, and the seasons, all of which are used by James to create an atmosphere of death and suspense. Alternatively, I ask students to gather all the words and phrases with religious connotation and analyze Bly as the Garden of Eden. Finally, the element of surprise, an essential component of any mystery tale, is achieved through the use of vocabulary that deviates from the expected. The governess often startles the reader not with the events that she narrates but with her choice of words. Like Mrs. Grose, students are shocked by her use of "contaminate" and "corrupt" to describe Miles's alleged misdeeds at school (35). Other puzzling phrases that students are asked to explain are "expiatory victim" (51), the possessives in "They're his and they're hers" (76), "infernal imagination" (78), "unnamed and untouched" (78), and "executioner" (119). In my teaching I try not to impose either the apparitionist or the hallucinationist approach to the novella. Many students are content to read it as a gripping, straightforward supernatural tale. Most, however, adopt the hallucinationist approach, since the psychological suspense that it offers is more appealing to their age group. Moreover, they find this approach more challenging, as it defies their initial expectations.

Once the close reading is over, I assign a writing task that demands analysis and argumentation. I usually ask students to consider the governess's doubt about herself in chapter 24:

> I seemed to float not into clearness, but into a darker obscure, and within a minute there had come to me out of my very pity the appalling alarm of his being perhaps innocent. It was for the instant confounding and bottomless, for if he *were* innocent what then on earth was I? (119)

Arguing whether that doubt is well founded or not, they must reach a conclusion about her culpability in Miles's death. The students have to read between the lines to uncover aspects of character that lead her to make the wrong assumptions about the children. What they must determine, therefore, is whether the narrative proves or disproves that the children see the ghosts.

The Turn of the Screw offers plenty of opportunities to practice strategies of argumentation. In their preliminary outline students have to note down at least three flaws in the governess's character and behavior that can be used as evidence against her. These flaws are later incorporated in carefully constructed topic sentences, all supporting the thesis statement of the student essay. The first character feature that makes the governess susceptible to apparitions is her overactive imagination, a result of the Romanticism with which she initially invests Bly and of the love she secretly harbors for the uncle in Harley Street. Her imagination makes her suspect Flora's confidence and openness and Mrs. Grose's gladness on meeting her. This susceptibility to flights of fancy causes her to dream of chance encounters in the grounds of Bly and even hear the cries of a child on her first night there. Students usually argue that since she likens her situation to fictional representations she recalls from her readings ("Was there a 'secret' at Bly—a mystery of Udolpho or an insane, an unmentionable relative kept in unsuspected confinement?" [41]), it is plausible that the ghosts are equally figments of her imagination. Her hasty inferences about the children's association with the world of the dead can also be attributed to an overactive imagination that craves to supply the romance and mystery that are missing from the setting and her occupation.

Another character feature of the governess that students point to in support of the hallucinationist interpretation is inflated vanity. Evidence of her self-esteem, which rises from the moment she is assigned "supreme authority," can be located easily (27). Students are invited to look at her fluttered reaction to the grand welcome she receives on her arrival and trace her numerous utterances of self-admiration, noting that they are always followed by a yearning for public recognition:

> I dare say I fancied myself in short a remarkable young woman and took comfort in the faith that this would more publicly appear. (39)

> [B]ut I was in these days literally able to find a joy in the extraordinary flight of heroism the occasion demanded of me. I now saw that I had been asked for a service admirable and difficult; and there would be a greatness in letting it be seen—oh in the right quarter!—that I could succeed where many another girl might have failed. (53)

> Then, with all the marks of a deliberation that must have seemed magnificent had there been any one to admire it, I laid down my book. (67)

While her actions indeed seem brave and self-sacrificing (some students praise her in their essays), they also tend to be self-imposed and exaggerated. As the ship image indicates, from her arrival she imagines her situation as perilous: "I had the fancy of our being almost as lost as a handful of passengers in a great drifting ship. Well, I was strangely at the helm!" (33). The word "lost" used here to describe not only herself but, peculiarly, Flora and Mrs. Grose as well, suggests that the governess considers them already in the midst of trouble and that unconsciously she assigns to them the corruption that she will describe in similar words later: "I don't save or shield [the children]! It's far worse than I dreamed. They're lost!" (59). By imagining her role as hazardous, she becomes the heroine she would like the children's uncle to think of her as. The appearance of the ghosts elevates what would otherwise be a routine and unnoteworthy occupation. To complete their argumentation against the governess, my students customarily concentrate on the overprotectiveness detected in her behavior and language, which they have been encouraged to study in the tasks described above. Students must structure their composition on these and other arguments, building topic sentences and finding textual justification in the form of examples and quotations.

One component that cannot be omitted from such a composition is the part where the students have to address the opposition. To make a strong case against the governess, they need to invalidate the opposing arguments used by the apparitionists. The strongest objections to the hallucinationist theory have always concentrated on Mrs. Grose's recognition of Quint from the governess's description, the supposedly demonic behavior of the children, and Flora's vulgarity in chapter 21. The second two issues can be addressed easily, and usually students find plausible explanations themselves, once they have finished reading. The children, having suffered the prisonlike overprotectiveness of their care provider, lash out, resorting to unruly behavior and playing tricks on the governess. Miles expresses his anxiety and suffocation near the end, when he craves to walk in the grounds, far from the oppressive enclosure imposed by the governess. As for Flora, her close association with her brother, who, as we learn at the end "said things" (118), could very well have resulted in her appropriation of the coarse language she uses to denounce the governess to Mrs. Grose.

Mrs. Grose's identification of Quint is not so easily bypassed or justified. A reading of Harold C. Goddard's step-by-step analysis of this point sheds light on this complex issue and also provides students with a useful example of argumentation, which they study and gradually learn to imitate. Goddard's belief that the governess's words, "He's a horror" (47), predispose Mrs. Grose to think of an intruder from the world of the dead is still one of the best explanations for this puzzle. Moreover, Stanley Renner's article from Peter G. Beidler's Bedford second edition, based on the governess's utterance, "he's like nobody" (48), documents the "physiognomical stereotypicality of the fearful male figure" (276) that matches the description of Quint and provides students with an interpretation that is historically grounded. Combining these two readings, one can argue that Mrs. Grose, rather than visualizing Quint from the governess's words, matches evil with evil in an abstract way. Finally, as many critics have noticed, the pronoun "you" in Miles's final words, "Peter Quint—you devil!" (120), is more likely to find a referent in the governess, who, as the narrative itself acknowledges, is the only person he can actually see.

The Turn of the Screw, with its many layers of meaning and the multitude of interpretations it invites, allows teachers to provide stimuli without stifling initiative. It shows learners the value of reading and interpreting for themselves. As a result, their imaginative response is so varied that their essays are often original and fun to read. Once students recognize the limits of subjectivity and the significance of recurrent images and words, they can work out for themselves an interpretation to support in a carefully planned and argued composition. All students benefit from this exercise in establishing, expressing, and proving a thesis. But international students gain a further advantage, as, through this dense and challenging text, they learn how to make associations on a semantic level in order to achieve not only a literary but also a linguistic appreciation of James's novella.

Driving Miss Daisy: Peter Bogdanovich's *Daisy Miller*

Mark A. Eaton

Peter Bogdanovich's film *Daisy Miller* (1974) provides an interesting pedagogical test case for teaching students how to go beyond simplistic approaches to film adaptations as more or less faithful versions of literary texts. Although students tend to perceive film adaptations as shortcuts to understanding the story—visual Cliffs Notes, if you will—*Daisy Miller* can be put to better use as a means of inculcating habits of cultural criticism that help place both literary works and movies in their relevant historical contexts.

Cultural critics have long recognized that historical representations are sometimes "more about the moments of their production than about the period they purportedly represent" (Kodat 79). Vivian Sobchack attests, "we have become increasingly aware of the highly invested and hardly objective nature of representation of *any* kind—and of historical representation in particular" (301–02). Films about the past, no less than literary or other texts, can be seen as palimpsests of sociohistorical meanings. Film noirs, for instance, are often said to embody anxieties about changing gender roles in the postwar era, and many historical epics such as *Spartacus* (1960) demonstrably reflect cold-war politics. A neo-noir like *Chinatown* (1974) expressed a growing distrust of authorities engendered by Watergate; twenty years later, *Forrest Gump* (1994) struck a chord with viewers who during the Clinton era were ready to reject such 1960s-style cynicism and disillusionment. Even a seemingly straightforward war film like *Saving Private Ryan* (1998), Catherine Gunther Kodat cogently argues, "simultaneously expresses and seeks to contain the sharp political and economic anxieties peculiar to its moment of production" (78–79).

Film adaptations similarly reflect their historical moment. As much as they faithfully (or not) reproduce the literary work in question, they also comment, however obliquely, on the world inhabited by the filmmakers. This reflection is easy to see in adaptations like *Clueless* (1995), *William Shakespeare's Romeo and Juliet* (1996), or *Ten Things I Hate about You* (1999), where the changed historical setting foregrounds issues and problems raised by the original literary work but recontextualizes them. Even film adaptations that remain faithful to the period represented in a literary text bear traces of the historical moment in which they are produced. Cultural studies scholars have taught us to be self-conscious about the many layers of historical specificity embedded in literary and filmic representations.

Daisy Miller is a provocative film to show in American literature surveys or specialized American literature courses because it draws viewers into the distant world of James's late-nineteenth-century European milieu and at the same time evokes changing attitudes about gender and sexuality during the 1970s, when the film was made. Bogdanovich was clearly looking at the rarefied Europe of James's novella through his own sexual-revolution-tinted glasses. The director cast his girlfriend, Cybill Shepherd, in the starring role as Daisy Miller, going so far as to claim, in a moment of typical Bogdanovich bravado, that "Henry James had Cybill in mind when he wrote it. I thought, if James had gone to all the trouble to write this story for Cybill, the least I could do was to film it" (qtd. in McCormack 34). Bogdanovich sees James's 1870s setting, somewhat anachronistically, as fertile ground for analyzing the changing ideologies of gender and sexuality in the 1970s. Today's undergraduates will bring their own ideas about courtship, gender, and sexuality to their viewing of this film, thus putting a third time period—ours—into play as one among several historical contexts to be considered.

To guide students in this kind of sophisticated cultural analysis, we might ask them to consider, first, whether Bogdanovich's *Daisy Miller* is as much about 1974 as it is about 1878, and second, to what extent the textual world of this novella and the filmic world of this film each differ from the world of its creator. Susan M. Griffin suggests such an approach to *Daisy Miller* when she writes that James and Bogdanovich in effect created two American girls, each reflecting her respective time period. By "creating icons of the American girl," Griffin points out,

> James and Bogdanovich . . . stage political, gendered dramas of American identity. These two Daisy Millers, in turn, had widely differing effects on their creators' professional careers. Encountering novella and film in the 1990s, . . . students provide a third critical audience, reading the cultural meanings of the American artist and his girl.
>
> ("Introduction: Making Movies" 3–4)

In what follows, I pursue a reading of James's and Bogdanovich's *Daisy Millers* that attempts to tease out the cultural meanings of American girlhood in two different time periods—the 1870s and the 1970s. The purpose of such a contextualized reading is to go beyond the tired question most often put to film adaptations, namely, that of fidelity to the original; instead, the reading should model a kind of cultural analysis that pays sufficient attention to the historical contexts of an exemplary literary work and its film adaptation. My approach to the two Daisy Millers is obviously indebted to current trends in new historicism and cultural studies, which have taught us to juxtapose literary texts to related cultural forms. This multilayered approach should encourage students to think critically about the cultural meanings of female adolescence at the start of the twenty-first century. I trust that it will likewise provoke them to examine American mass culture's near-total fixation on young, sexualized women, for today, as Nancy Bentley rightly suggests, "watching lovely women has become a mainstay of mass entertainment . . . a central preoccupation of the celluloid world" (127).

The American girl was James's specialty, as well as something of a national obsession in the late nineteenth century. When *Daisy Miller* was first published in *Cornhill* magazine in 1878 and then in book form by Macmillan in 1879, it was by far James's most popular work to date, and it established his reputation as an expert on the subject of American girlhood. Indeed, as Martha Banta points out, James was "largely responsible for creating the literary type of the American Girl" and Daisy Miller was "the prototype of the American Girl Abroad" (*Imaging* 289). Yet Miss Daisy was also an enigma—both in the story and to her readers. "[F]or a society that preferred to rely on clear identifications of type," says Banta, "Daisy was a problem . . . because types are supposed to be clear in their assigned meaning, and she was not" (49). The problem with Daisy Miller, then, was that she simply didn't fit the ideal type of American girl. She can almost be seen as an antitype, defying convention at every turn. Most college students have not yet heard of, much less read, *Daisy Miller*, so it's worth rehearsing the reception history of the text, particularly the fact that the name Daisy Miller became for a time after the novella's publication virtually synonymous with the American girl, instigating a vociferous public debate as to her problematic status. If students wonder what all the fuss was about, it may be because they are puzzled by the notion that a character in literature, of all things, could attract so much attention.

The anxieties Daisy Miller provoked in her day are best elucidated through a careful examination of James's text. Working inductively from textual details to the larger historical debate about the American girl abroad, I start by having students conduct a minidebate of their own about the meanings of Daisy Miller. This debate leads to a viewing of the film adaptation, which provokes further analysis of the dynamic meanings of adolescence, gender, and sexuality in the 1970s. Today's students are typically fascinated with the late 1960s and early 1970s, a fascination fed by their steady diet of popular music from the time as well as by the periodic revival of 1970s fashions. Not incidentally, that decade was also likely the time when their parents were adolescents. The film *Daisy Miller* lends itself to showing extended clips (any number of scenes will do) if time does not permit a full screening. I also strongly encourage students to rent and watch, outside class, Bogdanovich's earlier film *The Last Picture Show* (1971), which not only provides a subtext of the director's dangerous liaison with Cybill Shepherd but also gives them greater insight into the imminent sexual revolution: that film, set in the 1950s, indexes an increased laxity in sexual mores in small-town America. The current obsession with the 1960s surely has much to do with that decade's purported sexual promiscuity, as the *Austin Powers* films not so subtly suggest. Using Bogdanovich's *Daisy Miller* as a pretext for discussing changing standards of sexual behavior is less circuitous than it might seem. Ultimately, I urge students to reflect on their own attitudes about female identity, gender roles, and sexuality—gauging through their encounter with both James and Bogdanovich whether our society's gender ideologies are similar to or different from those of the 1870s and the 1970s, respectively.

James's *Daisy Miller* frames the question of female socialization in decidedly nationalist terms. "American girls are the best girls," declares Frederick Winterbourne at the outset, when young Randolph Miller announces the arrival of his older sister, Daisy, by exclaiming, "Here comes my sister! . . . She's an American girl" (50). Winterbourne has lived in Europe for many years and realizes immediately, on meeting Daisy, that "he had become dishabituated to the American tone. Never, indeed, . . . had he encountered a young American girl of so pronounced a type as this" (57). Like James, he fancies himself something of an expert on the subject: "He had a great relish for feminine beauty; he was addicted to observing and analyzing it" (53). Yet while Winterbourne might well prefer to remain a detached observer, Daisy discombobulates him with her frank familiarity: "She talked to Winterbourne as if she had known him a long time" (56). With her "perfectly direct and unshrinking" glance, her "wonderfully pretty eyes," and "her bright, sweet, superficial little visage," she strikes him as a "pretty American flirt" (53, 57). The last adjective is redundant, though, for as Winterbourne later points out, "Flirting is a purely American custom; it doesn't exist here" (99). Daisy exports this purely American custom to Europe.

Throughout the story, James is much concerned with the discrepancy between American and European manners, in particular with how much Daisy's manners, if she can be said to have any, diverge from those in Europe, for it is clear from the start that her behavior doesn't conform to the custom of the country. With "her habitual sense of freedom," Daisy basically does whatever she wants, no matter how outré by society's standards (75). Winterbourne is alarmed by "a certain laxity of deportment" (57) in Daisy and tells her so. When you "deal with the natives," he instructs her, "you must go by the custom of the place" (99). Nearly everyone in the novella disapproves of her behavior, yet she appears to be oblivious or is at least brazenly unapologetic: "this was simply her habit, her manner" (53). Daisy becomes ever more defiant as the plot progresses inexorably toward its tragic, if implausible, conclusion: "I don't see why I should change my habits for *them*" (99). Her mother, meanwhile, appears to be completely indifferent to the situation, allowing Daisy free rein to flirt with every man she meets. This neglect is obviously, from the author's point of view, a serious derogation of Mrs. Miller's maternal obligation to train her daughter in the ways of the world. Leaving Daisy to her own devices, Mrs. Miller allows her to exercise a degree of self-determination that was unknown to earlier generations, making Daisy a harbinger of changes to come.

Students who came of age in the 1990s or later may well relate to this lack of parental supervision if not to the strict societal expectations and the supercilious upper-class European setting. Yet they probably will not fully appreciate, without some guidance in unpacking the story's historical context, the scandal of maternal negligence that so worried James's contemporaries. I begin by pointing out that the European grand tour was, in James's time, de rigueur for upper-class Americans. "European travel," Richard Broadhead observes, "became one of the chief ways of displaying upper-class prerogatives of wealth and leisure after 1860" (97). For young American girls especially, it was a means of acquiring the symbolic capital of European high culture. As Lynn Wardley points out, "Daisy's European tour is the *rite de passage* of an aspiring young woman of her class. This rite of conspicuous acculturation loses none of its significance as a passage into adult sexuality" (238). After establishing that European travel was a necessary if risky proposition for young women of James's time, I historicize the novella further by distributing a bunch of quotations drawn from etiquette manuals, thus giving students an example of how to draw new-historicist parallels between literature and other discourses of the period. "The one essential thing for every American girl . . . who travels abroad to remember," according to the writer of a conduct manual titled *The Book of Good Manners* (1923), "is that men in Europe, generally speaking, have a different attitude toward women than that of men in America. They inevitably associate the freedom from accepted European conventions which marks the independence of the American woman as license." The problem with European travel, then, was how to acquire culture in a chaste way, lest acculturation involve a loss of sexual innocence. The writer continues:

> Especially where the young girl is concerned, their more exactly observed etiquette in all matters relating to chaperonage, moving about unattended in public, etc., is apt to lead them to erroneous conclusion. Therefore, lest her character be misunderstood, the American woman traveling in Europe . . . cannot be too circumspect in her conduct.
>
> (qtd. in Montgomery 108–09)

With the prevalence of carriages in many European cities, mothers were hard pressed to keep track of their young charges. "Every careful mother," advised the writer of one etiquette book published in 1913, "will know when, where and with whom her young daughter motors. She will see to it that all her motoring is done in accordance with established laws of chaperonage and good breeding" (qtd. in Montgomery 115). While these manuals postdate *Daisy Miller* by several decades, the quotations give students a glimpse of the social context in which Daisy's behavior could have caused such a scandal.

Taking a cue from the title of a popular play and movie from several years ago, I go on to trace a central thematic thread in James's novella that I like to call "driving Miss Daisy." Bogdanovich's film adaptation accentuates that theme in a series of carriage rides that together mark the major transitions in Daisy's romantic career. I outline here a few passages in the text that belong to this thread, commenting along the way on how the scenes are handled in the film. When Daisy proposes making a "very pretty excursion" to the Château de Chillon, she offers the services of her family's courier Eugenio to drive them "right up to the castle" (58). Winterbourne is astounded that Daisy's mother does not intend to chaperone: "[he] observed to himself that this was a very different type of maternity from that of the vigilant matrons" he was used to in Europe, where "a young man was not at liberty to speak to a young unmarried lady except under certain rarely-occurring conditions" (71, 51). Announcing that "she had a passion for steamboats" (74), Daisy persuades Winterbourne to accompany her, alone, across the lake to the castle. The film captures Daisy's flirtatiousness on the steamer as it ferries them across the lake to the castle. Winterbourne remarks, "I was never so pleased in my life," and Daisy replies, with a flutter of her eyelashes, "I like to make you say such things." After they visit the castle, however, he blows their first date by announcing, apparently for lack of anything better to say, that he will be returning to Geneva the next day. Daisy practically gives him up right on the spot: "I have half a mind to leave you here and go straight back to the hotel alone" (77). But she doesn't go alone; he accompanies her in the car, and their drive is conspicuous for her sulking all the way back to the hotel: "Winterbourne took a carriage, and they drove back to Vevey in the dusk; the young girl was very quiet" (78). This drive proves to be their last together, and Bogdanovich highlights the importance of that fact by fading to black before opening up on the next scene in Italy.

Now in Rome, we discover that Daisy is "quite carried away" with an Italian named Giovanelli, a "low-lived foreigner" of obscure origins (83, 90). Since Giovanelli looks perfectly respectable and well dressed in the film, students need to be reminded of the overly fine, invidious distinctions often made in James's fiction. An ambivalent arbiter of such distinctions, Winterbourne tries unsuccessfully to convince Daisy that her very reputation is at stake, urging her to come away from the young Italian in the streets of Rome and take a ride in Mrs. Walker's carriage: "He looked at her exquisite prettiness; and then he said, very gently, 'I think you should get into the carriage' " (93). This time Daisy refuses him, saying in the film, "I've never allowed any gentleman to dictate anything I do." Here Bogdanovich deliberately invites comparison between Daisy Miller and the so-called third-wave feminists of his time, or women's libbers in the parlance of the early 1970s. Despite the lavish costumes and sumptuous settings of this gorgeously shot period film (the cinematographer was Alberto Spagnoli), Daisy Miller sounds at certain moments like the protofeminist that she is, and the film offers an implicit commentary on what she might have to say to Bogdanovich's 1960s generation.

A final carriage ride clinches the rather contemporary self-determination Daisy enjoys, in the novella and in the film. When Winterbourne spots her coming out of Saint Peter's, she climbs "into an open cab with her accomplice and roll[s] away through the cynical streets of Rome" (104–05). Then, at the Colosseum, he notices "an open carriage—one of the little Roman street-cabs," waiting, apparently, for Daisy and her male companion (110). Bogdanovich stations the horse-drawn cab front and center at the Colosseum, using a wide-angle lens to highlight the immensity of the Roman ruins. In the film's climactic scene, Winterbourne confronts Daisy with the rashness of her behavior: "think simply of the craziness, from a sanitary point of view, of a delicate young girl lounging away the evening in this nest of malaria" (111). He refers, of course, to Roman fever, an obscure illness that isn't, as he puts it, "very pretty" (112). In the film, he gives it a name, malaria, and Bogdanovich includes mosquitoes buzzing in the background, though in James's time it was not known how the disease was passed. Sitting next to her beau in the cab, Daisy replies indignantly, "I don't care . . . whether I have Roman fever or not!" (113), and as the driver pulls away, Shepherd continues to gaze seductively at the camera, in an exquisite point-of-view shot from Winterbourne's perspective. Her fateful comment lingers as she is driven away, and the next day we learn that "the little American flirt was alarmingly ill . . . dangerously ill" (113–14). So ill, in fact, that she dies two days later, and Winterbourne is told that "it had been a terrible case of the fever" (114–15).

However incredulous students are nowadays about the deadly effects of Roman fever, the ending makes more sense when read as a cautionary tale of sorts. Yet the powerful erotic charge of Shepherd's gaze in this shot and throughout the film clearly undercuts James's attempt to circumscribe the dangerous energies and implications of Daisy's sexuality. Bogdanovich has nicely captured, in a series of close-ups on Shepherd's face, the way Daisy appropriates the male gaze: "she avoided neither his eyes nor those of anyone else; she blushed neither when she looked at him nor when she saw that people were looking at her" (75). Embodying the erotic potential of a young American woman, Shepherd seems to grow into the role as the film progresses. Initially she delivers her lines in a hurried, frenetic fashion, which may approximate the speech patterns James was trying to capture in the novella; after all, Winterbourne describes Daisy's voice as having an "odd mixture of audacity and puerility" (101). Shepherd's voice in the film nonetheless seems forced and stilted at first, and it comes across to my students at least as hopelessly comic. Encourage them to stick with it. Shepherd's performance, not to mention the film itself, grows on the viewer. Toward the end, thanks in part to the series of close-ups I have just discussed, Shepherd has matured in such a way that her newfound confidence intimates sexual experience as well. Her steady, unflinching gaze at the camera in a number of scenes precedes by almost twenty years Jane Campion's much-remarked-on use of the direct, returned gaze in her film *The Portrait of a Lady* (1993). Campion's ambitious if flawed adaptation foregrounds the same questions about historical anachronism and female sexuality that I ask in my interrogation of *Daisy Miller*.

Not James's late-nineteenth-century Europe but Bogdanovich's 1970s Hollywood was the reference point for many contemporary reviewers of the film, as Peggy McCormack has persuasively argued. Critics almost uniformly attacked Bogdanovich for casting his twenty-four-year-old girlfriend in the role of Daisy Miller. The director, who was thirty-five when the film was made, had met Shepherd three years earlier on the set of his second movie, *The Last Picture Show*. Married to his set decorator at the time, he fell in love with Shepherd and carried on a very public affair with her while making the film (Biskind 127–28). His marriage, predictably, ended in divorce. Shepherd appeared as a coldhearted sexual manipulator in that film, and some reviewers had difficulty separating the role from her glamorous life. Over the next few years, the famous couple appeared regularly on the *Tonight Show* with Johnny Carson and, in May 1974, on the cover of *People Magazine* with the headline "Peter and Cybill: Who Needs Marriage?" Two months later, *Daisy Miller* was released to decidedly mixed reviews (see Canby for a positive review, Cocks for a negative one). McCormack concludes that

> when Bodganovich cast Shepherd as Daisy Miller, audiences reacted not to the actual quality of her performance as James's ingenious, young American girl, but rather to the perception created by the couple's own public performance as reckless, star-crossed lovers. (35)

I am less interested in how contemporary reactions to *Daisy Miller* were colored by the real-life love affair between a maverick film director and his leading lady—that is an old story in Hollywood, after all—than in how the film invokes the changing sexual politics of the late 1960s and early 1970s. When teaching *Daisy Miller* to undergraduates who grew up in the 1990s and after, the question that inevitably comes up about Daisy Miller is, Did she or didn't she? "Which is 'the fast girl' and which is 'the free American?' " writes Banta. "This is, of course, 'the Daisy Miller question' " (*Imaging* 49). Flirty and vivacious as she is, however, Daisy definitely doesn't in James's text. In this, at least, she does conform to the social expectation that, while she may be "wonderfully pretty" or even "alluring," the American girl "possess[ed] no strong sexual appetites" and left no doubt "on the score of her chasteness" (48). Writing in 1976, the literary critic Cathy Davidson referred to Daisy Miller as "the patron saint of a repressed sexuality" (qtd. in Weisbuch 80). Still, the question, Did she or didn't she?, is interesting in light of Bogdanovich's extramarital affair with his blonde leading lady, and I believe Bogdanovich means to suggest that Daisy *has* had intimate relations with Giovanelli in the film, thus reminding viewers how much the culture's sexual mores have changed during the era of free love.

The sexual revolution is, in fact, the explicit subject of *The Last Picture Show*, an illuminating intertext when juxtaposed with James's *Daisy Miller*, on one hand, and Bogdanovich's *Daisy Miller*, on the other. *The Last Picture Show* represents precisely the moment in the 1950s when sexual practices were decisively altered by the pill. Tad Friend has noted that Bogdanovich's films from the early 1970s, like *The Last Picture Show*, "transported audiences to a time before drugs, race riots, and polyester pants—a time when you drove your jalopy with high hopes to the spring dance" (36–37). Bogdanovich's remarkable film portrays how two modern technologies—moving pictures and automobiles—accelerated changes in sexual codes that were already well under way by the early 1950s (the film's setting) and more or less codified by the early 1970s (the film's production). Sexuality is thoroughly enmeshed in the class structure of this mid-1950s Texas cow town, much as it was in James's late-nineteenth-century Europe. The cross-generational affairs, the fast teenage girls: these features of the mid-twentieth-century milieu may seem at first glance vastly different from the world of James's fiction, but they are actually quite reminiscent of the class and gender politics of that earlier time. Clearly both times are undergoing a process of transition with regard to gender identities and sexuality. Interestingly, Bogdanovich cast Eileen Brennan, who had played the adulterous, childless wife of the football coach in *The Last Picture Show*, as Daisy's feckless mother in *Daisy Miller*, a casting decision that brings home the complicated sexual tensions in both films.

A multilayered approach to Bogdanovich's *Daisy Miller* demands that students bracket off the traditional question of greater or lesser fidelity to the original text and ask instead nuanced questions about the complex, almost symbiotic relation between film and literature. The more remote in time the setting of the text being adapted, the more audiences will perceive differences as well as similarities between their world and that of the film. Filmmakers can either accentuate those differences or emphasize the continuities between past and present; whatever approach they take, audiences will always respond to the filmic world from the perspective of their own experiences.

Students typically respond best to those movies—and books, for that matter—that somehow speak to them on their own level. My approach gives students a greater appreciation of how customs and manners change over time yet, for all the change, remain strikingly similar. Teaching Bogdanovich's *Daisy Miller* allows students to rethink their favored dating and courtship rituals, which they tend to think of as entirely appropriate and natural, by considering how such rituals can and do change over time. This exercise in cultural criticism gives students a sense of the mutability of social customs and practices surrounding sex, reminding them that teen sexuality especially has long been a locus of cultural anxiety in America.

"A Matter of Appreciation, Speculation, Imagination": Interpreting *The Turn of the Screw* and Film Adaptations

Monika Brown

Few works of literature have generated more critical controversy or inspired more films and television dramas (thirteen to date) than Henry James's enigmatic tale *The Turn of the Screw*. At the remote Bly estate, something disquieting is going on, but what is its nature? On the surface the memoir of a governess who discovers and combats a supernatural threat to two innocent children, James's tale is equally plausible as a case study of the narrator's psychological breakdown, as an exploration of Victorian class and gender tensions, or even as an unresolvable critical conundrum. The novella seems designed to invite opposing and multiple interpretations as well as multiple adaptations, as James himself suggests in his preface to the 1908 New York edition of *The Turn of the Screw*:

> There is for such a case no eligible *absolute* of the wrong; it remains relative to fifty other elements, a matter of appreciation, speculation, imagination . . . in the light of the spectator's, the critic's, the reader's experience. (Beidler [2nd ed.] 185)

The Turn of the Screw is ideal for college study: James's compact tale invites students to develop skills of literary interpretation and argument; to explore modern critical perspectives; and to appreciate the art of film adaptation, itself a type of criticism, and the potential of a film to illuminate its literary original. I teach *The Turn of the Screw* and some of its film adaptations in two advanced literature seminars—Modern Fiction, Literature in Music and Film—and will adapt my approach for a general education course entitled Literature and Film. Drawing on my course experiences and the Bedford series Case Studies in Contemporary Criticism edition of the novella, I present here a two-week sequence of instructional activities suited to a variety of literature courses, whether they emphasize formalist analysis or application of critical theories, whether they call for only a few film scenes or close study of adaptations.

Interpretations of James's Tale: What Happens at Bly and Why?

When assigning *The Turn of the Screw*, I suggest that students focus on the main characters, the framing and point of view, and the ending. I also ask them to write brief answers to two questions: What happens at Bly? Why does it happen, or who is responsible? At the start of a class devoted to the novella, a few volunteers read their answers, then other students share similar interpretations or contribute new positions. Typically, a few class members accept the ghost story at face value. By their accounts, echoing words used by the narrator, the "kind" or "heroic" governess discovers that two "angelic" children have been "contaminated" by "evil spirits," and she struggles to save them. Thus it is the ghosts, or Quint alone, who bear responsibility for the children's strange behavior and Miles's death. Most students, familiar with unreliable narrators, read the tale as a study of psychological delusion. They blame the governess for the escalating tension and for Miles's death, citing her inflated self-image as romance heroine and savior ("She's full of herself"), or her "hysteria" and overactive imagination, or her repressed sexuality or class snobbery. A few decide, as one student put it, "We have to have two views."

Small groups of students with similar views now meet to clarify their interpretations and select supporting scenes and passages. The governess is heroic, the children innocent victims, and the ghosts real and evil, because the frame narrator's friend Douglas admires the woman who later became his sister's tutor, and because Flora seems to be angelic, Miles behaves well but was expelled from school, each child at times acts possessed, and Mrs. Grose identifies the man described to her as Peter Quint. The governess must be or become delusional, because she "jumps to conclusions" and attributes "negative" and "evil" motives to the children and because no one else, not even Mrs. Grose by the lake, admits to seeing an apparition. The reason for her hysteria may be sexual and class anxiety, since she longs for her employer's approval, is "too proud" to ask for help, and is shocked by Miles's school expulsion and by the liaison between a respectable governess and a seductive valet. After each group presents its interpretation, the class applies this perspective to explain the death of Miles, sometimes with critical quotations from Peter G. Beidler's "A Critical History of *The Turn of the Screw*" ([2nd ed.] 205-10). To wrap up this stage of interpretation, we browse subheads in the "Critical History" and recognize our positions: the "psychological case study," the "reactions against the psychoanalytic reading" that allow for a supernatural evil, "having it both ways," or "Marxist and gender-based readings."

A follow-up writing assignment allows students to extend their interpretations while practicing and demonstrating critical skills they will need for their seminar papers: reading, summarizing, and quoting from criticism. Students select a critical approach related to their interpretation of the novella, read the critical perspective introduction and article from the Bedford (or Norton) second edition of *The Turn of the Screw*, and write a 750-word report on a critical article. Part 1 of the report is a partial summary of the article: students select and explain, incorporating a few short quotes, three or four central insights from the essay. Part 2 is a concise summary or paraphrase (with short quotes and a block quotation) of a key section of the article, often its analysis of the death of Miles. Part 3 is a brief critique that evaluates features of the article: interpretive insights, application of critical approach(es), or use of evidence from the novella or from other critics.

From the Beidler edition, students interested in the psychology of the governess may report on Stanley Renner's psychoanalytic examination of her "sexual hysteria" and effort to block the children's "normal sexual development" (286), on Sheila Teahan's Lacanian perspective on the young woman's "mirror stage" of divided identity ("I Caught Him" 351), or on Priscilla L. Walton's more sympathetic feminist description of her struggle to find a female role outside those prescribed by Victorian patriarchy ("He Took"). For a psychological reading that accounts for the governess's social insecurities, students turn to Bruce Robbins's Marxist analysis of how the governess responds to class and gender relations at Bly or Teahan's explanation of the ambiguous social status of the Victorian governess. Students who read *The Turn of the Screw* as a gothic tale with ghosts and conflicts of good and evil, a genre suited to formalist and myth criticism, may go to my reserve collection and consult a classic Robert B. Heilman article: either his refutation of psychoanalytic interpretations ("Freudian Reading") or "*The Turn of the Screw* as Poem," which compares conditions at Bly to Eden and the Fall. In class, after brief group consultations, the articles are presented orally: students read aloud or talk about the most effective sections of their reports on critical articles. These critical articles, even when they meet with skepticism, affirm the variety of interpretations this text can support.

Class interpretation of the tale also includes formal analysis, a prerequisite for film study. Students identify features of James's novella that create its central ambiguity (Are the ghosts real? Where does the threat lie?) and varied readings. The double frame, with Douglas's editorial remarks, raises questions about reliability. The tale itself is unsettling because of its isolated setting, its vaguely sketched characters, and its repetitious plot, whose short chapters of alternating action and reflection involve shadowy secrets, apparent supernatural events, and class and gender conflicts. At the center of the novella's mystery, of course, are the personality and language of the novella's central character and first-person narrator. Female, youthful, naive, and imaginative, this parson's daughter creates an aura of mystery and terror by her vague descriptions of characters and settings; by her precipitate emotional reactions and moral judgments; and by her imagery and allusions from nature, the Bible, and heroic romances—areas of experience open to intrusions of the supernatural. For one student the "unsettled atmosphere" of the governess's narrative passages actually makes her "thoughts and feelings" seem by contrast "more real" and believable. Certainly the narrator's elusive language allows James to meet his objective, expressed in the 1908 preface, to create an overall impression of "portentous evil." "Only make the reader's general vision of evil intense enough," he writes. "Make him *think* the evil, make him think it for himself, and you are released from weak specifications" (Beidler [2nd ed.]

185). Can such narrator-mediated, verbally unspecified evil, the core of the novella's openness to interpretation, be sustained in the visual medium of film?

Film Adaptations and Scenes: What Happens in Films about Bly and Why?

Two principles from film-adaptation theory prepare the class for study of selected films. First, viewers must not expect a film to be entirely faithful to the literary original. "Faithful to what?" asks Donna Marie Nudd about films of *Jane Eyre*:

> Is Brontë's . . . novel a romance? a melodrama? a gothic mystery? a Christian morality tale? a feminist classic? a fictionalized autobiography? From the onset, it seems quite unreasonable to expect a film or televi sion adaptation to capture all these qualities. (523)

Such a comment may apply also to *The Turn of the Screw*. We can hardly expect a two-hour film to be as elaborate or as open to interpretations as James's tale. But we can legitimately ask whether a film preserves the novella's essential characters and incidents (from the governess's accepting her position to the death of Miles), suggests some ambiguity about the presence of evil spirits, and supports or extends particular critical interpretations of the novella (or even suggests new ones).

A second relevant principle is that an adaptation is not simply a translation from one medium to another: each film uses the medium of film for a creative reinterpretation. James's novella, with its spare plot, ambiguity of character and theme, and lack of specification, offers wide latitude for creativity to directors and actors and thus, like other mystery classics, has inspired many successful adaptations. Those who adapt fictional works, explains Brian McFarlane in *Novel to Film*, distinguish between features that can be "transferred" without much alteration into the film's visual action and dialogue and those that require modification, which McFarlane calls "adaptation," to fit time constraints as well as the discourse of film (21–22). Students recognize that characters and themes from James's tale—conflicts of good and evil, transitions from innocence to experience or sanity to madness, sexual tension and danger to children, mystery and the supernatural—can be transferred to the new medium, though interpretive choices are required about how to present them. But some literary techniques that create the novella's ambiguity must be modified (adapted) for film. James's multiple-frame stories may be reduced to one, and in place of a first-person point of view a film may suggest subjectivity by voice-over passages, point-of-view shots, and reaction shots. Students recognize that the creators of a film must transpose some of the narrator's musings into dialogue, add invented scenes in which the governess teaches her pupils, and find a visual way to present Miles's death as believable. Linguistic allusions and symbols may be expressed in visual form, while cinematography and a musical sound track may suggest subjectivity and vagueness.

Aware of these principles, students now list key scenes from *The Turn of the Screw* that they expect a film to include. These are scenes that illuminate the governess's character, the nature of the children, and the spectral appearances: the opening interview with her employer and acceptance of her position, her arrival at Bly and explorations with Flora (ch. 1), her meeting Miles (ch. 3), her sightings of Quint atop a tower and at a window (chs. 3, 4) and of Miss Jessel next to a lake and a desk (chs. 6, 15, 20), a few early dialogues with Mrs. Grose (chs. 2, 5, 7), Miles's night excursion (chs. 10–11), and of course Miles's death (ch. 24). For the arrival at Bly and the first two appearances of Quint, I show a storyboard analysis of how James presents each scene, then we talk about how a film might suggest a first-person perspective and support particular interpretations. As homework, students review other key novella scenes and reflect about how each might be presented on film to reflect their group's interpretation.

In two class sessions I introduce three to five films of *The Turn of the Screw*, showing from each a few key scenes (as two- or three-minute clips). Every film version we study includes most of the key episodes, shows ghosts on screen, and also (like each critical article) offers a coherent and to varying degrees ambiguous interpretation of why the governess sees ghosts and how their intrusions contribute to Miles's death. Each film frames the narrative in some way, and each uses resources of the film medium—especially settings, costumes, cinematography (colors, lighting), shots (e.g., a first-person feel created by closeups, reaction shots, and the constant presence of the central character), pacing and editing, and musical sound tracks with recurring motifs—to adapt literary techniques in ways that suit its interpretation(s) of James's novella.

Our film study begins with one or both of two fine adaptations that preserve the ambiguity of James's tale. Optional is a recent, very faithful, stage-play-like television film directed by Ben Bolt (UK, 1999). (I no longer use Tom McLoughlin's *The Haunting of Helen Walker*, which follows James's plot and dialogue but seems a pastiche of effects from other films). In the Bolt film, Jodhi May's serious and caring young governess has much the same experiences as James's protagonist: after sightings of two people she believes to be dead and tense dialogues with Mrs. Grose, she becomes obsessed with fear for the children and concern about what their guardian thinks of her. I show her interview with the aristocratic young master (Colin Firth), her encounter through a window with a contrasting male (Jason Salkey as a leering Quint), and one outdoor scene with both children.

Also true to James's ambiguity, and a work of art in its own right, is Jack Clayton's *The Innocents* (1961), a horror film classic that I have students view outside class (by lending videos and arranging an afternoon screening). Based on William Archibald's 1950 Broadway play, Clayton's black-and-white film lets supernatural events emerge naturally from its folktale settings but also suggests that the governess, Miss Giddens, played by a mature Deborah Kerr, is so unsettled by her responsibilities and sexual anxieties that she may see what is not present. Throughout *The Innocents*, Clayton and the cinematographer Freddie Francis create a visual experience of "dizziness, disorientation, and emptiness" (Mazzella 18) that is analogous to the governess's vague style of narration. Action shots are by turns sharp and vague, with lighted centers surrounded by darkness; interspersed are shots of dark spaces or empty spaces; and frequent dissolves blur scene transitions. Symbolic images with Freudian and mythic overtones accompany sightings of the ghosts, which seem by turns objective realities and subjective projections (Palmer 199-209; Mazzella 10–26).

When presenting *The Innocents* in class, I show first the opening sequence: a prelude that frames the governess's tale through her words, the movement of her hands at the edge of a dark screen, and a haunting original folklike ballad sung by an unseen girl, "O Willow Waly." (Paul Dehn's lyrics appear, with several inaccuracies, in Mazzella 27.) Comments follow, and clips from early scenes: the employment interview, the carriage ride to Bly, and the threshold crossing to Flora. I then show how the first Quint sighting supports both main readings of the story: in a scene rich with Freudian symbols, the governess sees the distant figure on top of a tower against "glaring sunlight . . . giving the image a hallucinatory quality" (Boyum 94). Students now recall later sightings from the film—when the governess sees Quint outside the window and Miss Jessel at the lake—and comment on how these scenes balance supernatural effects with hallucinatory elements and Freudian motifs. In each of the scenes and throughout Georges Auric's sound track, the opening ballad melody is a leitmotif, evoking both impending danger and the governess's obsessive fears.

Two television films from the mid-1970s, less faithful than Bolt's and less ambiguous than *The Innocents*, are of interest because they offer opposite answers to James's central question. Dan Curtis's television film *The Turn of the Screw* (1974) features Lynn Redgrave in an interpretation of James's novella that students after a scene or two can identify as a psychological reading. The film's visuals and spoken language maintain the point of view of its governess, Miss Cubberly, through extensive voice-overs and shots of what she alone observes. The governess attributes evil to the children that is not reflected in their behavior, though Miles and Flora do tease and frighten her and the adolescent boy behaves seductively. This film makes the ghosts into hallucinations by showing them frequently, each time preceded and followed by shots of the governess's terrified reaction. In the composer Robert Cobert's intermittent musical sound track, contrasting motifs (eerie fragmented sound effects for moments of terror and a hopeful pastoral melody for periods of calm) seem to emanate from inside the governess and increase our suspicion that, as she loses her sanity, more and more of the film's visual action also takes place in her mind (Brown 67–68). Worth showing are an early sighting of Quint and a few hallucinatory moments not from James's novella: Miss Cubberly sees Quint's expression on Miles's face as he leans over the tower parapet, her reflection in the mirror becomes Miss Jessel's image, and her dream of being kissed by Quint dissolves into Miles standing by her bed. Curtis's film, a showcase of techniques for bringing to screen psychological breakdown and efforts to reassert normality, contrasts with the subtlety of James's narrative and *The Innocents*. Curtis's film is, however, more effective than a later feature film about the governess's psychological breakdown that I do not include: Rusty Lemorande's *The Turn of the Screw*, featuring Patsy Kensit as a very young 1960s psychotic reminiscing during therapy, overwhelms viewers with surrealist horrors, camera distortions, and an insistent melody in the Simon Boswell sound track.

By contrast to Curtis's psychological study, Graeme Clifford's *The Turn of the Screw*, an episode of Showtime's Nightmare Classics, is a gothic horror film with a much altered plot, whose governess, played by Amy Irving, is a prim Victorian schoolmarm who combats real dangers to herself and the children. Clifford foregrounds, as students recognize, gender and social class issues that James and most adapters keep in the background. Here the repressed governess is everywhere beset by dangers. The decadent sensual uncle tries to seduce her at their interview and has filled a room at Bly with pornographic art. Miles, a seductive teen, rides a stallion, is on friendly terms with the aging groundskeeper, and deliberately shocks the governess with his language and behavior. And the ghosts, who appear menacingly on screen even when the governess is absent, are sexual lovers who seek revenge for injuries done to their living counterparts. In the musical sound track, J. Peter Robinson systematically integrates two motifs with the visual action: one announces gothic horrors; the other, an echo of Beethoven's "Moonlight Sonata," is connected to threatening male sexuality (Brown 68–69). With brief excerpts from early scenes, I show how explicit gothic horror, sexuality, and marked social class divisions set this film apart from other adaptations and from James's novella. When Quint appears outside a window and leers at the viewer after the governess flees, students recognize that he is real, of lower class, and sexually threatening.

A more satisfying interpretation emerges from our final adaptation, a work as significant in artistry and interpretive richness as *The Innocents*: a film of one of the great modern operas, Benjamin Britten's *The Turn of the Screw* (1954). In the opera, itself a subject of conflicting interpretations, the existence of the ghosts is not in question. Quint and Miss Jessel appear on stage; have substantial singing parts, with texts by the librettist Myfanwy Piper; and interact musically with the children, so as to suggest homosexual relations, and with the governess, in contests for the children. Left open, as in James's tale, is the question of where danger lies. Does the governess lose control and become actively evil herself (Mellers), or does she fail to perceive the nature of the danger and so become enmeshed in its power (Howard; Corse; Brown)? Is the opera the children's bildungsroman, whose ghosts offer an appealing alternative to the repressive values of the governess (Hindley), or an account of innocence—of the children and of the governess—corrupted by evil forces (Law)?

Interpretations of the opera as a study of innocence corrupted anticipate the approach taken by the Czech film director Petr Weigl, who in 1983 superimposed his purely visual film for German television over a recorded 1982 performance of Britten's opera conducted by Colin Davis at the Royal Opera House. Weigl's lush settings, beautiful actors, and elaborate visual symbolism present the opera (and James's tale) as a myth about an already fallen Eden, with seductive ghosts who interact with the children and draw the governess into their corruption. In class I show first the opening framing sequence, which crosscuts between the story's London employment interview, with the governess dressed in white, and her frantic later return to the same house, dressed all in black. A brief explanation of three musical motifs—the unsettling twelve-tone screw theme whose intensifying variations bridge scenes and create an atmosphere of evil, Quint's elaborate seduction melody, and Miles's mysterious "Malo" song—helps students appreciate this moving film, for which I next show the governess's first encounters with Quint: the tower scene, enhanced by the lovely Magdalena Vasaryova's movement through nature and the lyric soprano Helen Donath's innocent singing, is even more magical than in *The Innocents* (see Brown 72–77). I show also two scenes that characterize the innocent-corrupted children and present Quint (tenor Robert Tear) as a musical seducer.

Our film study, like our first class on the novella, concludes with depictions of Miles's death. I show two- or three-minute clips and let students recognize that every film ends with a scene well suited to its interpretation of James's novella. In the playlike Ben Bolt version, Quint is a physical presence inside the room, and the protective May holds a terrified Miles so closely that he appears to suffocate. In the Freud-overlaid folktale *The Innocents*, Miles's collapse amid bullying from the protective Kerr and terrifying Quint may result from an exorcism or from terror. In the film about descent into madness, Redgrave confronts Miles on a staircase, sees him for an instant transformed into Quint, and so pushes the boy downstairs to his death. In the gothic Irving film, the teenage Miles responds to Quint's physical attack on Flora by throwing himself and Quint from a tower. In the Britten-Weigl opera film, Miles's death—but also Quint's defeat—occurs at the moment when the corrupted governess, the soprano Donath acted by Vasaryova dressed in black, invokes for herself the power of the opera's ghostly screw theme, then sings Miles's

"Malo" in unison with Quint (Howard 101). Weigl's moving ending reminds us that his sources have religious significance: Piper's libretto, Britten's music, and even—for all the skepticism of recent critics—the text of James's *The Turn of the Screw*.

Through study of *The Turn of the Screw*, critical analyses, and several film versions, students learn that just as Henry James's text, by literary craft, supports various interpretations, so creators of a film adaptation use resources of their medium to convey their interpretations, which resemble those of particular literary critics or, as in *The Innocents* and the Britten-Weigl opera film, present a fresh perspective on the original text. Occasionally a student is inspired to write a seminar paper on the novella. One such paper made a strong case for a psychological breakdown, in both the novella and *The Innocents*, by noting that even James and the governess admit to doubts about the ghosts.

After exploring many critical and cinematic interpretations of *The Turn of the Screw*, a class may appreciate quotations from critics who affirm the value of our enterprise. Terry Heller celebrates the tale's resistance to a fixed interpretation: "*The Turn of the Screw* is special among literary works mainly because it insistently raises for all its readers questions that cannot be settled" (24). The tale thus

> educates the imagination for a moral life in a world where meanings are provisional and limited. By leading the reader into rereading, this story provides more than the usual practice in the construction of others' perspectives . . . [and] stimulates an awareness of meanings as constructs rather than givens. (139-40)

Where Heller values tolerance for ambiguity, Wayne Booth finds ethical significance in choosing one interpretation over another (e.g., identifying with a courageous heroine or passing judgment on the governess and her defenders). Booth also assures readers that the hours we spend "engaged with the imaginative richness" of James and his interpreters are hours well spent. "To wrestle with minds and hearts like that, to make . . . sense out of one rich piece of the world," may make us better readers not only of imaginary characters but of the morally ambiguous people in our own lives (253). Or we may be content to accept James's invitation and to experience his story, repeatedly, with "appreciation, speculation, imagination."

NOTE

The film analyses are adapted and abridged from my article "Film Music as Sister Art."

A Visual Approach to *The Turn of the Screw*

Sue Sorensen

Although Henry James's verbal dexterity is daunting—and no instructor should neglect to congratulate students on rising to the challenges of one of literature's most difficult writers—James did strive to infuse his writing with visual qualities. In his 1884 essay "The Art of Fiction," he refers to psychological subjects in fiction as "adorably pictorial" ([*Critical Muse*] 202) and draws many connections between painting and fiction. But he has a reputation for obscurity, both thematic and stylistic. The governess in *The Turn of the Screw* tells us that her situation is "[h]ideous and obscure" (105) and later reports herself sailing "into a darker obscure" (119). In his 1908 preface, James regretted tales of suspense where "some grand form of wrong-doing" was reduced to the "compass of some particular brutality, some particular immorality, some particular infamy" ([Beidler (2nd ed.)] 185). *The Turn of the Screw* is one work in which the tension between particularity and suggestion resolves in an uneasy but splendid equilibrium. In this essay, I discuss James's particular vision language—that is, images of seeing and perceiving—then some of the ways that film directors have developed this imagery as they make the story of the strange doings at Bly visible to modern audiences. James, in an apparent apology for the tale to his friend F. W. H. Myers in a letter written shortly after *The Turn of the Screw* was published, wrote that the story was "an inferior, a merely *pictorial*, subject" (178). He need not have apologized. The pictorial qualities of the story are part of what has given it a lasting appeal, both on the page and on the screen.

Many students are keenly attuned to visual learning. If they claim to find James convoluted and abstract, they can search out the constant references to vision in his narrative: verbal action involving staring, perceiving, spectating, and viewing occurs frequently. James's figurative language (less original and profuse here than in other works but still important) is another element that adds visual excitement and thematic depth. Students will have no trouble responding to this description of Flora: "these three words from her were in a flash like the glitter of a drawn blade, the jostle of a cup that my hand for weeks and weeks had held high and full to the brim and that now, even before speaking, I felt overflow in a deluge" (101). They can identify the violence of the blade image; the sexual agitation suggested by the overflowing cup; the rather frenzied quality, typical of the governess, of "flash." They may recognize a eucharistic metaphor (does the governess see herself as a priest? as Christ himself?) or a grail image, befitting the Romantic persona she has constructed for herself.

In analyzing the story's visual qualities, readers will eventually come across passages that ironically use visual ideas to convey obfuscation: "I was a screen—I was to stand before them" (53); "We lived in a cloud of music and affection and success" (65). The doubleness inherent in this imagery—that knowledge is tantalizingly held out as visible and yet, almost immediately, is also identified as untrustworthy or obscured—parallels, of course, the doubleness in the plot. Do the ghosts exist, or is the governess deluded? Is the evil real, or is it in her imagination? (My students are keen neither to pin blame on Mrs. Grose nor to stray from the binary of real ghosts / hallucinating governess, and my inclinations run close to theirs. The prospect that Mrs. Grose is the villain lacks "charm," to borrow a Jamesian word.)

One of my goals in teaching James is to encourage students to see that his style has a profound purpose. Yes, the sentences are complicated, but the moral and psychological issues involved are also complicated. The language promises clarity of vision, but nothing of the sort is forthcoming. It does not take students long to recognize the powerful impact of James's "excursion into chaos" that yet aims at "absolute singleness, clearness, and roundness," as he says in his preface (*Turn* [Beidler (2nd ed.)] 182).

When I teach *The Turn of the Screw* in my introductory literature class, I provide background about James before I focus on visual matters, giving an overview of his life, themes, style, and major works. In total, I spend about three hours on the novella. One particular point that is useful to make is the powerful hold that spiritualism had on nineteenth-century minds. Some students, studying William James in psychology courses, are interested to learn that Henry's brother (along with other respected intellectuals) followed the proceedings of the Society for Psychical Research with great seriousness.

I then ask students to name common qualities of horror movies or gothic literature. Although I have little acquaintance with horror—my affection for *The Turn of the Screw* is based on the author, not the genre—students tend to be knowledgeable here and gain confidence as they compile a list of gothic and horror signposts to be found in James's tale. Many of these are visual: the physical beauty of the children, an isolated mansion in the country, a tower, a mysterious and handsome master. They might also list as familiar elements an independent-minded governess (preferably an orphan), cliff-hanger chapter endings, and the Faustian-bargain plot. Students familiar with *Jane Eyre* can draw parallels between the two stories. The main action of *The Turn of the Screw* is set near the publication date of Charlotte Brontë's novel (1847), so the governess, a reader of romances, could be an early reader of *Jane Eyre*. Even students who have never read a gothic novel will be able to identify the hallmarks of the genre. I encourage them to realize that the governess is as familiar with these conventions as we are and to see how she comforts and indeed aggrandizes herself with Romantic ideas. She wastes no time in constructing a self-sacrificing persona, indulging in self-descriptive phrases like "extraordinary flight of heroism" (53) and, as early as chapter 2, relating her "curiosity that, all the next hours, was to deepen almost to pain" (34), which has appropriately Romantic coloring. (The paintings of Casper David Friedrich, with their melodramatic qualities, can provide a visual correlative to this discussion.)

A possible classroom exercise is to study the origins of words involving spiritualism and sight. This exercise has the advantage of exposing students to the *Oxford English Dictionary*. *Ghost*, for example, is an extremely old word and over the centuries has had many uses, both negative and positive ("Holy Ghost" being an example of a positive use). In its original meaning *ghost* is associated with fury and rage. Students may want to discuss the governess's mental state when they gain this information. The verbs *to look* and *to see*—used many times in this tale—are apparently straightforward words, but the *OED* entries remind us that *look* can mean not only "to direct one's sight" but also "to seek, search for" and "to have the appearance of." *To see* is not only to "perceive . . . with the eyes" but also "to behold . . . in imagination, or in a dream or vision." The word *vision*, too, contains this doubleness, and the *OED* reveals an amazing bit of information: the more concrete meaning ("the action of seeing with the bodily eye") was first recorded in 1491, but as early as 1290 the sense of vision as "something which is apparently seen otherwise than by ordinary sight" was known. I was surprised to find that the otherworldly sense pre-dates the physical one. This exercise introduces students to etymology and encourages them to consider the full force even of everyday words.

A focus on the vision language of James's tale exposes the fact that many of the words we commonly use to discuss ghostly experiences and those we use to discuss sight—something apparently trustworthy and empirical—overlap. James makes good use of this feature of language; the governess trusts the evidence of her eyes, but the language of sight long ago intermingled with the language of spirit. As an exercise, have students *speculate* on and then research the origin of the words *apparition* and *spectre*—all three terms are rooted in the language of sight.

In the next class, we perform close readings of passages that refer to vision. Students respond well to close readings of James, because his sentences are so rich and intricate. Nearly any sentence in *The Turn of the Screw* yields beautifully to careful analysis, showing how James weaves multiple meanings throughout the narrative. One sentence that works as a beginning exercise is the last one in chapter 6, where the governess is about to have her first sighting of Miss Jessel: "Then I again shifted my eyes—I faced what I had to face" (55). Students will pick up on the instability of "shifted" and may notice that the governess is already, at this early point in the story, steeling herself histrionically not merely to face (to look at) an adversary but to "face up to," or oppose and defy her. Another intriguing Jamesian vision word, used many times, is *fixed* ("She gave me never a glance. She only fixed the child" [57]). Here we have a double meaning of "intense look" and, as an ironic twist, "make stable" or "repair." Quint also "fixes" the governess twice in the last paragraph of chapter 3 and twice more at his third appearance, in chapter 9.

James uses words like *stare* and *look* in erotically suggestive ways. Although students in an introductory course can be resistant to psychosexual interpretation, they will hardly deny the suggestiveness of "our straight mutual stare" and Quint "looking at me hard all the while" (40, 41) in chapter 3. A key passage is "it was as if I had been looking at him for years and had known him always" (44); it yields all sorts of information about the governess—her identification with Quint, the quickness of her fancy, and the instantaneous manner in which she makes dubious equivalencies between sight and certain knowledge. It is the steady accumulation of emphasis in phrases like "we faced each other in our common intensity" (67) and "our long gaze at such close quarters" (68) that creates a highly charged erotic atmosphere rather than any one particular reference. Advanced students can discuss feminist ideas about the power of the gaze proposed by film theorists like Laura Mulvey. Whereas women have often been objectified by the male gaze, in *The Turn of the Screw* the governess and Quint engage in a mutual staring contest, which can be read as evidence of her determination to gain moral, social, and sexual power.

Students who enjoy close reading can tackle more difficult and ambiguous references to sight in the text:

> The more I go over it the more I see in it, and the more I see in it the more I fear. I don't know what I *don't* see, what I *don't* fear! (57)

> I saw neither of them [Flora and Mrs. Grose] on my return, but on the other hand I saw, as by an ambiguous compensation, a great deal of Miles. I saw—I can use no other phrase—so much of him that it fairly measured more than it had ever measured. (104)

James often uses "it" in this wonderful and maddening way. An instructor should compile on the chalkboard a list of suggestions from the class about what "it" seems to be, asking what hard visual or sensory evidence supports the various claims.

In the same class it may be possible to move on to an examination of metaphors. James's vivid figurative language builds tension even though the literal facts allow only a "general vision of evil" without "weak specifications," as he says in the preface ([Beidler (2nd ed.)] 185). For example, the governess says that an idea "brushed my brow like the wing of a bat" (61). A sense of her mental frustration is communicated by her metaphors of blind alleys and "doors we had indiscreetly opened" closing "with a little bang" (78). Arriving at Bly, she describes her new circumstances in a concrete manner: "I walked round them, gazed up at them, took them in." They have "an extent and mass" that make her "a little scared not less than a little proud" (32). She has given her situation a physical shape in order that she might look it over. Her ideas have nearly as definite a visual and tactile reality as the house does, and this correspondence will strike students as significant when they try to decide on her reliability as a narrator.

No discussion of vision would be complete without asking students to find the references to failure of vision as the tale winds down. The governess has a "flash of something it would scarce have done to call light" and feels the need to "shut my eyes as tight as possible to the truth" (111). In the final chapter she makes a "mere blind movement" of getting hold of Miles and feels elation that he sees "nothing" at the window (116, 117). One of the most difficult and important sentences in the entire tale involves sight, and it occurs near the conclusion. I spend a good deal of time untangling the following:

> I saw him [Miles], from the midst of my act, meet it with a divination, and on the perception that even now he only guessed, and that the window was still to his own eyes free, I let the impulse flame up to convert the climax of his dismay into the very proof of his liberation. (120)

Students confident about close reading can attempt a translation of this passage into their own words, or an instructor can map the sentence on the chalkboard. One notes the religious language ("divination," "flame," "convert") that the governess has dangerously claimed. What does she mean by "proof"? It could indicate either "evidence" or "test." Foremost for me is the incredible simultaneity—in one sentence—of four states of being: she sees, she realizes, she decides, she acts. Sight, for her, is coexistent with response. An interpreter can use this sentence as evidence of her acute intelligence and capability or, equally, as a sign of excessive mental activity and distress.

One of the most enjoyable classroom exercises divides up the sightings of Quint and Miss Jessel as group work, giving students fifteen minutes to discuss among themselves the evidence in each section. Then they report to the class whether the ghost sighting in that passage seems dependable or hallucinatory. There are eight of these, four each for Quint and Miss Jessel. I call these Q1 to Q4 and J1 to J4 and note the page numbers on the chalkboard. Students will note that Q1 is preceded by longing for the master, and then Quint suddenly appears. The coincidence makes the occurrence suspicious—yet later the governess is able to describe Quint, a man she never met, exactly to Mrs. Grose. Q2 is a different affair; the governess is not overwrought but on a sensible quest for gloves when she sees Quint through the window. In J1, the governess has been playing a role in Flora's fantasy; in J2 she is actually roaming the hallways expecting to see Quint.

All these episodes can be searched for hard evidence, and in my opinion only Q1 and Q2 have much going for them. But it is eye-opening how stubbornly readers cling to the ghosts; even after considerable discussion of the scarcity of concrete proof for the ghosts, a show of hands will likely demonstrate that a sizable portion of the class believe in the ghosts and a considerable number are undecided or unsure. Here is proof of one thing—James's great skill, which gives the unseen real presence.

Showing film clips from several of the many adaptations of *The Turn of the Screw* provides an opportunity to compare the elegance of James's scenes and metaphors with the sometimes brutally transparent interpretations of directors. One scene that works well is the schoolroom scene. Most film treatments emphasize the children's visible badness here, a simplistic approach markedly different from the novella's extravagant insistence (far more provocative) on the purity and perfection of Miles and Flora. If one is short of time, Miles's death scene is the key one for comparative analysis. For example, the conclusion of the 1989 film with Amy Irving, directed by Graeme Clifford, does attempt a dual reading. The ghosts seem real both to the governess and Miles, suggesting that we can acquit her of wrongdoing. Yet in the final frame, she adopts a look that is hard and uncanny, even murderous. Unfortunately, the resulting impression is largely one of confusion. Students may offer the criticism that although Miles utters "the cry of a creature hurled over an abyss" (120) in the text, it does not signify that he really is hurled over a parapet, as happens in this film. Making James's figurative language plainly literal usually has painful results. The version with Jodhi May, directed by Ben Bolt, is more carefully done, and students should be able to find textual evidence in the last few pages for the accidental strangulation of Miles that Bolt and the screenwriter Nick Dear propose. This conclusion is plausible, but it lacks the majestic, open-ended horror of James's conclusion.

Film analysis works well as an essay topic that asks students to investigate what has been lost or gained en route from book to film. The overall impression recorded by my students is that if the film makes the evil too obvious, the story is cheapened and becomes unintentionally laughable. James's subtle sexual suggestions (e.g., the sentence at the end of chapter 22 comparing Miles and the governess with a young couple on their wedding journey) are crude when presented in the form of naughty paintings, drunkenness, or lascivious kisses given by a minor.

The most convincing film version, *The Innocents*, with Deborah Kerr, contains a number of effective visual elements. The governess's dresses gradually shift from light colors to black, the shift symbolizing either her contamination by the spirits or her sorrow, and excellent cinematic use is made of shadows. Windows are emphasized: they can exist equally to be looked through and to show the reflection of the one who looks. Scenes dissolve slowly one into another, a visual counterpart of mental disintegration. Anthony J. Mazzella provides a helpful analysis in the volume *Henry James Goes to the Movies*; he points out the director Jack Clayton's creation of empty screen space, a space that "the others" might inhabit. When Clayton and the screenwriters make changes to James's tale, the additions are intriguing, such as the teardrop—rather striking ocular proof—that a weeping Miss Jessel leaves behind in the schoolroom.

In studying *The Turn of the Screw* students eventually gain an appreciation for James's expert ability to balance vividness and openness. Most will agree with his opinion in the preface that the reader's own mind "will supply him quite sufficiently with all the particulars" (185). James has provided just enough visual cues to set our imaginations in motion, and I make sure that students know what a compliment he has paid them with his trust that they are worthy to work alongside him in creating the meaning of this tale.

NOTES ON CONTRIBUTORS

Peter G. Beidler is the Lucy G. Moses Professor of English at Lehigh University. He is the author of books and essays on subjects ranging from Henry James to Geoffrey Chaucer to Louise Erdrich to pedagogy. He is general editor of the series Manual of the Writings in Middle English. He was named CASE National Professor of the Year in 1983, appointed Fulbright Professor at Sichuan University in China in 1987–88, and was Robert Foster Visiting Professor at Baylor University in 1995–96.

Kristin Boudreau is associate professor of English at the University of Georgia. She is the author of *Sympathy in American Literature: American Sentiments from Jefferson to the Jameses* and has written essays on Henry James, William James, and Alice James as well as on Nathaniel Hawthorne, Toni Morrison, Louisa May Alcott, and Ralph Waldo Emerson. She is currently at work on a book entitled "Capital Deliberations: Literary Responses to American Executions."

Monika Brown is professor of English at the University of North Carolina, Pembroke. She has published essays on Henry James, Gustave Flaubert, Joseph Conrad, George Eliot, and Victorian criticism. Her research interests include the nineteenth-century British novel and criticism of the novel and adaptations of literature into film and opera. She is currently working on Polanski's *Tess* and Gounod's *Faust*.

Gert Buelens is associate professor of English at Ghent University. He has published *Enacting History in Henry James*, *Henry James and the "Aliens,"* and numerous essays on James and other authors. He serves as editorial board member of *The Henry James Review*, *Comparative American Studies*, *The Canadian Review of American Studies*, *MELUS*, and *Queeries*. He is president of the Henry James Society for 2005.

Anna Despotopoulou is lecturer in the Faculty of English Studies at the University of Athens, Greece. She has published, in English-language and Greek literary periodicals, essays on Henry James, Jane Austen, Joseph Conrad, and film. Her current research focuses on the literary representation of London in late Victorian and early modernist fiction from a theoretical and sociological perspective.

Sallie Duhling is emerita chair of the Division of Humanities and Fine Arts at Gainesville College and emerita professor of English. She is the coauthor of *The Catfish Grammar: A Guide to Grammar and Composition*, an auto-instructional text for pre-college students.

Mark A. Eaton is associate professor at Azusa Pacific University and the author of essays on Henry James, Don DeLillo, Cormac McCarthy, Joseph Conrad, and Theodore Dreiser. His current teaching and research interests are American, African American, and ethnic literatures; American studies; cultural studies; and film studies. His screenplay *Klamath Falls* was a semifinalist for the 2003 Nicholl Fellowship.

Diane Long Hoeveler is professor of English and coordinator of Women's Studies at Marquette University. The author of *Gothic Feminism: The Professionalization of Gender from Charlotte Smith to the Brontës*, and *Charlotte Brontë*, she has coedited two volumes in the MLA series Approaches to Teaching World Literature, one on teaching *Jane Eyre*, the other on teaching the gothic. She is currently coediting a book entitled "Interrogating Orientalism: Contextual Approaches and Pedagogic Practices."

Philip Horne is professor of English at University College London. He is the author of *Henry James and Revision: The New York Edition*, *Henry James: A Life in Letters*, an edition of *A London Life / The Reverberator* for Oxford University Press, and an edition of *The Tragic Muse* for Penguin Classics. He is currently preparing a new edition of *The Portrait of a Lady* for Penguin Classics.

Dawn Keetley is associate professor of English at Lehigh University. She has published essays on American literature and coedited a three-volume documentary history of United States feminism entitled *Public Women, Public Words*. She is working on a book about invention of men's homicidal jealousy in nineteenth-century America.

Marian Kelly is a doctoral candidate at Tulane University. She has published on Elizabeth Bowen and is currently working on a dissertation on James Joyce and Toni Morrison, their responses to nationalism, and their revisions of traditional novelistic forms.

Pericles Lewis is associate professor of English and comparative literature at Yale University. He is the author of *Modernism, Nationalism, and the Novel* and the forthcoming *Cambridge Introduction to Modernism* as well as essays on Henry James, Joseph Conrad, Bram Stoker, Marcel Proust, James Joyce, Virginia Woolf, Walter Benjamin, and Theodor Adorno. He is currently working on a book on religious experience in the modern novel.

Collin Meissner is assistant professor of American studies at the University of Notre Dame. His publications include *Henry James and the Language of Experience* and essays on James. He is currently working on two book projects, one tentatively entitled "Capital Crimes: The Role of Money in American Literature and Culture," the other "Reading and the Public Sphere."

Michelle E. Moore is assistant professor of English at the College of DuPage. She has published essays on Bharati Mukherjee and the films of Todd Solondz. Her research and teaching interests include American literature and popular culture, European modernism, and film. She is writing a study on the figure of the vampire in modernist texts.

Sean Palmer is visiting assistant professor of English at Memorial University of Newfoundland. He has written essays on Henry James. He is currently working on essays on James's *The Golden Bowl*, Elizabeth Gaskell's *Sylvia's Lovers*, and George Eliot's *Felix Holt*.

Kimberly C. Reed is professor of English and foreign languages at Lipscomb University and director of study abroad. She has written on Henry James, Honoré de Balzac, and memoirists of the French Revolution as well as on contemporary British novelists. She is currently working on two projects: one on James's ghostly narratives; the other on a text for American university students living, studying, and working in London.

Warren Rosenberg is professor of English at Wabash College and the author of *Legacy of Rage: Jewish Masculinity, Violence, and Culture*; *American Voices: A Thematic/Rhetorical Reader* (coauthored); and essays on Norman Mailer, Philip Roth, and Bernard Malamud. He is researching the role of emotion in class discussion and writing an essay on Michael Chabon.

Eric Savoy is Professeur agrégé de littérature comparée at Université de Montréal. He has published on queer-theoretical approaches to Henry James and is completing a book on James and queer formalism. With Sheila Teahan he organized "Theory-analysis: Henry James and New Formalisms," a workshop conference held in May 2004 at Université de Montréal.

Sue Sorensen is assistant professor of English at Canadian Mennonite University. She has published essays on Susan Sontag, A. S. Byatt, and film adaptations of James's and Byatt's novels. Her current projects focus on biblical narratives in Guy Vanderhaeghe's short stories and the depiction of photography in film.

Sheila Teahan is associate professor of English at Michigan State University. She is the author of *The Rhetorical Logic of Henry James* and essays on James. She is working on a scholarly edition of James's biography of William Wetmore Story and on a book on rhetoric and representation in late James.

Robert Andrew Wilson is an instructor at Cedar Crest College and a doctoral candidate at Lehigh University. He is completing a dissertation entitled "As Good as Gold: Money, the Market, and Morality in American Literature, 1857–1914."

Nicolas S. Witschi is associate professor of English at Western Michigan University. He is the author of *Traces of Gold: California's Natural Resources and the Claim to Realism in Western American Literature* as well as essays on the American West. Among his projects are a biocritical introduction to the life and works of the California Gold Rush chronicler and satirist Alonzo Delano and the revisionist Hollywood westerns of the 1990s.

Patricia Worrall is associate professor of English at Gainesville College. She has written essays on Shakespeare and technology, late-medieval culture, and collaborative technology. Her research and teaching interests are electronic pedagogy, service learning in the composition classroom, and interdisciplinary learning communities.

Greg W. Zacharias is professor of English and director of the Center for Henry James Studies at Creighton University. He also is executive director of the Henry James Society. The author of essays on Henry James, Mark Twain, John Milton, and documentary editing theory and practice, he published *Henry James and the Morality of Fiction* and is the coeditor of the ongoing project *The Complete Letters of Henry James*.

SURVEY PARTICIPANTS

Evan H. Antone, *University of Texas, El Paso*
Ted Billy, *Saint Mary's College*
Kristin Boudreau, *University of Georgia*
Monika Brown, *University of North Carolina, Pembroke*
Gert Buelens, *Ghent University*
Anna Despotopoulou, *Deree College*
Sallie Duhling, *Gainesville College*
Mark A. Eaton, *Azusa Pacific University*
Wendy Graham, *Vassar College*
Mary Y. Hallab, *Central Missouri State University*
Richard D. Hathaway, *State University of New York, New Paltz*
Diane Long Hoeveler, *Marquette University*
Philip Horne, *University College London*
Dawn Keetley, *Lehigh University*
Marian Kelly, *Tulane University*
Elizabeth Keyser, *Hollins University*
Joan Lescinski, *Saint Mary-of-the-Woods College*
Pericles Lewis, *Yale University*
Robert K. Martin, *Université de Montréal*
Collin Meissner, *University of Notre Dame*
Richard Menke, *University of Georgia*
Michelle E. Moore, *State University of New York, Binghamton*
Sean Palmer, *University of Windsor*
Warren Rosenberg, *Wabash College*
Elizabeth Sabiston, *York University*
Eric Savoy, *Université de Montréal*
Margaret Senatore, *University of Southern Colorado*
Sue Sorensen, *University of Winnipeg*
Sheila Teahan, *Michigan State University*
Robert Andrew Wilson, *Lehigh University*
Nicolas S. Witschi, *Western Michigan University*
Patricia Worrall, *Gainesville College*
Greg W. Zacharias, *Creighton University*

WORKS CITED

Abrams, M. H. *The Mirror and the Lamp: Romantic Theory and the Critical Tradition.* New York: Oxford UP, 1953.

Adorno, Theodor W. "On Lyric Poetry and Society." *Notes to Literature.* Vol. 1. Trans. Shierry Weber Nicholsen. New York: Columbia UP, 1991. 37–54.

Anderson, Nancy Fix. *Woman against Women in Victorian England: A Life of Eliza Lynn Linton.* Bloomington: Indiana UP, 1987.

Armstrong, Paul. *The Challenge of Bewilderment: Understanding and Representation in James, Conrad, and Ford.* Ithaca: Cornell UP, 1987.

Bakhtin, Mikhail. "Discourse in the Novel." *The Dialogic Imagination: Four Essays by M. M. Bakhtin.* Ed. Michael Holquist. Trans. Caryl Emerson and Holquist. Austin: U of Texas P, 1981. 259–422.

Bal, Mieke. *Narratology: Introduction to the Theory of Narrative.* 2nd ed. Toronto: U of Toronto P, 1997.

Banta, Martha. *Henry James and the Occult: The Great Extension.* Bloomington: Indiana UP, 1972.

———. *Imaging American Women: Idea and Ideals in Cultural History.* New York: Columbia UP, 1987.

Barthes, Roland. *S/Z.* 1970. New York: Hill, 1974.

Beerbohm, Max. "The Mote in the Middle Distance." *A Christmas Garland.* Heinemann: London, 1912. 13–14.

Beidler, Peter G. "A Critical History of *The Turn of the Screw.*" H. James, *Turn* (Beidler [1st ed.]) 127–51; (2nd ed.) 189–222.

———. *Ghosts, Demons, and Henry James: "The Turn of the Screw" at the Turn of the Century.* Columbia: U of Missouri P, 1989.

———. "Introduction: Biographical and Historical Contexts." H. James, *Turn* (Beidler [1st ed.]) 127–51; (2nd ed.) 3–21.

———. " 'With Holes of Different Sizes Made in Them, to Admit of Sticks': Phallic Playthings in Henry James's *The Turn of the Screw.*" *ANQ: A Quarterly Journal of Short Articles, Notes, and Reviews* 117.3 (2004): 47–52.

Bell, Millicent. "Class, Sex, and the Victorian Governess: James's *The Turn of the Screw.*" Pollack 91–119.

———. *Meaning in Henry James.* Cambridge: Harvard UP, 1991.

Benjamin, Walter. "The Storyteller." *Illuminations.* Trans. Harry Zohn. Ed. Hannah Arendt. New York: Schocken, 1968. 83–109.

Bennett, Andrew, and Nicholas Royle. *Introduction to Literature, Criticism, and Theory: Key Critical Concepts.* 2nd ed. New York: Prentice, 1999.

Bentley, Nancy. "Conscious Observation: Jane Campion's *Portrait of a Lady.*" Griffin, *Henry James* 127–46.

Bernard, Jessie. *The Future of Motherhood.* New York: Dial, 1974.

Berne, Suzanne. *A Perfect Arrangement.* Chapel Hill: Algonquin, 2001.

Bevington, Merle. *Saturday Review*. New York: AMS, 1966.

Biskind, Peter. *Easy Riders, Raging Bulls: How the Sex-Drugs-and-Rock 'n' Roll Generation Saved Hollywood*. New York: Simon, 1998.

Bloch, Ruth. "American Feminine Ideals in Transition: The Rise of the Moral Mother, 1785–1815." *Feminist Studies* 4 (1978): 101–26.

Booth, Wayne C. " 'He Began to Read to Our Hushed Little Circle': Are We Blessed or Cursed by Our Life with *The Turn of the Screw*?" H. James, *Turn* (Beidler [2nd ed.]) 239–53.

———. *The Rhetoric of Fiction*. 2nd ed. Chicago: U of Chicago P, 1983.

Boyum, Joy Gould. *Double Exposure: Fiction into Film*. New York: NAL, 1985.

Bradley, John R., ed. *Henry James and Homo-erotic Desire*. London: Macmillan, 1999.

Breuer, Joseph, and Sigmund Freud. *Studies on Hysteria*. 1895. London: Hogarth, 1955.

Bridges, Robert. "Henry James as a Ghost Raiser." H. James, *Turn* (Esch and Warren) 153–54.

Britten, Benjamin. *The Turn of the Screw, Op. 54: An Opera in a Prologue and Two Acts*. Libretto by Myfanwy Piper. London: Boosey, 1966.

Broadhead, Richard H. *Culture of Letters: Scenes of Reading and Writing in Nineteenth-Century America*. Chicago: U of Chicago P, 1993.

Brooke-Rose, Christine. *A Rhetoric of the Unreal*. New York: Cambridge UP, 1981.

Brooks, Peter. *The Melodramatic Imagination: Balzac, Henry James, Melodrama, and the Mode of Excess*. New York: Columbia UP, 1984.

———. *Reading for the Plot: Design and Intention in Narrative*. Cambridge: Oxford UP, 1984.

Brown, Monika. "Film Music as Sister Art: Adaptations of *The Turn of the Screw*." *Mosaic: A Journal for the Interdisciplinary Study of Literature*. Interarts Project, Part 1: Establishing Frameworks. 31.1 (1998): 61–81.

Buelens, Gert. "Henry James's Initiation: Letter to the Editor." *Times Literary Supplement* 17 Jan. 1997: 17.

———. "Henry James's Oblique Possession: Plottings of Desire and Mastery in *The American Scene*." *PMLA* 116 (2001): 300–14.

———. "In Possession of a Secret: Rhythms of Mastery and Surrender in 'The Beast in the Jungle.' " *Henry James Review* 19 (1998): 17–35.

Butler, Judith. *Gender Trouble: Feminism and the Subversion of Identity*. New York: Routledge, 1990.

Canby, Vincent. "*Daisy* is an Unexpected Triumph." Rev. of *Daisy Miller*, dir. Peter Bogdanovich. *New York Times* 16 June 1974, sec. 11: 1+.

Caruth, Cathy. *Unclaimed Experience: Trauma, Narrative, and History*. Baltimore: Johns Hopkins UP, 1996.

Cocks, Jay. "Culture Shock." *Time* 3 June 1974: 56–57.

Cohen, Paula Marantz. "Freud's *Dora* and James's *The Turn of the Screw*: Two Treatments of the Female 'Case.' " *Criticism* 28 (1986): 73–87.

Conrad, Joseph. *The Secret Sharer*. Ed. Daniel R. Schwarz. Boston: Bedford–St. Martin's, 1997.

Cornwell, Neil, and Maggie Malone, eds. The Turn of the Screw *and* What Maisie Knew: *Contemporary Critical Essays*. New York: St. Martin's, 1998.

Corse, Sandra. "From Narrative to Music: Benjamin Britten's *The Turn of the Screw*." *University of Toronto Quarterly* 51 (1981–82): 161–74.

Cranfill, Thomas Mabry, and Robert Lanier Clark. *An Anatomy of* The Turn of the Screw. Austin: U of Texas P, 1965.

Crews, Frederick. *Postmodern Pooh*. New York: North Point, 2001.

Culler, Jonathan. *Literary Theory: A Very Short Introduction*. Oxford: Oxford UP, 1997.

Daisy Miller. Dir. Peter Bogdanovich. Director's Company, 1974.

de Man, Paul. *The Resistance to Theory*. Minneapolis: U of Minnesota P, 1986.

Dunlop, M. H. *Gilded City: Scandal and Sensation in Turn-of-the-Century New York*. New York: Perennial, 2000.

Edel, Leon. *Henry James: A Life*. New York: Harper, 1985.

———, ed. *Henry James: Letters*. 4 vols. Cambridge: Harvard UP, 1974–84.

———, ed. *Henry James: Selected Letters*. Cambridge: Harvard UP, 1987.

———. *Henry James: The Conquest of London, 1870–1881*. New York: Lippincott, 1962.

———. "Henry James: The Dramatic Years: An Introductory Essay." H. James, *Complete Plays* 19–69.

———. *Henry James: The Master, 1901–1916*. Philadelphia: Lippincott, 1972.

Edgeworth, Maria. "It Is the Worst Thing in the World to Leave Children with Servants." 1798. H. James, *Turn* (Beidler [2nd ed.]) 123–27.

Edgeworth, Maria, and Richard Lovell Edgeworth. *Practical Education*. 2 vols. London, 1798. Facsim. ed. New York: Garland, 1974.

Eliot, T. S. *Selected Prose of T. S. Eliot*. Ed. Frank Kermode. New York: Harcourt, 1975.

———. *T. S. Eliot: The Complete Poems and Plays, 1909–1950*. New York: Harcourt, 1971.

Ellmann, Richard. "James amongst the Aesthetes." Bradley 25–44.

Felman, Shoshana. "The Grasp with Which I Recovered Him: A Child Is Killed in *The Turn of the Screw*." H. James, *Turn* (Beidler [1st ed.]) 193–206.

———. "Turning the Screw of Interpretation." *Yale French Studies* 55–56 (1977): 94–207. Rpt. in *Writing and Madness: Literature/Philosophy/Psychoanalysis*. Ithaca: Cornell UP, 1985. 141–247.

Fishbach, Stephen. "The Interpretation of the Human." Unpublished essay, 2001.

"Flirt." *The American Heritage Dictionary*. 2nd college ed. 1982.

Fogel, Daniel Mark, ed. *A Companion to Henry James Studies*. Westport: Greenwood, 1993.

———. Daisy Miller: *A Dark Comedy of Manners*. Boston: Twayne, 1990.

Fowler, Virginia C. *Henry James's American Girl: The Embroidery on the Canvas*. Madison: U of Wisconsin P, 1984.

Freedman, Jonathan, ed. *The Cambridge Companion to Henry James*. Cambridge: Cambridge UP, 1998.

Freud, Sigmund. "The Uncanny." 1919. *Art and Literature*. Ed. Angela Richards et al. Harmondsworth: Penguin, 1953. 335–76. Vol. 14 of *The Penguin Freud Library*.

Friend, Tad. "The Moviegoer." *New Yorker* 8 Apr. 2002: 36–43.

Fussell, Edwin. "The Ontology of *The Turn of the Screw*." *Journal of Modern Literature* 8 (1980): 118–28.

G., Mrs. "What Has Happened to the Children?" 1889. H. James, *Turn* (Beidler [2nd ed.]) 157–61.

Gale, Robert. *Henry James Encyclopedia*. Westport: Greenwood, 1989.

Goddard, Harold C. "A Pre-Freudian Reading of *The Turn of the Screw*." H. James, *Turn* (Esch and Warren) 161–68.

The Golden Bowl. Dir. James Ivory. Videocassette. Merchant-Ivory Productions, 2000.

Graham, Wendy. "Bringing It All Back Home: Henry James and the Mother-Complex." *Arizona Quarterly* 54.1 (1998): 27–64.

Griffin, Susan, ed. *Henry James Goes to the Movies*. Lexington: UP of Kentucky, 2002.

———. Introduction. *Forum on Teaching James*. Spec. issue of *Henry James Review* 17 (1996): 211–12.

———. "Introduction: Making Movies with Henry James." Griffin, *Henry James* 1–7.

The Hand That Rocks the Cradle. Dir. Curtis Hanson. 1992. DVD. Buena Vista Home Entertainment, 1998.

The Haunting of Helen Walker. Dir. Tom McLoughlin. Rosemont, 1995.

Hawthorne, Nathaniel. *The Scarlet Letter*. Columbus: Ohio State UP, 1962. Vol. 1 of *The Centenary Edition of the Works of Nathaniel Hawthorne*. Ed. William Charvat, Roy Harvey Pearce, and Claude M. Simpson. 20 vols. 1962–88.

Hayes, Kevin J., ed. *Henry James: The Contemporary Reviews*. New York: Cambridge UP, 1996.

Heilman, Robert. "The Freudian Reading of *The Turn of the Screw*." H. James, *Turn* (Esch and Warren) 177–83.

———. "*The Turn of the Screw* as Poem." *U of Kansas City Review* 14 (1948): 277–89.

Heller, Terry. The Turn of the Screw: *Bewildered Vision*. Boston: Twayne, 1989.

Helsinger, Elizabeth, Robin Sheets, and William Veeder. *The Woman Question: Society and Literature in Britain and America, 1837–1883*. New York: Garland, 1983.

Hindley, Clifford. "Why Does Miles Die? A Study of Britten's *The Turn of the Screw*." *Musical Quarterly* 74.1 (1990): 1–17.

Hoople, Robin P. *Distinguished Discord: Discontinuity and Pattern in the Critical Tradition of* The Turn of the Screw. Lewisburg: Bucknell UP, 1997.

Horne, Philip, ed. *Henry James: A Life in Letters*. New York: Viking, 1999.

———. *Henry James and Revision: The New York Edition*. Oxford: Clarendon, 1990.

———. "Henry James at Work: The Question of Our Texts." Freedman 63–78.

Howard, Patricia. *Benjamin Britten*, The Turn of the Screw. Cambridge Opera Guides. Cambridge: Cambridge UP, 1985.

Howells, William Dean. *Life in Letters of William Dean Howells*. Ed. Mildred Howells. Vol. 1. New York: Russell, 1968.

Hoxie, Elizabeth F. "Mrs. Grundy Adopts Daisy Miller." *New England Quarterly* 19 (1946): 474–84.

Hrdy, Sarah Blaffer. "Mothers and Others." *Natural History* May 2001: 50–63.

Hughes, Kathryn. *The Victorian Governess*. London: Hambledon, 1993.

The Innocents. Dir. Jack Clayton. Fox Video. Twentieth-Century Fox, 1961.

James, Henry. "Albert Rhodes." H. James, *Literary Criticism* 1: 580–81.

———. *The Ambassadors*. Boston: Houghton, 1960.

———. "The Art of Fiction." H. James, *Literary Criticism* 1: 44–65.

———. "The Art of Fiction." *The Critical Muse: Selected Literary Criticism*. Ed. Roger Gard. London: Penguin, 1987. 186–206.

———. *The Art of the Novel: Critical Prefaces*. Ed. R. P. Blackmur. New York: Scribner's, 1939.

———. "The Author of Beltraffio." 1884. *Eight Tales from the Major Phase: In the Cage and Others*. Ed. Morton Dauwen Zabel. New York: Norton, 1969. 29–78.

———. *Autobiography*. Ed. F. W. Dupee. New York: Criterion, 1956.

———. "The Beast in the Jungle." H. James, *Tales* 277–312.

———. *Collected Travel Writings: Great Britain and America*. Ed. Richard Howard. New York: Lib. of Amer., 1993.

———. *Collected Travel Writings: The Continent*. Ed. Richard Howard. New York: Lib. of Amer., 1993.

———. *The Complete Notebooks of Henry James*. Ed. Leon Edel and Lyall H. Powers. New York: Oxford, 1987.

———. *The Complete Plays of Henry James*. Ed. Leon Edel. New York: Oxford UP, 1990.

———. *Daisy Miller*. 1878. London: Penguin, 1986.

———. *Daisy Miller: A Comedy in Three Acts*. H. James, *Complete Plays* 117–76.

———. "Daisy Miller: A Study." H. James, *Tales* 3–50.

———. "Four Meetings." *Complete Stories, 1874–1884*. Ed. William L. Vance. New York: Lib. of Amer., 1999. 191–218.

———. *Literary Criticism*. 2 vols. Ed. Leon Edel. New York: Lib. of Amer., 1984.

———. "Modern Women." H. James, *Literary Criticism* 1: 19–26.

———. *Notes of a Son and Brother*. New York: Scribner's, 1913.

———. Preface. *The Portrait of a Lady*. Penguin Classics. London: Penguin, 1984. 41–55.

———. Preface to *The American*. H. James, *Literary Criticism* 2: 1053–69.

———. Preface to "The Lesson of the Master." H. James, *Literary Criticism* 2: 1225–37.

———. Preface to *Roderick Hudson*. H. James, *Literary Criticism* 2: 1039–52.

———. Preface to *The Turn of the Screw*. H. James, *Literary Criticism* 2: 1173–91. Excerpt in *Turn* (Beidler [2nd ed.]) 179–86.

———. *A Small Boy and Others*. London: Macmillan, 1914.

———. *Tales of Henry James*. 1st ed. Ed. Christof Wegelin. Norton Critical Ed. New York: Norton, 1984.

———. "Travelling Companions." *Complete Stories, 1864–1874*. Ed. Jean Strouse. New York: Lib. of Amer., 1999. 495–542.

———. *The Turn of the Screw*. Ed. Peter G. Beidler. 1st ed. Boston: Bedford, 1995. 2nd, rev. ed. 2004.

———. *The Turn of the Screw*. Ed. Deborah Esch and Jonathan Warren. 2nd ed. New York: Norton, 1999.

———. *What Maisie Knew*. Oxford: Oxford UP, 1966.

———. *The Wings of the Dove*. London: Penguin, 1986.

James, William. *The Letters of William James*. Vol. 2. Boston: Atlantic Monthly, 1920.

———. *Pragmatism*. 1907. Ed. Bruce Kuklick. Indianapolis: Hackett, 1981.

———. *Principles of Psychology*. 2 vols. 1890. New York: Dover, 1950.

———. *The Varieties of Religious Experience*. Ed. Martin E. Marty. Harmondsworth: Penguin, 1982.

Jameson, Anna. "The Occupation of Governess Is Sought Merely through Necessity." 1846. H. James, *Turn* (Beidler [2nd ed.]) 128–32.

Jameson, Fredric. *The Political Unconscious: Narrative as a Socially Symbolic Act*. Ithaca: Cornell UP, 1982.

Kaplan, Alice. *French Lessons*. Chicago: U of Chicago P, 1993.

Kaplan, Fred. *Henry James: The Imagination of Genius*. New York: Morrow, 1992.

Kehler, Dorothy. "Teaching *Romeo and Juliet* Historically." *Approaches to Teaching Shakespeare's* Romeo and Juliet. Ed. Maurice Hunt. New York: MLA, 2000. 78–84.

Kodat, Catherine Gunther. "Saving Private Property: Steven Spielberg's American DreamWorks." *Representations* 71 (2000): 77–105.

Krook, Dorothea. "Intentions and Intentions: The Problem of Intention and Henry James's *The Turn of the Screw*." *The Theory of the Novel: New Essays*. Ed. John Halperin. New York: Oxford UP, 1974. 353–72.

The Last Picture Show. Dir. Peter Bogdanovich. BBS Productions, 1971.

Law, Joe K. "The Dialogics of Operatic Adaptation: Reading Benjamin Britten." *Yearbook of Interdisciplinary Studies in the Fine Arts* 1 (1989): 407–27.

Leavis, F. R. *The Great Tradition: George Eliot, Henry James, Joseph Conrad*. New York: New York UP, 1960.

———. "Reply to Bewley's 'Rejoinder.' " *Scrutiny* 17 (1950): 263.

Levenson, Michael H. *A Genealogy of Modernism: A Study of English Literary Doctrine, 1908–1922*. Cambridge: Cambridge UP, 1984.

Lewis, Jan. "Mother's Love: The Construction of an Emotion in Nineteenth-Century America." *Social History and Issues in Human Consciousness: Some Interdisciplinary Connections*. Ed. Andrew E. Barnes and Peter N. Stearns. New York: New York UP, 1989. 209–29.

Lewis, R. W. B. *The Jameses: A Family Narrative*. New York: Farrar, 1991.

Linton, Eliza. "The Exclusiveness of Women." *Saturday Review* Feb. 1870: 242–43.

———. "The Girl of the Period." *Saturday Review* Mar. 1868: 339–40.

———. "The Modern Mother." *Saturday Review* July 1875: 109–10.

———. "The Tyranny of Mothers." *Saturday Review* Feb. 1875: 211–12.

———. "The Wild Women." *Saturday Review* Jan. 1870: 14–15.

———. "Woman and the World." *Saturday Review* Apr. 1868: 479–80.

———. "Women's Weapons." *Saturday Review* Oct. 1869: 440–41.

Lodge, David. *Changing Places: A Tale of Two Campuses*. London: Penguin, 1978.

———. *Small World: An Academic Romance*. London: Penguin, 1985.

Longman Dictionary of English Language and Culture. 2nd ed. Harlow: Addison, 1998.

Lukacher, Ned. *Primal Scenes: Literature, Philosophy, Psychoanalysis*. Ithaca: Cornell UP, 1986.

Lustig, T. J. *Henry James and the Ghostly*. Cambridge: Cambridge UP, 1994.

Machor, James L., and Philip Goldstein, eds. *Reception Study: From Literary Theory to Cultural Studies*. New York: Routledge, 2001.

Marx, Karl, and Friedrich Engels. *Communist Manifesto. Economic and Philosophic Manuscripts of 1844* [by Marx] *and the* Communist Manifesto. Trans. Martin Milligan. Amherst: Prometheus, 1988. 203–43.

Maurice, Mary. "Many Were the Daughters of Clergymen." 1847. H. James, *Turn* (Beidler [2nd ed.]) 133–34.

———. "There Is a Strong Prejudice against Governesses." 1849. H. James, *Turn* (Beidler [2nd ed.]) 134–35.

Mazzella, Anthony J. " 'The Story . . . Held Us': *The Turn of the Screw* from Henry James to Jack Clayton." Griffin, *Henry James* 9–31.

McCarthy, Justin. "American Women and English Women." *Galaxy* July 1870: 25–36.

McCormack, Peggy. "Reexamining Bogdanovich's *Daisy Miller*." Griffin, *Henry James* 34–59.

McFarlane, Brian. *Novel to Film: An Introduction to the Theory of Adaptation*. New York: Oxford UP, 1996.

McGann, Jerome. *The Beauty of Inflections: Literary Investigations of Historical Method and Theory*. Oxford: Clarendon, 1985.

McMaster, Graham. "Henry James and India: A Historical Reading of *The Turn of the Screw*." *Clio* 18 (1988): 23–40.

McWhirter, David. *Henry James's New York Edition: The Construction of Authorship*. Stanford: Stanford UP, 1995.

———. "In the 'Other House' of Fiction: Writing, Authority, and Femininity in *The Turn of the Screw*." Pollack 121–48.

Meissner, Collin. *Henry James and the Language of Experience*. Cambridge: Cambridge UP, 1999.

Mellers, Wilfrid. "Turning the Screw." *The Britten Companion*. Ed. Christopher Palmer. Cambridge: Cambridge UP, 1984. 144–52.

Meyer, Cheryl L., and Michelle Oberman. *Mothers Who Kill Their Children: Understanding the Acts of Moms from Susan Smith to the "Prom Mom."* New York: New York UP, 2001.

Miller, D. A. "Anal Rope." *Inside/Out: Lesbian Theories, Gay Theories*. Ed. Diana Fuss. New York: Routledge, 1991. 118–41.

Montgomery, Maureen E. *Displaying Women: Spectacles of Leisure in Edith Wharton's New York*. New York: Routledge, 1998.

Mulvey, Laura. "Visual Pleasure and Narrative Cinema." *Screen* 16 (1975): 6–18.

Nudd, Donna Marie. "The Pleasure of Intertextuality: Reading *Jane Eyre* Television and Film Adaptations." *Jane Eyre*. By Charlotte Brontë. 3rd ed. Ed. Richard J. Dunn. Norton Critical Ed. New York: Norton, 2000. 522–29.

Oates, Joyce Carol. "Accursed Inhabitants of the House of Bly." *Haunted: Tales of the Grotesque*. New York: Plume, 1995. 254–83.

———. "The Short Story." *Southern Humanities Review* 5 (1971): 213–14.

The Oxford English Dictionary. 2nd ed. 1989.

Pace, Barbara G. "Resistance and Response: Deconstructing Community Standards in a Literature Class." *Journal of Adolescent and Adult Literacy* Feb. 2003: 408–11.

Palmer, James W. "Cinematic Ambiguity: James's *The Turn of the Screw* and Clayton's *The Innocents*." *Literature/Film Quarterly* 5 (1977): 198–215.

Parkinson, Edward J. The Turn of the Screw: *A History of Its Critical Interpretations, 1898–1979*. 11 June 2003. 26 Oct. 2004 <http://www.turnofthescrew.com>.

Penn, Arthur. "Fanny Kemble's Journal." *Scribner's Monthly Magazine* May 1879: 157–59.

Person, Leland. "Homo-erotic Desire in the Tales of Writers and Artists." Bradley 25–44.

"Peter and Cybill: Who Needs Marriage?" *People Magazine* 13 May 1974: 19–22.

Peterson, M. Jeanne. "The Victorian Governess: Status Incongruence in Family and Society." *Suffer and Be Still: Women in the Victorian Age*. Ed. Martha Vicinus. Bloomington: Indiana UP, 1972. 3–19.

Pollack, Vivian R., ed. *New Essays on* Daisy Miller *and* The Turn of the Screw. New York: Cambridge UP, 1993.

Poovey, Mary. *Uneven Developments: The Ideological Work of Gender in Mid-Victorian England*. Chicago: U of Chicago P, 1988.

The Portrait of a Lady. Dir. Jane Campion. Videocassette. PolyGram Filmed Entertainment, 1996.

Punter, David. *Literature of Terror: A History of Gothic Fictions from 1765 to the Present Day*. London: Longman, 1980.

Renner, Stanley. " 'Red Hair, Very Red, Close-Curling': Sexual Hysteria, Physiognomical Bogeymen, and the 'Ghosts.' " H. James, *Turn* (Beidler [2nd ed.]) 271–89.

Rhodes, Albert. "Shall the American Girl Be Chaperoned?" *Galaxy* Oct. 1877: 451–58.

Richter, David H., ed. *The Critical Tradition: Classic Texts and Contemporary Trends*. Boston: Bedford, 1998.

Ricoeur, Paul. *Hermeneutics and the Human Sciences*. Ed. and trans. John B. Thompson. Cambridge: Cambridge UP, 1981.

Riggio, Milla Cozart, ed. *Teaching Shakespeare through Performance*. New York: MLA, 1999.

Rivkin, Julie, and Michael Ryan, eds. *Literary Theory: An Anthology*. Oxford: Blackwell, 1998.

Robbins, Bruce. " 'They Don't Much Count, Do They?': The Unfinished History of *The Turn of the Screw*." H. James, *Turn* (Beidler [1st ed.]) 283–96; (2nd ed.) 333–46.

Rocklin, Edward L. "Performance Is More Than an 'Approach' to Shakespeare." Riggio 48–62.

Rosenwasser, David, and Jill Stephen. *Writing Analytically*. 3rd ed. Boston: Thompson Learning, 2003.

Rowe, John Carlos. "Henry James and the Art of Teaching." *Henry James Review* 17 (1996): 213–24.

———. "Screwball: The Use and Abuse of Uncertainty in Henry James's *The Turn of the Screw*." *Delta: Revue du Centre d'Etudes et de Recherche sur les Ecrivains du Sud aux Etats-Unis* 15 (1982): 1–31.

Schrero, Elliot M. "Exposure in *The Turn of the Screw*." *Modern Philology* 78 (1981): 261–74.

Sedgwick, Eve Kosofsky. "The Beast in the Closet: James and the Writing of Homosexual Panic." *Epistemology of the Closet.* Hemel Hempstead, Eng.: Harvester Wheatsheaf, 1991. 182–212.

Seltzer, Mark. *Henry James and the Art of Power*. Ithaca: Cornell UP, 1984.

Sewell, Elizabeth Missing. "She Is Perfectly Incompetent for Her Task." 1866. H. James, *Turn* (Beidler [2nd ed.]) 135–36.

Shand, G. B. "Reading Power: Classroom Acting as Close Reading." Riggio 244–55.

Skrupskelis, Ignas K., and Elizabeth M. Berkeley, eds. *William and Henry, 1861–1884*. Charlottesville: UP of Virginia, 1992. Vol. 1 of *The Correspondence of William James*.

Sobchack, Vivian. "What Is Film History?; or, The Riddle of the Sphinxes." *Reinventing Film Studies*. Ed. Christine Gledhill and Linda Williams. London: Arnold, 2000. 300–15.

Stafford, William T., ed. *James's* Daisy Miller: *The Story, the Play, the Critics*. New York: Scribner's, 1963.

Stead, William T. "I No Longer Felt I Belonged to Myself." 1896. H. James, *Turn* (Beidler [2nd ed.]) 163–71.

Stevens, Wallace. "The Snow Man." *Harmonium*. New York: Knopf, 1923. 24.

Swingers. Dir. Doug Liman. Miramax, 1996.

Tanner, Tony. *Henry James: The Writer and His Work*. Amherst: U of Massachusetts P, 1985.

Tarbox, Gwen Athene. *The Clubwomen's Daughters: Collectivist Impulses in Progressive-Era Girls' Fiction*. New York: Garland, 2000.

Teahan, Sheila. "Henry James at Moo U." *Henry James Review* 17 (1996): 242–47.

———. " 'I Caught Him, Yes, I Held Him': The Ghostly Effects of Reading (in) *The Turn of the Screw*." H. James, *Turn* (Beidler [2nd ed.]) 349–63.

Thomas, Brooke. "The Historical Necessity for—and Difficulties with—New Historical Analysis in Introductory Literature Courses." *College English* 49 (1987): 509–22.

Tintner, Adeline. *Henry James's Legacy: The Afterlife of His Figure and Fiction*. Baton Rouge: Lousiana State UP, 1998.

———. *The Museum World of Henry James*. Ann Arbor: UMI Research, 1986.

———. *The Pop World of Henry James: From Fairy Tales to Science Fiction*. Ann Arbor: UMI Research, 1989.

The Turn of the Screw. Dir. Ben Bolt. Videocassette. Exxon Mobil Masterpiece Theatre. 2000.

The Turn of the Screw. Dir. Graeme Clifford. Cannon Video. Showtime, 1989.

The Turn of the Screw. Dir. Dan Curtis. ABC, 1973. MPI Home Video, 1992.

The Turn of the Screw. Dir. Rusty Lemorande. Electric Pictures, 1992.

The Turn of the Screw. Dir. Petr Weigl. Unitel Munich and WDR, 1982.

Van Thal, Herbert. *Eliza Lynn Linton: The Girl of the Period*. London: Allen, 1979.

Vatas-Simpson, Mrs. "There Must Be Some Foundation for the Rumours." 1885. H. James, *Turn* (Beidler [2nd ed.]) 151–55.

Walton, Priscilla L. *The Disruption of the Feminine in Henry James*. Toronto: U of Toronto P, 1992.

———. " 'He Took No Notice of Her; He Looked at Me': Subjectivities and Sexualities in *The Turn of the Screw*." H. James, *Turn* (Beidler [2nd ed.]) 305–16.

Wardley, Lynn. "Reassembling Daisy Miller." *American Literary History* 3 (1991): 232–54.

Weber, Max. *The Protestant Ethic and the Spirit of Capitalism*. Trans. Talcott Parsons. London: Routledge, 2001.

Weisbuch, Robert. "Winterbourne and the Doom of Manhood in *Daisy Miller*." Pollack 65–89.

Westcott, B. F. "A Sufficient Number of Clear and Well-Attested Cases." 1851. H. James, *Turn* (Beidler [2nd ed.]) 144–45.

White, Allon. *The Uses of Obscurity: The Fiction of Early Modernism*. London: Routledge, 1981.

Widdowson, H. G. *Stylistics and the Teaching of Literature*. Essex: Longman, 1975.

Wilson, Edmund. "The Ambiguity of Henry James." *Hound and Horn* 7 (1934): 385–406. Rpt. in H. James, *Turn* (Esch and Warren) 170–73.

The Wings of the Dove. Dir. Iain Softley. Videocassette. Miramax Home Entertainment, 2003.

INDEX

Modern Language Association of America

Approaches to Teaching World Literature

Joseph Gibaldi, series editor

Achebe's Things Fall Apart. Ed. Bernth Lindfors. 1991.

Arthurian Tradition. Ed. Maureen Fries and Jeanie Watson. 1992.

Atwood's The Handmaid's Tale *and Other Works*. Ed. Sharon R. Wilson, Thomas B. Friedman, and Shannon Hengen. 1996.

Austen's Emma. Ed. Marcia McClintock Folsom. 2004.

Austen's Pride and Prejudice. Ed. Marcia McClintock Folsom. 1993.

Balzac's Old Goriot. Ed. Michal Peled Ginsburg. 2000.

Baudelaire's Flowers of Evil. Ed. Laurence M. Porter. 2000.

Beckett's Waiting for Godot. Ed. June Schlueter and Enoch Brater. 1991.

Beowulf. Ed. Jess B. Bessinger, Jr., and Robert F. Yeager. 1984.

Blake's Songs of Innocence and of Experience. Ed. Robert F. Gleckner and Mark L. Greenberg. 1989.

Boccaccio's Decameron. Ed. James H. McGregor. 2000.

British Women Poets of the Romantic Period. Ed. Stephen C. Behrendt and Harriet Kramer Linkin. 1997.

Brontë's Jane Eyre. Ed. Diane Long Hoeveler and Beth Lau. 1993.

Byron's Poetry. Ed. Frederick W. Shilstone. 1991.

Camus's The Plague. Ed. Steven G. Kellman. 1985.

Cather's My Ántonia. Ed. Susan J. Rosowski. 1989.

Cervantes' Don Quixote. Ed. Richard Bjornson. 1984.

Chaucer's Canterbury Tales. Ed. Joseph Gibaldi. 1980.

Chopin's The Awakening. Ed. Bernard Koloski. 1988.

Coleridge's Poetry and Prose. Ed. Richard E. Matlak. 1991.

Conrad's "Heart of Darkness" and "The Secret Sharer." Ed. Hunt Hawkins and Brian W. Shaffer. 2002.

Dante's Divine Comedy. Ed. Carole Slade. 1982.

Defoe's Robinson Crusoe. Ed. Maximillian E. Novak and Carl Fisher. 2005.

Dickens' David Copperfield. Ed. Richard J. Dunn. 1984.

Dickinson's Poetry. Ed. Robin Riley Fast and Christine Mack Gordon. 1989.

Narrative of the Life of Frederick Douglass. Ed. James C. Hall. 1999.

Eliot's Middlemarch. Ed. Kathleen Blake. 1990.

Eliot's Poetry and Plays. Ed. Jewel Spears Brooker. 1988.

Shorter Elizabethan Poetry. Ed. Patrick Cheney and Anne Lake Prescott. 2000.

Ellison's Invisible Man. Ed. Susan Resneck Parr and Pancho Savery. 1989.

English Renaissance Drama. Ed. Karen Bamford and Alexander Leggatt. 2002.

Works of Louise Erdrich. Ed. Gregg Sarris, Connie A. Jacobs, and James R. Giles. 2004.

Dramas of Euripides. Ed. Robin Mitchell-Boyask. 2002.

Faulkner's The Sound and the Fury. Ed. Stephen Hahn and Arthur F. Kinney. 1996.
Flaubert's Madame Bovary. Ed. Laurence M. Porter and Eugene F. Gray. 1995.
García Márquez's One Hundred Years of Solitude. Ed. María Elena de Valdés and Mario J. Valdés. 1990.
Gilman's "The Yellow Wall-Paper" and Herland. Ed. Denise D. Knight and Cynthia J. Davis.
Goethe's Faust. Ed. Douglas J. McMillan. 1987.
Gothic Fiction: The British and American Traditions. Ed. Diane Long Hoeveler and Tamar Heller. 2003.
Hebrew Bible as Literature in Translation. Ed. Barry N. Olshen and Yael S. Feldman. 1989.
Homer's Iliad *and* Odyssey. Ed. Kostas Myrsiades. 1987.
Ibsen's A Doll House. Ed. Yvonne Shafer. 1985.
Henry James's Daisy Miller *and* The Turn of the Screw. Ed. Kimberly C. Reed and Peter G. Beidler. 2005.
Works of Samuel Johnson. Ed. David R. Anderson and Gwin J. Kolb. 1993.
Joyce's Ulysses. Ed. Kathleen McCormick and Erwin R. Steinberg. 1993.
Kafka's Short Fiction. Ed. Richard T. Gray. 1995.
Keats's Poetry. Ed. Walter H. Evert and Jack W. Rhodes. 1991.
Kingston's The Woman Warrior. Ed. Shirley Geok-lin Lim. 1991.
Lafayette's The Princess of Clèves. Ed. Faith E. Beasley and Katharine Ann Jensen. 1998.
Works of D. H. Lawrence. Ed. M. Elizabeth Sargent and Garry Watson. 2001.
Lessing's The Golden Notebook. Ed. Carey Kaplan and Ellen Cronan Rose. 1989.
Mann's Death in Venice *and Other Short Fiction.* Ed. Jeffrey B. Berlin. 1992.
Medieval English Drama. Ed. Richard K. Emmerson. 1990.
Melville's Moby-Dick. Ed. Martin Bickman. 1985.
Metaphysical Poets. Ed. Sidney Gottlieb. 1990.
Miller's Death of a Salesman. Ed. Matthew C. Roudané. 1995.
Milton's Paradise Lost. Ed. Galbraith M. Crump. 1986.
Molière's Tartuffe *and Other Plays.* Ed. James F. Gaines and Michael S. Koppisch. 1995.
Momaday's The Way to Rainy Mountain. Ed. Kenneth M. Roemer. 1988.
Montaigne's Essays. Ed. Patrick Henry. 1994.
Novels of Toni Morrison. Ed. Nellie Y. McKay and Kathryn Earle. 1997.
Murasaki Shikibu's The Tale of Genji. Ed. Edward Kamens. 1993.
Pope's Poetry. Ed. Wallace Jackson and R. Paul Yoder. 1993.
Proust's Fiction and Criticism. Ed. Elyane Dezon-Jones and Inge Crosman Wimmers. 2003.
Rousseau's Confessions *and* Reveries of the Solitary Walker. Ed. John C. O'Neal and Ourida Mostefai. 2003.
Shakespeare's Hamlet. Ed. Bernice W. Kliman. 2001.
Shakespeare's King Lear. Ed. Robert H. Ray. 1986.

Shakespeare's Romeo and Juliet. Ed. Maurice Hunt. 2000.
Shakespeare's The Tempest *and Other Late Romances.* Ed. Maurice Hunt. 1992.
Shelley's Frankenstein. Ed. Stephen C. Behrendt. 1990.
Shelley's Poetry. Ed. Spencer Hall. 1990.
Sir Gawain and the Green Knight. Ed. Miriam Youngerman Miller and Jane Chance. 1986.
Spenser's Faerie Queene. Ed. David Lee Miller and Alexander Dunlop. 1994.
Stendhal's The Red and the Black. Ed. Dean de la Motte and Stirling Haig. 1999.
Sterne's Tristram Shandy. Ed. Melvyn New. 1989.
Stowe's Uncle Tom's Cabin. Ed. Elizabeth Ammons and Susan Belasco. 2000.
Swift's Gulliver's Travels. Ed. Edward J. Rielly. 1988.
Thoreau's Walden *and Other Works*. Ed. Richard J. Schneider. 1996.
Tolstoy's Anna Karenina. Ed. Liza Knapp and Amy Mandelker. 2003.
Vergil's Aeneid. Ed. William S. Anderson and Lorina N. Quartarone. 2002.
Voltaire's Candide. Ed. Renée Waldinger. 1987.
Whitman's Leaves of Grass. Ed. Donald D. Kummings. 1990.
Woolf's To the Lighthouse. Ed. Beth Rigel Daugherty and Mary Beth Pringle. 2001.
Wordsworth's Poetry. Ed. Spencer Hall, with Jonathan Ramsey. 1986.
Wright's Native Son. Ed. James A. Miller. 1997.